IAN HARRISON

INTRODUCING
ACCOUNTING

FOR AS

SECOND EDITION

HODDER
EDUCATION
AN HACHETTE UK COMPANY

Orders: please contact Bookpoint Ltd, 130 Milton Park, Abingdon, Oxon OX14 4SB. Telephone: (44) 01235 827720. Fax: (44) 01235 400454. Lines are open from 9.00–5.00, Monday to Saturday, with a 24-hour message answering service. You can also order through our website www.hoddereducation.co.uk.

British Library Cataloguing in Publication Data
A catalogue record for this title is available from the British Library

ISBN: 978 0340 959404

First Published 2008
Impression number   10 9 8 7 6
Year   2014 2013 2012

Copyright © 2008 Ian Harrison

Cover photo © Adam Gault/Digital Vision/Getty.
Typeset by Fakenham Photosetting Limited, Fakenham, Norfolk.
Illustration on page 7 by Oxford Designers and Illustrators Ltd.
Printed in Dubai for Hodder Education, an Hachette UK Company, 338 Euston Road, London NW1 3BH

CONTENTS

Introduction		v
Chapter 1	The balance sheet	1
Chapter 2	Profits	10
Chapter 3	The trading account	16
Chapter 4	The profit and loss account	26
Chapter 5	The final accounts	33
Chapter 6	Double-entry bookkeeping	42
Chapter 7	Books of prime entry	52
Chapter 8	The trial balance	65
Chapter 9	The ledger accounts in detail	85
Chapter 10	The two-column cash book	92
Chapter 11	The three-column cash book	103
Chapter 12	Bank reconciliations	110
Chapter 13	Control accounts	127
Chapter 14	Accruals and pre-payments	143
Chapter 15	Closing down the double-entry system	154
Chapter 16	Depreciation of fixed assets	175
Chapter 17	Bad debts and provision for doubtful debts	187
Chapter 18	The final accounts revisited	199
Chapter 19	Accounting concepts	209
Chapter 20	The final accounts of limited companies	216
Chapter 21	Accounting ratios	243
Chapter 22	Budgeting and budgetary control	264
Answers		273
Index		297

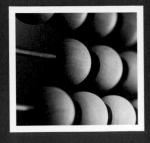

INTRODUCTION

The aim of this book is to explain the topics that you will encounter during your first year of studying accounting. It is designed to help you understand the topics that may be examined at AS level.

Each chapter contains a list of objectives that identify the key points covered. There are also references to the sections of the AQA and OCR specifications covered in each chapter.

Each time a new term is introduced it will appear in a definition box. Examination tips are provided as you work through the chapters. Each chapter will explain the topic then give worked examples of the type of questions that may be asked in the exam. You should cover the example answer with a sheet of paper before you attempt the question. If you cannot complete a question you can take a look at the answer and find how to proceed so that you can attempt the question again.

Practice questions appear throughout the text. The questions are graded so that you begin with simpler questions and build up to more complex questions as you progress through the chapter.

It is important in your study of accounting that you gain as much practice as possible. You will need to learn, by heart, layouts and definitions so do not be afraid to revisit topic areas that you may have forgotten. You may also find it useful to go over certain examples and questions more than once as practice.

At the end of most chapters there are self-test questions. Answers to these questions can be found by a thorough examination of the chapter.

The examination at AS level is of one-and-a-half hours' duration and there will be four questions on each paper. All questions are compulsory so it is important that you do not skip any topics.

'Accounting' is the term used to cover bookkeeping and accounting.

Bookkeeping records all the financial transactions undertaken during a period. This is necessary in order that the owner of a business can control how the business is performing. It also ensures the owner can provide:

■ records of the information required by HM Revenue and Customs for tax purposes and VAT returns
■ records required by the suppliers of additional finance.

Bookkeeping records the details of all:

■ expenditures incurred during the accounting period
■ incomes receivable during the accounting period
■ the profit (or loss) made during the period
■ amounts owed by debtors
■ amounts owed to creditors
■ the value of assets owned by the business and any changes in the values during the period
■ the value of liabilities owed by the business and any changes in the value during the period.

Accounting deals with the final presentation of the details gathered in the bookkeeping system.

■ It summarises the fine detail used.
■ It deals with the classification of the information and presents the information in such a way that it will be useful to any readers and users of the information.
■ It takes into account any standards laid down by the accounting bodies
■ It takes into account the legal requirements that must be adhered to.

Financial accounts are used by many groups of people, so it is important that the information shown in the accounts is:

■ Relevant – readers should be able to assess whether the business managers are using the resources at their disposal wisely. It is important that readers can also make informed economic decisions regarding the business.

- Reliable – the financial information should be free from bias; it should be free of errors and must be prepared prudently.
- Comparable – the use of appropriate accounting policies in the production and presentation of accounting information can identify similarities and differences that may account for differences in performance.
- Understandable – the information presented in the accounts should be able to be understood by a reader with 'reasonable' knowledge of business and accounting.

CHAPTER
ONE

The balance sheet

Most people who have read a newspaper or who have seen the news on television will have seen and heard the term 'balance sheet' at some time.

Some balance sheets are very complicated and need a great deal of experience and technical know-how to read and interpret. Do not let this put you off. Everything appears daunting when first encountered. The first time you rode a bicycle it was difficult. The first time that you tried to walk you did not succeed!

Like all areas of study, accounting has its own jargon. When a new word or term is introduced an explanation will be given in a box like this:

> **Assets** are resources that are owned by an organisation. They are used to help the organisation survive and function.

Assets used in a business could include premises, machinery, vehicles, computers, etc. Assets used in a rugby club might include the ground, lawnmowers, bar equipment, and so on.

> **Liabilities** represent the debts owed by an organisation.

The liabilities owed by a business could include a mortgage and money owed to the suppliers of goods and services. For example, the liabilities of a local garage may include money owed to the Ford Motor Company for spare parts, to the supplier of electricity, to the supplier of office stationery, and so on. The liabilities of the rugby club could include money owed to a local garage for repairs to the mowers, money owed to the brewery for supplies of beer and money owed to the ground staff for last week's work, and so on.

A balance sheet simply lists all the assets that are owned by the organisation and all the liabilities that are owed by the organisation. A balance sheet can be prepared for any type of organisation from a business to a squash club; you can even draw up your own personal balance sheet. The only difference between your personal balance sheet and that of Barclays Bank plc, for example, is the types of assets owned and the magnitude of the figures used.

From now on, we will make most of our references to businesses.

Self-test questions appear both throughout the chapter and at the end of each chapter. These questions are designed to test whether you have understood the new concepts that have been introduced in the text.

QUESTION 1

Which items from the following list are liabilities of Anne's Mini-Market?

- Stock
- Money owed to Kelloggs for the supply of breakfast cereals
- A van used for collecting goods from the local cash and carry
- An HP debt owed to Bent Finance Ltd for a van purchase
- Three freezer cabinets
- Six display units
- Money owed by the Crown Hotel for goods supplied by Anne

Specification coverage:
AQA Unit 1
OCR Unit 1

By the end of this chapter you should be able to:
- prepare a simple balance sheet
- calculate capital
- solve problems associated with the accounting equation.

> **Trade debtors** are people (or organisations) that owe money to a business, because they are customers that have not yet paid for the goods or services provided.

> **Trade creditors** are people (or organisations) which the business owes money to, because they have supplied goods and services that the business has received but as yet has not paid for.

Initially, you may get the terms 'debtors' and 'creditors' confused. Try to find a way of memorising which is which. In all subjects there are facts or concepts that have simply got to be learned and accounting is no different.

QUESTION 2

You owe your Mum £10. Is she a debtor or a creditor?
Your brother owes you £1. Is he a debtor or a creditor?

Balance sheets are presented in two main ways. At the moment we shall use what is known as the 'horizontal layout'. Later, we will use a 'vertical layout'.

The horizontal layout lists the assets of a business on the left of the page. It lists the liabilities opposite the assets on the right of the page.

EXAMPLE

A balance sheet for Anne's Mini-Market might look like this:

	£		£
Premises	45,000	Mortgage on premises	25,000
Shop fittings	18,000	Hire purchase owed on van	12,000
Van	16,000	Trade creditors	890
Stock	1,670		
Trade debtors	140		
Bank balance	900		

All balance sheets must 'balance'. This means that the assets must add to the same total as the liabilities.

It is fairly obvious that Anne's balance sheet, as shown above, does not balance.

To make it balance we need to insert a missing figure on the liabilities side. If we include £43,820 as a liability the two sides would add to the same total of £81,710.

What is this missing figure? What does it represent?

> **Capital** is the term used to describe how much a business is worth. It represents how much the owner(s) have invested in the business.

Anne's business is worth £43,820. The business has assets totalling £81,710 and the business debts amount to £37,890.

If Anne decided to stop trading she would sell her assets, settle her debts and take £43,820 out of the business, as this is the amount the business owes the owner. It is the amount invested in the business, by Anne, on the date the balance sheet was drawn up. This is Anne's capital.

Note: This assumes that the business assets could be sold for their balance sheet values. In reality the assets may be sold for more or less than their balance sheet values and we will consider this at a later stage in our studies.

WORKED EXAMPLE

If we include the capital figure that we previously calculated, Anne's balance sheet will 'balance' and will look like this:

	£		£
Premises	45,000	Mortgage on premises	25,000
Shop fittings	18,000	Hire purchase owed on van	12,000
Van	16,000	Trade creditors	890
Stock	1,670		
Trade debtors	140	**CAPITAL**	**43,820**
Bank balance	900		
	81,710		81,710

A balance sheet will always balance because the capital figure is always the 'missing figure'.

What does Anne's balance sheet show us?

- It shows us what Anne's business is worth.
- It shows us the resources (assets) that are in use in Anne's business.
- It shows us who has provided the funds to acquire those resources.
- It shows Anne's capital.

The funds that have financed the acquisition of the assets used in the business have been provided by:

- the business providing the finance for the hire purchase
- the bank or building society
- the creditors
- Anne.

Notice that capital is a liability. Initially this concept can be quite difficult to come to terms with. Capital is what the business owes the proprietor.

If you are unsure about the calculation of the capital figure (or that capital is a liability), imagine that Anne decided to close her business down. The business assets would be sold – they should fetch £81,710. This would be used to pay off the hire purchase debt (£12,000), the bank or building society (£25,000) and the creditors (£890). The cash left (£43,820) is what Anne would receive.

The **accounting equation** recognises that the assets owned by a business are always equal to the claims against the business.

One side of the equation shows in monetary terms the assets that are owned by an organisation. The other side of the equation shows how these resources have been financed with funds provided by the owner(s) and others.

Balance sheets are the formal way of showing the accounting equation.

Liquid is the term used to describe how easily an asset can be turned into cash.

Stock is more liquid than premises. Stock can be turned into cash much more quickly than premises (ask anyone who has tried to sell a house!).

Machinery is less liquid than debtors. It is generally easier to obtain money from debtors than it is to obtain money from selling surplus machinery.

Fixed assets will be used by the business for more than one year. Examples might include business premises, factory machinery and delivery vehicles.

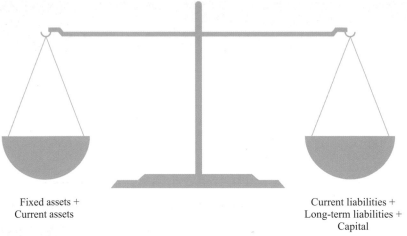

Fixed assets +	Current liabilities +
Current assets	Long-term liabilities +
	Capital

Figure 1.1 The accounting equation

Current assets are cash or assets that will be changed into cash within one year.

Examples might include stock, debtors, bank balances and cash in the till.

Assets are classified in balance sheets according to:

- how long they are likely to be used in the business
- how liquid they are.

Long-term liabilities are debts owed by a business that need to be paid after more than one year.

Examples might include a bank loan that needs to be repaid in four years' time. A 25-year mortgage would fall under this heading (except in its final year!).

Current liabilities are debts owed by a business that need to be repaid within one year.

Examples might include suppliers who are owed money for goods supplied (trade creditors) or money owed to a landlord for overdue rent.

In reality, many current liabilities need to be paid much more quickly – a supplier of goods is unlikely to allow a business 365 days before the debt is settled, for example.

Liabilities are classified according to the time allowed by the creditor to settle the debt.

THE ACCOUNTING EQUATION

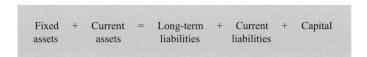

Fixed assets	+	Current assets	=	Long-term liabilities	+	Current liabilities	+	Capital

If we know four of the parts that make up the accounting equation, then we should be able to find out the missing one by completing the accounting equation.

QUESTION 3

Required Fill in the missing figures in the following table. Use the accounting equation to work out your answers.

Fixed assets £	Current assets £	Long-term liabilities £	Current liabilities £	Capital £
70,000	16,000	20,000	8,000	?
?	24,000	20,000	4,000	60,000
20,000	3,000	0	8,000	?
55,000	9,000	15,000	?	45,000
30,000	?	20,000	10,000	15,000

If we use the above asset classifications, the left side of Anne's balance sheet will look like this:

EXAMPLE

Fixed assets	£	Comment
Premises	45,000	Normally used for many years.
Shop fittings	18,000	Normally used for, say, 10 years.
Van	16,000	Normally in use for, say, 4 or 5 years.

Current assets	£	
Stock	1,670	Hopefully will become cash in the next few months.
Trade debtors	140	Hopefully will settle their debts within 30 days.
Bank balance	900	Almost as good as cash.

The order in which assets appear under their headings is known as the 'reverse order of liquidity'. This means that the most liquid of the assets appears last, while the least liquid appears first.

If we classify Anne's liabilities, the right side of her balance sheet would look like this:

Comment		£
Capital is normally the first item to appear.	Capital	43,820
	Long-term liabilities	
Mortgage is generally owed for a long time period, as also is money	Mortgage on premises	25,000
borrowed to purchase a vehicle. However, both of these would be	Hire purchase owed on van	12,000
classified as current liabilities in the final year of the debt.		
	Current liabilities	
Suppliers will normally expect payment within 30 days of the debt being incurred.	Trade creditors	890

Business transactions are normally recorded over a twelve-month period. This is known as the business's **financial year**. The process is then repeated for each subsequent year.

A business's financial year can start at any time during the calendar year. The financial year of a business may run from 1 February until the following 31 January; another business may have 1 October until the following 30 September as its financial year.

A balance sheet is prepared at one moment in time, usually at the end of the business's financial year. Anne's mini-market has a financial year end of 31 March. The balance sheet can only be prepared at one moment in time since some of its components will change on an hourly basis. Money will be going in and out of the bank account each day; stock will be sold and reordered regularly; Anne will be paying creditors on a regular basis, and so on.

The date shown in the heading for a balance sheet will reflect the fact that it is prepared at the end of one day. The heading will show the name of the business and the date when the balance sheet was prepared.

EXAMPLE

Here are some examples of headings that would appear on a balance sheet.

Angel's records
Balance sheet **at** 30 June 20**

Bill's Burger Bar
Balance sheet **at** 28 February 20**

Mrs Charlotte's Tea Room
Balance sheet **at** 31 October 20**

One final point to note before the two sides of the balance sheet are put together: assets are recorded on balance sheets at their **original cost**. This does initially cause a problem for some students of accounting. The reason for valuing assets at cost is quite simple – cost is the only **objective** valuation that can be applied to the assets that are owned.

Consider the van that Anne uses in her business. She paid £16,000 for it three years ago. She intends to use it for another two years. How can she determine the 'correct' value to include on her balance sheet?

She could take the van to her local garage for a valuation. Sounds simple but . . .

- the value placed on it would depend on whether it was a straight sale or a trade in
- if it was part of a trade in deal, the value would also change according to the selling price of the new vehicle
- another garage could give a better or worse allowance on Anne's three-year-old van.

Valuing assets can prove to be a minefield. The problem is solved by valuing all assets at cost.

We can now put the two sides of Anne's completed balance sheet together. It would look like this:

EXAMPLE

Anne's Mini-Market

Balance sheet at 31 March 20*8

	£	£		£	£
Fixed assets			**Capital**		43,820
Premises at cost		45,000			
Shop fittings at cost		18,000	**Long-term liabilities**		
Van at cost		16,000	Mortgage	25,000	
		79,000	Hire purchase debt	12,000	
Current assets					37,000
Stock	1,670		**Current liabilities**		
Trade debtors	140		Trade creditors		890
Bank balance	900				
		2,710			
		81,710			81,710

This layout is based on the accounting equation. In recent years there has been a move to present balance sheets in a vertical format. This simply means that the right-hand side of the accounting equation (the liabilities section) is shown under the left-hand side (the assets section).

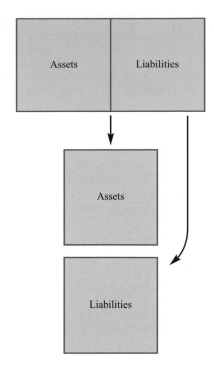

A useful analogy to remember when using the vertical format for a balance sheet is to think of the growth of a tree: there is the same amount of growth under the surface of the soil as there is above the surface and this is certainly the case with a balance sheet drawn up using the vertical layout.

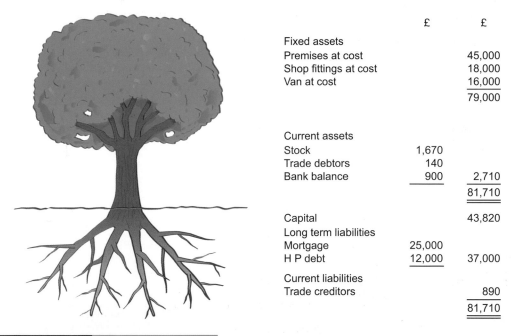

	£	£
Fixed assets		
Premises at cost		45,000
Shop fittings at cost		18,000
Van at cost		16,000
		79,000
Current assets		
Stock	1,670	
Trade debtors	140	
Bank balance	900	2,710
		81,710
Capital		43,820
Long term liabilities		
Mortgage	25,000	
H P debt	12,000	37,000
Current liabilities		
Trade creditors		890
		81,710

Chapter summary

- Balance sheets are prepared on one day.
- Balance sheets show the assets being used by a business on that day.
- Liabilities represent the indebtedness of the business to people or organisations outside the business on that day.
- Capital represents the indebtedness of the business to the owner of the business.
- The top part of a vertically presented balance sheet must total the same as the bottom part. They must always 'balance' because of the accounting equation.

SELF-TEST QUESTIONS

These questions are designed to test whether you have understood the new concepts that have been introduced in this chapter.

Answers can be found in the text.

- Define the term 'asset'.
- Explain why fixed assets are valued in a balance sheet at cost.
- What is meant by the term 'liability'?
- Give an example of a liability typically found in a retail shop selling DVDs.
- What is a debtor?
- What is a creditor?
- Why must a balance sheet always balance?
- What is the main difference between a fixed asset and a current asset?
- What is the main difference between a long-term liability and a current liability?
- Why is capital shown as a liability in a balance sheet?
- Could a business have a financial year end on 29 April?
- Could a business have a financial year which runs from 19 June until 30 May the following year?
- Would fixed assets appear in the top part of a vertically presented balance sheet?
- In which part of a vertically presented balance sheet would you expect to find trade debtors; machinery; a mortgage?

TEST QUESTIONS

QUESTION 4

Required Explain how one type of business can include a delivery van as a current asset on its balance sheet, and yet another type of business includes a similar delivery van as a fixed asset on its balance sheet.

QUESTION 5

Required Classify the following items into fixed assets and current assets for an electrical goods retailer:

	Fixed asset	Current asset
27 refrigerators for resale		
Delivery van		
Money owed by customers		
Money in till		
Display cabinets		

QUESTION 6

Required Classify the following items into fixed assets, current assets and current liabilities for a garage:

	Fixed asset	Current asset	Current liability
Electronic tuning equipment			
Money owed to BP plc			
Second-hand cars on forecourt			
Typewriters			
Breakdown vehicle			
Petrol			

QUESTION 7

Carole has the following assets and liabilities on 31 August 20*8:

Machinery at cost £120,000; vehicles at cost £70,000; stock £20,000; debtors £10,000; creditors £8,000; bank balance £2,000.

Required Calculate the amount of Carole's capital at 31 August 20*8.

QUESTION 8

Atul has the following assets and liabilities on 31 December 20*8:

Premises at cost £60,000; equipment at cost £25,000; stock £5,000; debtors £4,000; creditors £8,000; money owed to the bank £6,000.

Required Calculate the amount of Atul's capital at 31 December 20*8.

QUESTION 9

The following information is provided by Sandeep, a painter and decorator, at 31 January 20*8:

Capital £4,300; vehicle at cost £8,000; tools at cost £250, bank loan repayable in four years' time £4,000; stocks of paint £110; money owed to suppliers of paint £60.

Required Prepare the balance sheet at 31 January 20*8. Use a horizontal layout. Classify all assets and liabilities.

QUESTION 10

Archie, a newsagent, provides the following information at 30 September 20*8:

Capital £45,300; premises at cost £73,000; mortgage on premises £48,000; shop fittings at cost £14,000; vehicle at cost £3,000; stock £4,500; debtors £300; creditors £900; bank overdraft £600.

Required Prepare the balance sheet at 30 September 20*8. Use a horizontal layout. Classify all assets and liabilities.

QUESTION 11

Sandra has provided you with the following information which relates to her business at 31 March 20*8:

Premises at cost £40,000; machinery at cost £10,000; office equipment at cost £4,000; vehicle at cost £9,000; long-term bank loan £18,000; stock £4,000; debtors £1,200; creditors £500; bank balance £800. She is unable to tell you what her capital is currently.

Required Prepare the balance sheet at 31 March 20*8. Use a vertical layout.

QUESTION 12

Andrew is a door-to-door salesman selling cosmetics. He gives you the following information:

Car at cost £12,400; bank overdraft £1,800; stock £240; debtors £180; creditors £400.

Required Prepare Andrew's balance sheet at 29 February 20*8.Use a vertical layout.

QUESTION 13

Your Uncle Jack has recently had his balance sheet prepared by his accountant.

He cannot understand why his capital account is shown as a liability and asks you whether his accountant has got this wrong.

Required Explain to Uncle Jack whether the accountant is correct in showing the capital account as a liability.

QUESTION 14

Required Explain the circumstances that could result in a mortgage being shown as a current liability.

CHAPTER
TWO

Profits

The owners of a business are interested in what their business is worth. As we have seen, this can be determined by preparing a balance sheet or by using the accounting equation.

By the end of this chapter you should be able to:
- calculate the profit or loss made by a business using the net asset approach
- identify retained profits
- explain the terms 'drawings' and 'capital introduced'.

QUESTION 1

Required Explain if the owner of a business could prepare a balance sheet on 9 December, or 23 June, or today.

QUESTION 2

Required Explain what the * represents in the accounting equation.

Assets * Liabilities = Capital

Not only are the owners of a business interested in what their business is worth, they are also interested in how much their business is earning for them. They are interested in the *profitability* of their business.

We cannot tell whether a business is profitable by analysing a balance sheet. After all, it can only tell us what the business has in the way of assets and liabilities at one particular time. It may help to think of a balance sheet as being rather like a photograph—it only captures the moment when the balance sheet was prepared.

However, over a financial year it is likely that a balance sheet will change. Assets may increase or decrease. Liabilities may increase or decrease. These changes will take place due to business activity.

Profit is the excess of income over expenditure. A **loss** occurs when expenditure exceeds income.

If a business is profitable, one would expect that the assets owned by the business would increase, unless the owner of the business takes more cash and/or goods from the business than the profits warrant. If a business is unprofitable then one would expect that the business assets would decrease.

EXAMPLE

A business woman purchases goods costing £100 and incurs no other expenses. She sells these goods for £250. The profit earned is £150. Unless the woman withdraws some of that profit, the business assets must increase by £150

If you do not spend all your allowance and/or the wage you earn from your part-time job, your assets will increase. Imagine that you earn £2,400 over a year and you spend only £2,000. What happens to the difference? Your assets will show an increase of £400. The cash that you have will have increased by £400 or your savings account may have increased.

Net assets of a business are all assets less all liabilities, or:
fixed assets + current assets – (long-term liabilities + current liabilities), or:
net assets = **capital** (check this by referring to the accounting equation).

Profits increase the net assets of a business unless they are taken from the business by the owner.

The converse is also true. That is, if there is an increase in the net assets then this must be due to the business being profitable.

The only exception to this rule would be if extra assets were introduced into the business from outside, or if liabilities were paid off by money from outside the business. An example of this would be if the owner of the business injected more money into the business, or if more assets were introduced into the business from another source.

How can we calculate the profits?

WORKED EXAMPLE

Barker Dog Foods has the following assets and liabilities at 1 January 20*8:

fixed assets at cost £270,000; current assets £21,000; trade creditors £5,000.

One year later on 1 January 20*9, the business has the following assets and liabilities:

fixed assets at cost £290,000; current assets £27,000; trade creditors £8,000.

During the year there were no withdrawals or injections of money or assets by the owner.

Required   Calculate the profit earned by Barker Dog Foods for the year ended 31 December 20*8.

Answer   £

Barker Dog Foods net assets at 1 January 20*8	Fixed assets	270,000
	Current assets	21,000
		291,000
	less current liabilities	5,000
	Net assets (capital)	286,000
Barker Dog Foods net assets at 1 January 20*9	Fixed assets	290,000
	Current assets	27,000
		317,000
	less current liabilities	8,000
	Net assets (capital)	309,000

The net assets (capital) of the business have increased by £23,000 (£309,000 – £286,000) during the year. This is the profit that Barker Dog Foods has made during the year. It has to be profit since we were told that no money or assets had been introduced or withdrawn during the year.

Retained profits are profits that are kept in a business for expansion purposes. They increase the net assets of a business. They are sometimes said to be **'ploughed back'**.

Drawings is the term used to describe the withdrawal of resources (cash or goods) from the business by the proprietor for private use outside the business.

It is unrealistic to think that money or assets would not be injected into a business if this was necessary to safeguard the business or in order to expand the business.

It is also unrealistic to imagine that the owner of a business would not withdraw some cash from the business in order to pay for various items of private household expenditure during the year. This cash taken from the business is drawings.

It is also unrealistic to imagine that Brenda, who owns a garage, would send her car to another garage for servicing or for repairs. The value of servicing or repairing Brenda's car is drawings.

Any cash or goods taken from a business by the proprietor for private use are in fact withdrawals of profits!

In order to calculate business profits it is important that we only consider transactions that involve the business.

- Money won on the National Lottery and paid into the business bank account should not be included in any calculations to determine profits.
- Cash taken from the business and used to buy the week's groceries should not be used in a calculation of profits.
- A cheque for £2,300 drawn on the business bank account to pay for the family holiday is not part of the calculation.

WORKED EXAMPLE

Cora has been in business for a number of years. At 1 March 20*7 her business assets and liabilities were as follows:

fixed assets at cost £40,000; current assets £10,000; current liabilities £5,000.

One year later, on 28 February 20*8, her business assets and liabilities were:

fixed assets £45,000; current assets £9,000; current liabilities £6,000.

During the year she withdrew from the business cash of £14,500 for private use.

Required Calculate Cora's business profits for the year ended 29 February 20*8.

Answer

	£
Cora's net assets at 1 March 20*7 (£40,000 + £10,000 − £5,000)	45,000
Cora's net assets at 29 February 20*8	48,000
Increase in net assets over the year (*profits ploughed back into the business*)	3,000

	£
Increase in net assets over the year	3,000
Drawings (*profits withdrawn during the year*)	14,500
Business profit earned during the year	17,500

WORKED EXAMPLE

Chang had business net assets on 1 August 20*7 of £16,000. On 31 July 20*8 his business net assets stood at £45,000. During the year his Uncle George died and left Chang £20,000. The legacy was paid into the business bank account.

Required Calculate the profit that Chang's business made for the year ended 31 July 20*8.

Answer

	£
Chang's net assets at 1 August 20*7	16,000
Chang's net assets at 31 July 20*8	45,000
Increase in net assets over the year	29,000

Some of the increase in net assets is due to Uncle George's legacy. This has to be disregarded if we wish to determine the profits generated by the business, so:

	£
Increase in net assets over the year	29,000
Less capital introduced	20,000
Business profit earned during the year	9,000

WORKED EXAMPLE

Marc has been in business for a number of years. On 1 February 20*7 his capital account stood at £30,500. At 31 January 20*8 his business balance sheet showed the following:

WORKED EXAMPLE *continued*

fixed assets at cost £45,000; current assets £18,000; long-term liability £20,000; current liabilities £7000.

During the year he paid into the business bank account a National Lottery win of £10,000. His drawings for the year amounted to £21,000.

Required Calculate the profit or loss made by the business for the year ended 31 January 20*8.

Answer

	£
Marc's net assets (capital) at 1 February 20*7	30,500
Marc's net assets (capital) at 31 January 20*8	36,000
Increase in net assets over the year	5,500
Add drawings	21,000
	26,500
Less capital introduced	10,000
Business profit for the year ended 31 January 20*8	16,500

WORKED EXAMPLE

Helen's balance sheet at 1 May 20*7 showed:

fixed assets at cost £16,000; current assets £4,000; current liabilities £3,500; capital £16,500.

On 30 April 20*8 her balance sheet showed fixed assets £30,000; current assets £5,000; current liabilities £6,000; long-term liability £20,000.

During the year Helen paid into the business bank account a legacy of £18,000. Her drawings for the year amounted to £14,000.

Required Calculate the profit or loss made by Helen's business for the year ended 30 April 20*8.

Answer

	£	
Helen's net assets at 1 May 20*7	16,500	
Helen's net assets at 31 April 20*8	9,000	
Decrease in net assets over the year	(7,500)	Negative numbers
Add drawings for the year	14,000	are often shown
	6,500	in brackets.
Less capital introduced	18,000	
Loss made by Helen's business during the year	(11,500)	

Chapter summary

- Profit can be calculated quickly and accurately by comparing net assets held by a business at the end of a financial year with net assets held at the start of the year.
- The profit calculated is an accurate figure, provided that the values placed on assets and liabilities are accurate.
- Adjustments to the change shown have to be made by adding back drawings and eliminating any capital introduced during the year.

SELF-TEST QUESTIONS

- Define the term 'profits'.
- Define the term 'loss'.
- Explain what is meant by the term 'net assets'
- What is the connection between capital and net assets?
- Fixed assets £7,000; current assets £3,000; current liabilities £2,000. Calculate net assets.
- Fixed assets £100,000; current assets £20, 000; long-term liabilities £40,000; current liabilities £9,000. Calculate capital.
- What is meant by the term 'drawings'?
- Give an example of drawings that the proprietor of an electrical goods store could make.
- Is it possible to make drawings that exceed the profit earned in a year?
- Explain what is meant by 'capital introduced'.

TEST QUESTIONS

QUESTION 3
Ben runs a general store. Which of the following items are drawings?
- Money taken from till to pay staff.
- Money taken from till to buy Ben's wife a bunch of flowers for her birthday.
- Money taken from till to purchase stamps to send out bills.
- Crisps taken from shop for children's lunch box.
- Vegetables taken from shop for evening meal.

QUESTION 4
A business shows an increase in its net assets over the year of £12,300. During the year the proprietor made drawings to the value of £16,000.

Required Calculate the profit made during the year by the business.

QUESTION 5
A business's net assets reduced by £3,500 during the year. The proprietor's drawings amounted to £8,900.

Required Calculate the profit or loss made by the business during the year.

QUESTION 6
A business shows an increase in its net assets over the year of £35,000. During the year the proprietor paid an inheritance of £25,000 into the business bank account.

Required Calculate the profit or loss made by the business during the year.

QUESTION 7
A proprietor's capital account increased over the year by £12,700. She paid a £50,000 premium bond win into the business bank account during the year.

Required Calculate the profit or loss made by the business during the year.

QUESTION 8
Over a year the capital account shown in a business balance sheet has increased by £17,800. During the year the proprietor paid a legacy of £4,000 into the business bank account. His drawings for the year amounted to £19,500.

Required Calculate the profit or loss made by the business during the year.

QUESTION 9
The net assets of a business have increased over the year by £2,750. The proprietor paid into the business bank account £35,000, withdrawn from her personal building society account. During the year she withdrew £14,000 from the business for personal expenses.

Required Calculate the profit or loss made by the business during the year.

QUESTION 10

On 1 February 20*7 the net assets of Becky's business were £83,000. During the year ended 31 January 20*8 she withdrew £18,000 for her private use. She also paid into the business bank account a premium bond win of £20,000. At 31 January 20*8 the net assets of Becky's business amounted to £79,000.

Required Calculate the profit or loss made by Becky's business for the year ended 31 January 20*8.

QUESTION 11

On 1 November 20*7 the business assets of Charles were as follows:

Fixed assets £42,000; current assets £17,000, current liabilities £14,000.

A year later, on 31 October 20*8, the fixed assets of the business were £56,000; the current assets were £20,000; and the current liabilities were £15,000. In addition, the business had a long-term bank loan of £10,000 which is due to be repaid in 2023.

During the year ended 31 October 20*8, Charles paid a legacy of £12,000 into the business bank account. His personal drawings for the year amounted to £14,000.

Required Calculate the profit or loss made by Charles' business for the year ended 31 October 20*8.

QUESTION 12

The following information relates to Boogies Boutique:

	At 1 January 20*8 £	At 31 December 20*8 £
Fixed assets	70,000	72,000
Current assets	26,000	27,000
Long-term liability	–	20,000
Current liabilities	18,000	23,000

During the year ended 31 December 20*8, the proprietor of Boogies Boutique introduced a further £9,500 from a private source. She also withdrew £16,500 for personal expenditure.

Required Calculate the profit or loss for the year ended 31 December 20*8.

CHAPTER
THREE

The trading account

We have seen that we can calculate the profit or loss for a business over a period of time (usually a financial year), provided that we know:

- the net assets of the business at the start and
- the net assets of the business at the end of the time period in question.

Profits are generally calculated over a financial year but they can be calculated for any time period. We could calculate the profits earned by a business for a week or a month, for two months or 73 days if we wished to.

Many business owners calculate their profits half-way through the year as well as at their financial year-end in order to plot the progress of their business.

QUESTION 1

Required Fill in the gaps:

Net assets of a business is the same as the owner's ....; both show how much the business is ....

> **Final accounts** are the trading account, the profit and loss account and balance sheet of a business. (Technically, the balance sheet is not an account as you will discover later.)

The final accounts are usually produced at the financial year-end, but they could be produced at any time they might be required by the owner or managers of a business.

> A **trading account** is a statement that calculates the **gross profit** that a business has made by buying and selling its goods during a particular period of time.

> **Gross profit** is sales less the cost of those same sales

Although the net asset method of calculating the net profit of a business does calculate the net profit **easily** and **accurately**, it does have a major drawback. It does not give us any details of how the profit (or loss) was arrived at.

The details of how a profit has been earned or why a loss has been incurred are important to both the owner and any external providers of finance because:

- the owner will probably wish to make greater profits in the future
- lenders will wish to see that their investment is safe and that any interest due or repayments due will be able to be met by the business.

> **Revenue expenditure** is spending on everyday expenses.

> **Capital expenditure** is spending on fixed assets or the improvement of fixed assets.

Specification coverage:
AQA Unit 1
OCR Unit 1

By the end of this chapter you should be able to:
- prepare a trading account
- distinguish between capital and revenue expenditure
- distinguish between capital and revenue receipts
- calculate cost of sales
- determine gross profit
- incorporate returns and payments for carriage into a trading account.

> **Revenue receipts** are incomes derived from the 'usual' activites of the business.

> **Capital receipts** are derived from transactions that are not the usual activities of the business.

QUESTION 2

Required Place an x in the column which classifies the following receipts and payments made by Bloggs' Garage.

	Revenue expenditure	Capital expenditure	Revenue receipt	Capital receipt
Loan of money from the bank				
Sale of breakdown truck				
Petrol sales				
Assistant's wages				
Purchase of hydraulic jack				

Profits can be calculated by using the 'net asset method'. This method of discovering profit is like a forensic archaeologist discovering a skeleton. We are unable to see the details of how the profit was arrived at just as the archaeologist cannot determine whether the person was fat or thin or whether they were beautiful or plain from looking at their skeleton.

We need to put some flesh on our skeleton. We need to put some detail into our profit calculations.

The details of how profits are arrived at are shown in two statements:

- the trading account and
- the profit and loss account.

Both of these statements are fairly easy to understand.

THE TRADING ACCOUNT

The trading account shows how much it cost to buy the goods and how much they were sold for. The goods in question are the goods that the business buys and sells in its everyday activities.

The goods bought for resale are called 'purchases'.

The goods that are sold are called 'sales'.

QUESTION 3

A clothes shop buys the following items:

- jeans
- sweatshirts
- trainers
- a delivery van
- leather jackets.

Required Identify the items that are purchases.

QUESTION 4

A general store sells the following items:

- apples
- magazines
- a freezer cabinet that is no longer required

- fish fingers
- caramel toffees.

Required Identify the items that are sales.

A simple trading account compares the purchases and sales for a financial period. The difference between the two is the gross profit earned for the period.

The trading account is generally prepared to show the gross profit earned for a financial year. However, a trading account could be prepared for a week, a month, two months or 123 days.

EXAMPLE

Here are some examples of trading account headings.

Brian Bains
Trading account **for the year ended** 31 December 20*8

Brenda Binks
Trading account **for the three months ended** 30 June 20*8

Boris Bruker
Trading account **for the half year ended** 31 July 20*8

All the headings are for a period of time. The balance sheets we prepared earlier were prepared at **one moment** in time.

WORKED EXAMPLE

Betty owns a business selling magazines and books. She is able to give you the following information relating to her business for the year ended 31 December 20*8:

	£
Purchases of magazines and books	32,500
Purchase of cash register	840
Sales of magazines and books	65,800
Sales of shop fittings	1,200

Required Prepare the trading account for the year ended 31 December 20*8.

Answer
Trading account for the year ended 31 December 20*8:

	£
Sales	65,800
Less purchases	32,500
Gross profit	33,300

Notes
- The figures included in the trading account are figures for a year (the heading tells us this).
- The purchase of the cash register has not been included – it is capital expenditure.
- The sale of shop fittings has not been included – it is a capital receipt.
- Purchases are revenue expenditure. They are part of the everyday costs associated with running Betty's business.
- Sales are revenue receipts. These receipts are from Betty's normal trading activities.
- The gross profit is found by deducting the value of purchases from the value of the sales.

The trading account is prepared by using purchases and sales, which are examples of revenue expenditure and revenue receipts.

> **Stock** (or **stock in trade**) is the term applied to goods bought for resale, which have not been disposed of during the financial year. Like fixed assets, it is valued at cost price (but see Chapter 15).

The preparation of a trading account is so simple, there has to be a complication! There always is!

As you can appreciate, very few businesses sell all the goods that they purchase each day. At the end of every day there will be goods left on the shelves, in the display cabinets and in the stock room.

Generally, there will be stock left unsold at the end of any financial year. The last millisecond of the last day of the financial year is (almost) the same time as the first millisecond of the new financial year.

So, the stock value at the end of one financial year is the stock value at the start of the following financial year.

The stock held by a business at 31 May 20*8 is the stock held on 1 June 20*8.

Stock at 30 November 20*8 is stock at 1 December 20*8.

The stocks held at the start of a financial year are sometimes referred to as 'opening stock'. The stocks held one year later at the end of the financial year are sometimes referred to as 'closing stock'.

What effect will opening and closing stock values have on a trading account?

We need to calculate the value of the goods that have been sold during the year.

> **Cost of sales** is deducted from net sales to calculate the gross profit earned by a business.
> Cost of sales = opening stock + purchases − closing stock

I am on a diet! My wife (she never eats bread) is counting the number of slices of bread that I eat during the day. How does she find out how many slices I have eaten today? She knows that there were 8 slices in the bread bin this morning. I bought a loaf (only 14 slices) this afternoon and there are now 13 slices left.

How many slices have I eaten?

Answer: Too many for my diet! Actually, only 9 slices.

If you calculated my bread consumption accurately then the trading account should pose no problems for you.

Opening stock of bread	8 slices	
Purchases of bread	<u>14 slices</u>	
I could have eaten	22 slices	
However, there were	<u>13 slices</u>	left
So, I must have eaten	9 slices	

WORKED EXAMPLE

Becky has a market stall selling jeans. She provides the following information:

Stock of jeans at 1 September 20*7: £345
Purchases of jeans for the year ended 31 August 20*8: £18,450
Sales of jeans for the year ended 31 August 20*8: £42,750
Stock of jeans at 31 August 20*8: £400

Required Prepare the trading account for the year ended 31 August 20*8

Answer
We first have to find the value of the jeans that Becky sold during the year. We do this by applying the technique that was used to find how many slices of bread I ate today.

	£	
Becky started the year with	345	worth of jeans
She bought a further	18,450	worth of jeans
So she could have sold	18,795	worth ... but she didn't ... she had some left.
She had	400	worth left.
So she must have sold	18,395	worth of jeans.

How much did she sell these jeans for? The answer is £42,750. Her gross profit for the year was £24,355.

Talk yourself through this example a few times. It is important that you understand the process which you have gone through.

The actual trading account should be presented like this

Becky
Trading account for the year ended 31 August 20*8

	£	£
Sales		42,750
Less cost of sales		
Stock 1 September 20*7	345	
Purchases	18,450	
	18,795	
Less stock 31 August 20*8	400	18,395
Gross profit		24,355

The description for £18,395 is 'cost of sales'. This is the value of the jeans that Becky sold during the year at cost price. The figure is the monetary value of the jeans sold at the price she paid for them. £42,750 is the monetary value of the SAME jeans at the price that the customers paid.

Notice the use of two columns. At first you may find this confusing. All that it does is to remove the calculation of the cost of sales out of the second column. After a few times using this technique you will see that it makes the calculation of gross profit much clearer.

QUESTION 5

The following information relates to the business of Biddulph, for the year ended 31 March 20*8:

Stock at 1 April 20*7 £4,560; stock at 31 March 20*8 £5,050; purchases for the year £47,800; sales for the year £84,350.

Required Prepare the trading account for the year ended 31 March 20*8.

QUESTION 6

Julie owns a small retail grocery store. She provides the following data:

purchase of goods for resale £49,000; purchase of delivery van £14,500; stock at 30 June 20*8 £890; stock at 1 July 20*7 £930; sale of unused shop fittings £320; sales of groceries £81,000.

Required Select the appropriate information and prepare a trading account for the year ended 30 June 20*8.

Note: You should not have included the purchase of the delivery van in your trading account, because it is capital expenditure. You should not have included the sale of unused shop fittings in your trading account because it is a capital receipt.

QUESTION 7

Clary provides the following information for the year ended 30 April 20*8:

stock 1 May 20*7 £340; stock 30 April 20*8 £530; purchases £23,560; sales £52,900.

Required Prepare a trading account for the year ended 30 April 20*8.

QUESTION 8

Eddie provides the following information for the year ended 31 July 20*8:

stock 1 August 20*7 £12,907; stock 31 July 20*8 £10,987; purchases £143,673; sales £243,561.

Required Prepare a trading account for the year ended 31 July 20*8.

QUESTION 9

Joe provides the following information for the year ended 31 December 20*8:

stock 1 January 20*8 £238; stock 31 December 20*8 £432; purchases £34,930; sales £54,760.

Required Prepare a trading account for the year ended 31 December 20*8.

The next step in the preparation of trading accounts is the one that seems to cause students a lot of headaches.

> **Sales returns** are goods that have been returned by the customer. They are also known as **returns in** or **returns inwards**.

> **Purchase returns** are goods that the business sends back to the supplier. They are also known as **returns out** or **returns outwards**.

Even in businesses that are extremely well run, some goods are returned by customers. The way that these sales returns are treated in the trading account seems fairly obvious: the total of sales returns is deducted from the total sales for the year.

No matter how good and how careful suppliers are, there will inevitably be occasions when a business has to return goods. Again, our treatment of any purchase returns seems fairly obvious: the total of purchase returns is deducted from the total purchases for the year.

WORKED EXAMPLE

The following information relates to the business of Bunty:

stock at 1 September 20*7 £1,200; stock at 31 August 20*8 £1,500; purchases £48,000; sales £72,380; returns inwards £180; returns outwards £360.

Required Prepare the trading account for the year ended 31 August 20*8.

Answer

Bunty
Trading account for the year ended 31 August 20*8

	£	£	£
Sales			72,380
Less returns inwards			180
			72,200
Less cost of sales			
Stock 1 Sept 20*7		1,200	
Purchases	48,000		
Less returns outwards	360	47,640	
		48,840	
Stock 31 Aug 20*8		1,500	47,340
Gross profit			24,860

Once again notice the way that the calculation to find the 'net' purchases figure has been set back from the second column. Accountants often use 'extra' columns so that the main column does not get too cluttered. You will soon get the hang of this.

QUESTION 10

The following information relates to the year ended 30 April 20*8 for the business of Sahera Patel:

stock at 1 May 20*7 £1,435; stock at 30 April 20*8 £1,265; purchases £34,328; sales £72,548; returns inwards £459; returns outwards £671.

Required Prepare the trading account for the year ended 30 April 20*8.

QUESTION 11

The following information relates to the year ended 30 November 20*8 for the business of Rob Berry:

stock at 1 December 20*7 £1,657; stock at 30 November 20*8 £2,004; purchases £54,672; sales £98,651; returns inwards £421; returns outwards £803.

Required Prepare the trading account for the year ended 30 November 20*8.

QUESTION 12

Kim Reddy provides the following information for the year ended 29 February 20*8:

stock at 1 March 20*7 £502; stock at 29 February 20*8 £677; purchases £85,207; sales £137,503; returns inwards £506; returns outwards £109.

Required Prepare the trading account for the year ended 29 February 20*8.

> **Carriage inwards** is a cost incurred when a supplier charges for delivery on the goods purchased.

> **Carriage outwards** *is an expense* which a business incurs when it pays for delivery of goods to a customer. It is sometimes referred to as **carriage on sales**.

Carriage inwards makes the goods that are purchased more expensive. It is added to the goods that appear as purchases on the trading account.

Carriage outwards is an expense that will be dealt with in Chapter 4.

WORKED EXAMPLE

The following figures relate to the business of Benji, who owns a hardware business:

stock at 1 October 20*7 £5,300; stock at 30 September 20*8 £4,900; purchases for the year £124,600; sales for the year £314,000; returns inwards for the year £930; returns outwards for the year £2,100; carriage inwards for the year £1,750.

Required Prepare the trading account for the year ended 30 September 20*8.

Answer

Benji
Trading account for the year ended 30 September 20*8

	£	£	£
Sales			314,000
Less returns inwards			930
			313,070
Less cost of sales			
Stock 1 Oct 20*7		5,300	
Purchases	124,600		
Less returns outwards	2,100		
	122,500		
Carriage inwards	1,750	124,250	
		129,550	
Stock 30 Sept 20*8		4,900	124,650
Gross profit			188,420

This example shows the most complicated form that a trading account can take. To make a more difficult example you could only be asked to manipulate larger numbers!

Notice once more the use of the three columns. This has enabled us to get one figure for the total cost of net purchases (£124,250) without lots of calculations in the main column.

When you attempt the test questions that follow you may have to refer to Benji's trading account to get a good layout. Don't worry about this. You will soon start to remember where to enter the various items.

Chapter summary

- The trading account is used to calculate gross profit by deducting the sales at cost price from the sales figure.
- Returns inwards are deducted from sales to find the net sales.
- Returns outwards are deducted from purchases to find the net purchases figure.
- Carriage inwards is a cost that makes purchases more expensive.
- Carriage outwards is also an expense but is not used in the trading account.

SELF-TEST QUESTIONS

- What is meant by the term 'final accounts'?
- Which statement would you prepare to calculate the capital of a business?
- Give two reasons why the owner of a business would prepare final accounts.
- Which statement would you prepare to calculate gross profit?
- Explain what is meant by the term 'revenue expenditure'.
- Give an example of a revenue receipt for a Chinese takeaway.
- Which statement would you prepare to calculate net assets?
- Explain what is meant by the term 'capital receipts'.
- Give an example of capital expenditure for a plumber.
- Which is the only statement prepared in the final accounts of a business that contains capital expenditure?

TEST QUESTIONS

QUESTION 13

Required Match the titles and the dates:

Trading account   at 30 June 20*8
Balance sheet   for the year ended 30 April 20*8

QUESTION 14

Required State whether the following headings are correct:

Balance sheet for the month ended 31 March 20*8	Yes/No
Trading account for the year ended 30 April 20*8	Yes/No
Balance sheet at 31 May 20*8	Yes/No
Trading account at 30 June 20*8	Yes/No

QUESTION 15

Required Complete the equations:

Sales – cost of sales = ?
£230,000 – £120,000 = ?

QUESTION 16

Required Complete the equations:

Cost of sales + gross profit = ?
£67,000 + £56,000 = ?

QUESTION 17

Required State which of the following could be found in a trading account:

- capital expenditure
- returns inwards
- carriage inwards
- opening stock.

QUESTION 18

Required State which of the following items could be found in a trading account:

- capital receipts
- returns outwards
- carriage outwards
- closing stock.

QUESTION 19

Required State how the value of goods available for sale is calculated.

QUESTION 20

Required State what is meant by cost of sales.

QUESTION 21

The following information is given for the year ended 30 June 20*8 for Trevor:

stock at 1 July 20*7 £256; stock at 30 June 20*8 £641; purchases £71,006; sales £108,975.

Required Calculate the value of goods available for sale for the year ended 30 June 20*8.

QUESTION 22

The following information relates to the year ended 29 February 20*8 for Rodney:

stock at 1 March 20*7 £230; stock at 29 February 20*8 £380; purchases £24,600; sales £39,400.

Required Prepare a trading account for the year ended 29 February 20*8.

QUESTION 23

The following information is given for the year ended 31 January 20*8 for Del:

stock at 1 February 20*7 £970; stock at 31 January 20*8 £1,050; purchases £35,780; sales £56,710.

Required Prepare a trading account for the year ended 31 January 20*8.

QUESTION 24

The following information relates to the year ended 31 March 20*8 for Belinda's business:

stock at 1 April 20*7 £6,500; stock at 31 March 20*8 £5,850; purchases £266,000; sales £412,000; purchase returns £470; sales returns £990; carriage inwards for the year £430; carriage outwards for the year £1,670.

Required Prepare a trading account for the year ended 31 March 20*8.

QUESTION 25

The following information relates to the year ended 31 January 20*8 for Natalie:

stock at 1 February 20*7 £1,560; stock at 31 January 20*8 £1,640; purchases £65,090; sales £176,040; returns inwards £360; carriage inwards £960; returns outwards £770; carriage outwards £430.

Required Prepare a trading account for the year ended 31 January 20*8.

QUESTION 26

The following information is given for the year ended 31 October 20*8 for Elsie:

stock at 1 November 20*7 £1,234; stock at 31 October 20*8 £1,357; purchases £48,961; sales £88,552; returns inwards £508; returns outwards £469; carriage inwards £48; carriage outwards £1,486.

Required Prepare a trading account for the year ended 31 October 20*8.

QUESTION 27

The following information is given for the year ended 31 December 20*8 for Mao:

stock at 1 January 20*8 £12,651; stock at 31 December 20*8 £11,537; purchases £175,873; sales £342,960; returns inwards £4,532; returns outwards £1,364; carriage inwards £733.

Required Prepare a trading account for the year ended 31 December 20*8.

QUESTION 28

The following information is available for the year ended 30 June 20*8 for Jay:

stock at 1 July 20*7 £12,641; stock at 30 June 20*8 £10,673; purchases £132,785; sales £410,006; purchase of office equipment £3,450; returns inwards £421; returns outwards £650; carriage inwards £48; carriage outwards £769.

Required Prepare a trading account for the year ended 30 June 20*8.

FOUR

The profit and loss account

A person who is in business will endeavour to generate profits. She will use some of those profits in order to pay for her housekeeping, holidays, hobbies and so on. She may 'plough back' some of the profits to make the business more efficient so that greater profits may be generated in the future.

You may use all your allowance or wage from a part-time job to buy DVDs, CDs, computer games or to download singles or albums to your iPod, or you may spend it on other everyday living costs.

But remember that sometimes things do not work out for the owner of a business and the business may actually run at a loss.

If your weekly income does not cover your weekly expenditure what do you do? You draw some money from your savings (if you have any) or you may borrow sufficient money to tide you over until your income is sufficient to cover your spending.

The same principle applies to someone in business. If the business is unprofitable, the owner may have to live off her savings or borrow money to help the business to survive.

We have just seen how to calculate the gross profit of a trading business. Put simply, the gross profit is the difference between the cost of goods sold by a business and the amount which the goods have been sold for. Clearly there are expenses that have to be paid out of this gross profit in order that the firm can continue in business.

> **Net profit** is calculated by deducting revenue expenditure incurred by the business from the gross profit that it has earned through buying and selling its goods.

Specification coverage:
AQA Unit 1
OCR Unit 1 and Unit 2

By the end of this chapter you should be able to:
- prepare a profit and loss account
- calculate net profit
- understand the different purposes for which accounts are prepared
- incorporate carriage outwards into the profit and loss account.

Denise buys 1,000 CDs for £4,000 and she sells them all for £6,990. She has made a gross profit of £2,990 on the sale. However, she will have incurred some expenses in selling the CDs. Can you list some expenses that Denise might have incurred?

Your answer could have included:

rent of a market stall; transport costs to get the CDs to the stall; wages of any sales assistants; wrapping materials, etc.

When all other expenses incurred in the sales have been taken into account the result is net profit.

If Denise ran the stall for a month and paid the following expenses:

- local council £400 for rent of the stall
- wages to her assistant £880
- wrapping materials £34
- electricity for lighting and heating £161

her net profit for the month would be £1,515.
Gross profit £2,990 – expenses £1,475
                (400 + 880 + 34 + 161)

> **A profit and loss account** is a statement that calculates the net profit that a business has made for a period of time (usually a financial year).

A profit and loss account details the incomes and expenditure incurred by the business during a particular period of time.

Why do we need to prepare a trading account and a profit and loss account? We have seen that we can calculate profits accurately and fairly quickly by comparing the net assets of a business at the beginning of a time period with the net assets at the end of the period.

As we explained earlier, calculating profit using the net asset method is like the archaeologist finding a skeleton. Managers or owners of a business generally need to know more than just the net profit figure in isolation.

> The **stewardship function** of accounting. Final accounts are produced to show the providers of finance that their funds are being used wisely by the managers or owner of the business in question.

The managers or owner of a business often use other people's money (from banks, building societies, relatives, etc.) to help provide some of the finance necessary to enable the business to operate.

A bank manager would not be able to say whether a profit of £12,765 would give him confidence that the money provided by his bank is secure and being used wisely. The profit figure in isolation does not show how the gross profit of the business is being used. It does not answer the question of how much the business is spending on wages, rent, insurance, and so on.

> The **management function** of accounting. Final accounts are also produced to enable the managers or owner of a business to gauge how well the business has performed and to provide information that might highlight areas in which improvements can be made in the way that the business is run.

The managers of a business will wish to improve the performance of the business. A profit figure alone will not highlight areas of good practice and identify areas that need to be improved. Details of all expenditure might show that a business is paying a high rent or has a large amount of vehicle expenses. If these could be reduced then profits would rise.

How could a business reduce rent paid and spend less on vehicle expenses?

Answers could have included:

- moving to smaller premises (if present premises are too large)
- moving to out-of-town premises (provided customers would not be lost)
- using diesel vehicles
- charging delivery to some customers.

QUESTION 1

Required List six items of revenue expenditure a supermarket would incur in an average month's trading.

QUESTION 2

Required State whether the following statements are true or false:

Capital expenditure is included in a profit and loss account.	True/False
Capital expenditure is not included in a profit and loss account.	True/False
Revenue expenditure is included in a profit and loss account.	True/False
Revenue expenditure is not included in a profit and loss account.	True/False
Capital receipts are included in a profit and loss account.	True/False
Capital receipts are not included in a profit and loss account.	True/False
Revenue receipts are included in a profit and loss account.	True/False

WORKED EXAMPLE

David owns and runs a greengrocer's shop. For the year ended 31 March 20*8 he made a gross profit of £21,500. During the same year he incurred the following expenditure:

	£
Rent and rates	750
Wages	8,000
Insurance	400
New weighing scales	2,340
Motor expenses	1,100
Light and heating expenses	500
Stationery and advertising	250
Bank charges	135
New delivery van	15,600
General expenses	185
Money spent on family holiday	2,300

Required Prepare a profit and loss account for the year ended 31 March 20*8.

Answer

David
Profit and loss account for the year ended 31 March 20*8

	£	£
Gross profit		21,500
Less expenses		
Rent and rates	750	
Wages	8,000	
Insurance	400	
Motor expenses	1,100	
Light and heating expenses	500	
Stationery and advertising	250	
Bank charges	135	
General expenses	185	11,320
Net profit		10,180

The weighing scales and the delivery van have not been included because they are both examples of capital expenditure. They will appear on David's balance sheet.

The money spent on the holiday has not been included since this is not a business expense. The profit and loss account refers only to business expenses.

The holiday would be drawings if the transaction had gone through the records of the business.

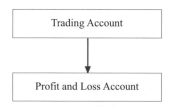

It is usual for businesses to combine the profit and loss account with the trading account.

WORKED EXAMPLE

Danielle is a trader of furniture. She supplies the following information relating to the year ended 31 May 20*8:

	£
Stock 1 June 20*7	27,268
Stock 31 May 20*8	28,420

Purchases	481,690
Sales	748,381
Wages	132,471
Rent and rates	26,402
Advertising and insurance	8,327
Motor expenses	10,513
Office expenses	12,468
Lighting and heating	11,235

Required Prepare the trading and profit and loss account for the year ended 31 May 20*8.

Answer

Danielle
Trading and profit and loss account for the year ended 31 May 20*8

	£	£
Sales		748,381
Less cost of sales		
Stock 1 June 20*7	27,268	
Purchases	481,690	
	508,958	
Less Stock 31 May 20*8	28,420	480,538
Gross profit		267,843
Less expenses		
Wages	132,471	
Rent and rates	26,402	
Advertising and insurance	8,327	
Motor expenses	10,513	
Office expenses	12,468	
Light and heat	11,235	201,416
Net profit		66,427

The trading account determined the gross profit of £267,843.

The profit and loss account shows what is left of the gross profit when all expenses for the year have been taken into account, i.e. the net profit.

REVISION TIP

Carriage IN.................TradINg account

Carriage Out...............PrOfit and loss account

Carriage outward is an expense borne by the business. It is sometimes referred to as carriage on sales. It is included in the *profit and loss account* with all other expenses incurred by the business.

Chapter summary

- A profit and loss account calculates the net profit of a business.
- It lists revenue expenditure incurred by the business.
- It provides the detail for the stewardship and management functions of accounting.
- Carriage inward appears in the trading account as an addition to purchases.
- Carriage outward appears in the profit and loss account as an expense.

SELF-TEST QUESTIONS

- Why is it important to make the distinction between capital and revenue expenditure?
- Give an example of revenue expenditure for a furniture shop.
- Give an example of capital expenditure for a book shop.
- Under what circumstances might the purchase of a commercial oven/cooker constitute revenue expenditure?
- How is gross profit calculated?
- How is carriage inward treated in a trading and profit and loss account?
- How is carriage outward treated in a trading and profit and loss account?
- How is net profit calculated?
- Why is gross profit different from net profit?
- Complete the following equations:
  Net profit + revenue expenditure = ?
  Gross profit – revenue expenditure = ?
  Gross profit – net profit = ?
- What do we mean by the term 'final accounts'?

TEST QUESTIONS

QUESTION 3

The following information is given for the year ended 31 December 20*8 for Pierre Roi:

stock at 1 January 20*8 £613; stock at 31 December 20*8 £770; purchases £14,661; sales £25,047.

Required Prepare a trading account for the year ended 31 December 20*8.

QUESTION 4

The following information relates to the year ended 31 July 20*8 for Pauline:

stock at 1 August 20*7 £429; stock at 31 July 20*8 £591; purchases £32,649; sales £71,544.

Required Prepare a trading account for the year ended 31 July 20*8.

QUESTION 5

Jack supplies the following information for the year ended 31 January 20*8:

gross profit £43,719; wages £15,437; motor expenses £2,864; rent and rates £1,442; insurances £3,669; general expenses £8,742.

Required Prepare a profit and loss account for the year ended 31 January 20*8.

QUESTION 6

The following information is given for the year ended 30 April 20*8 for Viv:

gross profit £45,892; wages £27,769; rent and rates £6,000; insurances £4,575; motor expenses £7,814; general expenses £2,390.

Required Prepare a profit and loss account for the year ended 30 April 20*8

QUESTION 7

Terry supplies the following information for the year ended 31 May 20*8:

stock at 1 June 20*7 £1,329; stock at 31 May 20*8 £1,275; purchases £23,664; sales £65,782; wages £12,674; motor expenses £6,710; general expenses £441; heating and lighting expenses £1,375; advertising £2,674.

Required Prepare a trading and profit and loss account for the year ended 31 May 20*8.

QUESTION 8

Pablo supplies the following information for the year ended 29 February 20*8:

stock at 1 March 20*7 £211; stock at 29 February 20*8 £485; purchases £27,665; sales £74,882; wages £32,559; motor expenses £11,456; rates £674; general expenses £5,391.

Required Prepare a trading and profit and loss account for the year ended 29 February 20*8.

QUESTION 9

The following information is given for the year ended 30 November 20*8 for Gwenelle:

stock at 1 December 20*7 £12,453; stock at 30 November 20*8 £10,661; purchases £157,994; sales £325,007; wages £56,743; rates £6,740; heating and lighting £5,441; advertising £1,250; insurances £6,750; general expenses £7,531.

Required Prepare a trading and profit and loss account for the year ended 30 November 20*8.

QUESTION 10

Bill supplies the following information for the year ended 30 June 20*8:

stock at 1 July 20*7 £438; stock at 30 June 20*8 £541; purchases £54,763; sales £99,063; returns inward £286; returns outward £421; wages £17,539; motor expenses £6,882; advertising £480; heat and light £2,856; rates £1,165; general expenses £6,423.

Required Prepare a trading and profit and loss account for the year ended 30 June 20*8.

QUESTION 11

Helen supplies the following information for the year ended 31 March 20*8:

stock at 1 April 20*7 £1,554; stock at 31 March 20*8 £977; purchases £23,887; sales £51,311; returns inward £367; returns outward £541; wages £8,712; rates £2,350; heat and light £1,458; advertising £2,350; insurances £2,005; general expenses £4,637.

Required Prepare a trading and profit and loss account for the year ended 31 March 20*8.

QUESTION 12

The following information is given for the year ended 31 October 20*8 for Les:

stock at 1 November 20*7 £3,419; stock at 31 October 20*8 £3,491; purchases £43,771; sales £74,911; returns inward £118; returns outward £489; wages £12,562; telephone £782; rates £1,750; motor expenses £6,488; general expenses £7,869.

Required Prepare a trading and profit and loss account for the year ended 31 October 20*8.

QUESTION 13

The following information is supplied for the year ended 31 August 20*8 for Janice:

stock at 1 September 20*7 £673; stock at 31 August 20*8 £891; purchases £29,041; sales £93,673; returns inward £276; returns outward £450; carriage inward £452; carriage outward £772; wages £23,774; general expenses £5,675; motor expenses £2,563; rent £3,600; rates £895; telephone £779; advertising £1,250; heat and light £2,588.

Required Prepare a trading and profit and loss account for the year ended 31 August 20*8.

QUESTION 14

Attil provides the following information for the year ended 31 December 20*8:

stock at 1 January 20*8 £207; stock at 31 December 20*8 £870; purchases £43,672; sales £91,211; returns inward £75; returns outward £671; carriage inward £317; carriage outward £139; wages £23,649; rates £1,764; heating and lighting £2,785; telephone £1,476; insurance £579; general expenses £4,361.

Required Prepare a trading and profit and loss account for the year ended 31 December 20*8.

QUESTION 15

The following information relates to the year ended 31 March 20*8 for Catherine:

stock at 1 April 20*7 £1,549; stock at 31 March 20*8 £1,471; purchases £54,772; sales £127,773; returns inward £321; returns outward £84; carriage inward £270; carriage outward £129; wages £41,005; motor expenses £2,756; rent £4,750; rates £1,254; insurance £2,674; advertising £1,547; heat and light £2,541; telephone £3,428; general expenses £6,539.

Required Prepare a trading and profit and loss account for the year ended 31 March 20*8.

QUESTION 16

The following information relates to the year ended 29 February 20*8 for Fred:

stock at 1 March 20*7 £2,765; stock at 29 February 20*8 £2,890; purchases £34,675; purchase of computer for shop £2,990; sales £71,320; returns inward £276; returns outward £100; carriage inwards £187; carriage outwards £908; wages £8,650; telephone £1,981; rent £6,000; heating and lighting £2,410; general expenses £7,845.

Required Prepare a trading and profit and loss account for the year ended 29 February 20*8.

CHAPTER
FIVE

The final accounts

Final accounts is the term often used to describe the trading account and profit and loss account and balance sheet produced by the owner of a business at the financial year end.

A full set of final accounts is produced at the end of the financial year. This enables the owner of the business to see:

- if the business has been running profitably during the year
- the assets and liabilities that the business owns at the end of the year.

Specification coverage:
AQA Unit 1
OCR Unit 1

By the end of this chapter you should be able to:
- prepare a full set of final accounts
- understand the relationship between the trading account, the profit and loss account and the balance sheet.

WORKED EXAMPLE

Edward has given you the following information that relates to his DIY shop.

All the figures in the lists relate to the year ended 29 February 20*8. All, that is, except the stock figure and the capital figure. These two figures are the value of the stock at the start of the year and Edward's capital at the start of the year.

Why? This will be explained later. Trust me – I'm an accountant!

	£
Premises at cost	80,000
Fixtures at cost	14,200
Vehicle at cost	8,700
Purchases	211,640
Sales	408,830
Stock at 1 March 20*7	26,480
Wages	152,610
Light and heat	8,420
Motor expenses	3,170
Drawings	18,500
Advertising	860
Insurance	1,540
General expenses	3,950
Debtors	1,340
Creditors	7,140
Bank balance	2,790
Capital at 1 March 20*7	118,230

The stock at 29 February 20*8 was valued at £24,560.

Required Prepare a set of final accounts for the year ended 29 February 20*8.

WORKED EXAMPLE *continued*

Answer

Edward
Balance sheet at 29 February 20*8

	£	£
Fixed assets		
Premises at cost		80,000
Fixtures at cost		14,200
Vehicle at cost		8,700
		102,900
Current assets		
Stock	24,560	
Debtors	1,340	
Bank balance	2,790	
	28,690	
Less current liabilities		
Creditors	7,140	21,550
		124,450
Capital (balancing figure)		124,450

We have calculated the capital figure (net assets) at the balance sheet date.
The list provided by Edward tells us that one year earlier Edward's capital (net assets) was £118,230.

Edward's business has £6,220 more net assets at the end of the financial year than at the start of the financial year. These assets have been provided by the profits retained in the business over the year.

Net assets at 29 February 20*8	124,450
Less Net assets 1 March 20*7	118,230
Net profit retained in business	6,220

But, Edward has been withdrawing profits all through the year in order to finance his life outside the business. He has been making *drawings* during the year.

These profits need to be added to the retained profits to tell us the total profit generated by the business during the year.

Net profit retained in the business	6,220
Net profit withdrawn by Edward	18,500
Total business profit for the year ended 29 February 20*8	24,720

This calculation does not provide us with the details that may be required for *management* and *stewardship* reasons. For this we must prepare a trading and profit and loss account for the year.

Edward
Trading and profit and loss account for the year ended 29 February 20*8

	£	£
Sales		408,830
Less cost of sales		
Stock 1 March 20*7	26,480	
Purchases	211,640	
	238,120	
Less Stock 29 February 20*8	24,560	213,560
Gross profit		195,270
Less expenses		
Wages	152,610	
Light and heat	8,420	
Motor expenses	3,170	
Advertising	860	
Insurance	1,540	
General expenses	3,950	170,550
Net profit		24,720

You should now be aware that if a business is making profits the net assets of the business will increase, provided those profits are reinvested ('ploughed back') into the business, and are not withdrawn from the business. You should understand that if the business is running at a loss the net assets will reduce. Spend a little time running through this in your mind – it is quite sensible – if you don't spend all of your income, the surplus must show up in your net assets.

REVISION TIP

When you have studied a topic, ask yourself this question:

'Could I explain what I have just learned to a relative who is not an accountant?'

If the answer is 'Yes, I think I could', then you understand the topic.

If the answer is 'No way!' then further work is required on your part.

Now for a small change in the presentation of the work that has already been covered.

Accountants generally present their final accounts in a set order. You should be reasonably confident on the preparation of the three statements that make up the final accounts.

The three statements are usually presented in this order

1   the trading account for the year
2   the profit and loss account for the year
3   the balance sheet at the end of the year.

● EXAMINATION TIP

Always give a full heading. Do not abbreviate any part of the heading. If the year end is 31 December 20*8, state this in full. Always use the business name in any heading.

To help in the preparation of the three statements, you may find it useful to go down the list of information and indicate alongside where each item will be used.

WORKED EXAMPLE

	£
Purchases	123,932
Sales	427,109
Wages	96,452
Drawings	23,600
Machinery at cost	100,000
Mortgage on premises	80,000
Carriage inward	675
Carriage outward	490

Required Indicate where each of the items shown above would be found in a set of final accounts.

Answer

Purchases	*Trading a/c*
Sales	*Trading a/c*
Wages	*P & L a/c*
Drawings	*Balance sheet*
Machinery at cost	*Balance sheet*
Mortgage on premises	*Balance sheet*
Carriage inward	*Trading a/c*
Carriage outward	*P & L a/c*

WORKED EXAMPLE

Erica owns and runs a small repair garage. She supplies the following information at 31 May 20*8:

	£
Premises at cost	180,000
Break down truck at cost	24,000
Office furniture at cost	8,000
Debtors	3,450
Creditors	1,673
Stock at 1 June 20*7	945
Purchases	48,620
Sales	92,431
Wages	23,789
Rates	872
Insurance	2,150
Advertising	450
Stationery	357
Mortgage on premises	160,000
Drawings	15,750
Bank balance	849
Capital	55,128

Erica has valued her stock on 31 May 20*8 at £1,045.

Required Prepare a trading and profit and loss account for the year ended 31 May 20*8 and a balance sheet at 31 May 20*8.

Answer

Erica
Trading and profit and loss account for the year ended 31 May 20*8

	£	£
Sales		92,431
Less cost of sales		
Stock 1 June 20*7	945	
Purchases	48,620	
	49,565	
Less Stock 31 May 20*8	1,045	48,520
Gross profit		43,911
Less expenses		
Wages	23,789	
Rates	872	
Insurance	2,150	
Advertising	450	
Stationery	357	27,618
Net profit		16,293

Balance sheet at 31 May 20*8

	£	£
Fixed assets		
Premises at cost		180,000
Break down truck at cost		24,000
Office furniture at cost		8,000
		212,000
Current assets		
Stock	1,045	
Debtors	3,450	
Bank balance	849	
	5,344	
Less current liabilities		
Creditors	1,673	3,671
		215,671

	£
Less long-term liability	
Mortgage on premises	160,000
	55,671
Capital (Balancing figure)	55,671

We can check to see whether or not we have arrived at the correct figure for Erica's profit. In Chapter 2 we used the net asset method of calculating profit. We shall use it to check the net profit that we calculated using the profit and loss account.

	£
Closing capital 31 May 20*8	55,671
Less opening capital 1 June 20*7	55,128
Profits retained in Erica's business	543
Plus profits taken out of the business (drawings)	15,750
Total profits generated by the business	16,293

These details are an important source of information, so they are usually incorporated into the balance sheet. From now on we shall include them in any balance sheet that is prepared.

The way that information is presented on the balance sheet is shown below.

	£	
Opening capital	55,128	(the worth of the business at the start of the year)
Add profit	16,293	(the increase in worth over the year)
	71,421	
Less drawings	15,750	(the decrease in worth during the year because of drawings of profits)
Closing capital	55,671	(the worth of the business at the end of the year).

Talk yourself through this new layout. It should make sense!

● EXAMINATION TIP

If an examination question asks you to *calculate* net profit, use the net asset method, because it is much quicker (you will probably have insufficient information to use any other method). If the question asks you to prepare a trading and profit and loss account, then that is precisely what the answer must show!

WORKED EXAMPLE

Drew has been trading as a florist for some years. The following information relates to his financial year-end at 31 August 20*8:

	£
Purchases	58,400
Sales	97,260
Stock at 1 September 20*7	230
General expenses	4,260
Rent and rates	5,500
Light and heat	2,300
Stationery and wrapping materials	8,700
Fixtures and fittings at cost	3,400
Van at cost	7,500
Debtors	85
Creditors	432
Drawings	13,200
Cash in hand	87

	£
Balance at bank	990
Capital at 1 September 20*7	6,960

The stock at 31 August 20*8 has been valued at £210.

Required Prepare a trading and profit and loss account for the year ended 31 August 20*8 and a balance sheet at that date.

Answer

Drew
Trading and profit and loss account for the year ended 31 August 20*8

	£	£
Sales		97,260
Less cost of sales		
Stock 1 September 20*7	230	
Purchases	58,400	
	58,630	
Less stock 31 August 20*8	210	58,420
Gross profit		38,840
Less expenses		
General expenses	4,260	
Rent and rates	5,500	
Light and heat	2,300	
Stationery and wrapping materials	8,700	20,760
Net profit		18,080

Balance sheet at 31 August 20*8

	£	£
Fixed assets		
Fixtures and fittings at cost		3,400
Van at cost		7,500
		10,900
Current assets		
Stock	210	
Debtors	85	
Balance at bank	990	
Cash in hand	87	
	1,372	
Less current liabilities		
Creditors	432	940
		11,840
Capital 1 September 20*7		6,960
Add profit		18,080
		25,040
Less drawings		13,200
		11,840

Chapter summary

- Final accounts comprise the trading account, the profit and loss account and the balance sheet.
- They are interconnected. Gross profit is transferred from the trading account to the profit and loss account. The net profit is transferred from the profit and loss account to the capital account shown on the balance sheet.

SELF-TEST QUESTIONS

- Identify the three statements that make up the final accounts of a business.
- Which statements are prepared for the year?
- Name the only statement in the final accounts that is prepared for one day of the financial year.
- You have been using a list of figures to prepare final accounts. Which stock figure appears in this list?
- Why are assets shown on a balance sheet at cost?
- Define 'drawings'.
- Sales – cost of sales = ?
- Sales – cost of sales – expenses = ?
- Closing capital – opening capital + drawings = ?
- List three items that could be classified as current liabilities.

TEST QUESTIONS

QUESTION 1

Ashley Peacock provides the following information for the year ended 30 June 20*8:

	£
Capital at 1 July 20*7	108,044
Premises at cost	150,000
Machinery at cost	45,000
Motor van at cost	17,500
Stock at 1 July 20*7	7,854
Debtors	13,563
Creditors	8,734
Bank balance	1,245
Purchases	70,031
Sales	175,672
Wages and general expenses	38,962
Repairs and renewals	7,459
Rent and rates	5,350
Insurance and advertising	5,312
Motor expenses	13,674
Drawings	16,500
Long-term loan	100,000
Stock at 30 June 20*8	9,004

Required Prepare a trading and profit and loss account for the year ended 30 June 20*8 and a balance sheet at that date.

QUESTION 2

Frank Sert provides the following information for the year ended 31 March 20*8:

	£
Land and buildings at cost	115,000
Machinery at cost	35,700
Vehicles at cost	52,500
Debtors	7,342
Creditors	6,721
Stock at 1 April 20*7	3,572
Bank balance	2,775
Drawings	14,000
Purchases	42,782
Sales	121,649
Carriage inward	541
Wages	34,669
Insurance	1,560
Motor expenses	5,231
Advertising	3,672

		£
General expenses		4,759
Capital at 1 April 20*7		195,733
Stock at 31 March 20*8		3,885

Required Prepare a trading and profit and loss account for the year ended 31 March 20*8 and a balance sheet at that date.

QUESTION 3

Leslie Harris provides the following information for the year ended 31 December 20*8:

	£
Machinery at cost	85,750
Vehicles at cost	50,000
Stock at 1 January 20*8	3,691
Debtors	5,367
Creditors	3,753
Purchases	48,775
Sales	102,367
Carriage inward	693
Carriage outward	528
Wages and salaries	28,570
Motor expenses	6,371
Heat and light	2,448
Advertising and insurance	3,691
General expenses	7,999
Drawings	21,700
Bank overdraft	872
Long-term loan	100,000
Capital at 1 January 20*8	58,591
Stock at 31 December 20*8	4,187

Required Prepare a trading and profit and loss account for the year ended 31 December 20*8 and a balance sheet at that date.

QUESTION 4

Joan Hornby supplies the following information for the year ended 30 September 20*8:

	£
Stock at 1 October 20*7	6,500
Purchases	205,985
Sales	450,064
Returns inward	412
Rent	5,480
Rates	3,420
Insurance	1,740
Light and heat	4,532
Wages	61,439
Motor expenses	5,300
General expenses	5,331
Carriage inward	461
Carriage outward	793
Debtors	34,671
Creditors	29,870
Land and buildings at cost	110,000
Plant and machinery at cost	43,500
Vehicles at cost	35,000
Bank balance	3,874
Cash in hand	769
Bank loan (repayable 2030)	50,000
Drawings	23,760
Capital at 1 October 20*7	23,033
Stock at 30 September 20*8	7,439

Required Prepare a trading and profit and loss account for the year ended 30 September 20*8 and a balance sheet at that date.

QUESTION 5

The following information is available for the year ended 31 March 20*8 for Dratesh Narewal:

	£
Motor vehicles at cost	35,000
Office equipment at cost	18,750
Premises at cost	65,000
Purchases	48,661
Sales	102,453
Returns inward	743
Returns outward	911
Carriage inward	1,539
Carriage outward	332
Salaries	28,749
Drawings	24,675
Motor expenses	5,673
Advertising	1,350
Insurances	3,764
Heat and light	2,479
Rates	1,245
General expenses	941
Debtors	4,601
Creditors	1,955
Stock at 1 April 20*7	995
Stock at 31 March 20*8	1,007
Bank overdraft	351
Long-term bank loan	40,000
Capital at 1 April 20*7	98,827

Required Prepare the trading and profit and loss account for the year ended 31 March 20*8 and a balance sheet at that date.

QUESTION 6

The following information relates to the year ended 29 February 20*8 for Rita Shah:

	£
Sales	238,965
Purchases	117,671
Carriage inward	563
Returns inward	631
Carriage outward	793
Returns outward	1,451
Drawings	24,700
Wages and salaries	74,378
Rent rates and insurance	8,765
Advertising and stationery	4,611
Motor expenses	11,453
General expenses	4,358
Premises at cost	91,000
Machinery at cost	42,000
Office equipment at cost	14,650
Motor vehicles at cost	47,000
Debtors	2,865
Creditors	3,428
Stock at 1 March 20*7	8,531
Stock at 29 February 20*8	8,002
Bank balance	4,662
Capital at 1 March 20*7	214,787

Required Prepare the trading and profit and loss account for the year ended 29 February 20*8 and a balance sheet at that date.

SIX

Double-entry bookkeeping

In the previous chapters you were presented with figures. Some of these figures were used to prepare balance sheets; some were used to prepare trading accounts that showed the gross profit; some figures were used to prepare profit and loss accounts so that the net profit of a business could be determined.

In the 'real world' these figures will be derived from many transactions undertaken by a business on a daily basis. There are two main ways in which businesses record their financial transactions. They use either:

■ a double-entry bookkeeping system; or
■ a single-entry bookkeeping system (you will encounter this system in the second year of your studies).

This chapter looks at the double-entry system that provides the accountant with the information needed in order to provide the data required to prepare the final accounts.

As the name implies, double-entry bookkeeping recognises that there are two sides or aspects to every business transaction.

I fill my car with diesel costing £20. The two aspects are:

■ I receive the diesel.
■ The filling station gives me the diesel.

I buy a pair of trainers costing £85:

■ I receive the trainers.
■ The sports shop gives me the trainers.

There are two more aspects to these transactions.

When I give the filling station attendant my £20 note:

■ She receives the cash.
■ I give the cash.

When I give the shop assistant my £85:

■ He receives the cash.
■ I give the cash.

This way of recording both sides of any transaction is known as the **dual aspect** principle of accounting.

> An **account** contains the detailed record of financial transactions undertaken by a business.

All financial transactions involving the business are recorded in a format called an **account**.

You will find each account on a separate page in the ledger. In fact, if a great many transactions of a similar nature were undertaken an account may spread over several pages.

> The **ledger** is the book where all accounts are kept.

For convenience's sake, this one book is divided into several smaller books. You can imagine that large businesses like Marks and Spencer or McDonalds could not possibly keep all their financial records in one book.

Specification coverage:
AQA Unit 1
OCR Unit 1

By the end of this chapter you should be able to:
■ use double-entry bookkeeping to record financial transactions
■ enter financial transactions into the ledger
■ understand the purpose of the ledger
■ understand and use debit and credit entries
■ understand why the ledger is divided into three parts.

Initially, to make our task a little simpler we shall keep all our records together. Later, the other books will be introduced and you will see that it does make sense to split the ledger into several different parts.

Don't worry if all this seems a little strange. You will soon get the hang of it but it does require *practice*. The key to success in accounting is practice.

An account looks like this:

Each account has two sides:

- the **left** side is known as the **debit** side
- the **right** side is known as the **credit** side.

An account

Debit	Credit
The debit side of an account is always the receiving side or the side that shows gains in value. Debit is often abbreviated to Dr.	The credit side of an account is always the giving or losing side – the side that shows value given. Credit is often abbreviated to Cr.

Dr	**An account**	**Cr**
Receives or Gains		Gives or Loses

An account in the ledger would be headed thus:

Dr	******* **account**	**Cr**

Note

There should always be a heading. If the account shown is not a personal account, the heading should include the word 'account'.

Purchases are any items that are purchased with the intention of selling them to customers. Purchases are an example of revenue expenditure.

Sales are any items that are sold in the normal course of business to customers. Sales are an example of revenue income.

The golden rule of the game of 'double-entry' is that every time you enter something on the debit side (left side) of an account, you must enter an equivalent amount on the credit side (right side) of another account.

This is all fairly straightforward, but it does require practice.

WORKED EXAMPLE

Barbara owns a butchery business. During one week the following financial transactions take place:

1 She purchases meat £210 from Scragg and Co. She will pay for the meat in a couple of weeks.
2 Barbara's cash sales for the week amount to £742.
3 Barbara supplies meat to the Grand Hotel £217. They will pay for the meat at the month end.
4 Barbara pays her shop rent £75.
5 She pays her telephone bill £43.

Required Enter the transactions in Barbara's ledger.

Answer
1 Barbara receives meat . . . and Scragg and Co. 'loses' the meat.

Dr	Purchases account	Cr	Dr	Scragg and Co	Cr
	£ 210				£ 210

2 Barbara 'loses' (sells) the meat . . . and gains cash.

Dr	Sales account	Cr	Dr	Cash account	Cr
		£ 742		£ 742	

3 Barbara 'loses' meat and the Grand Hotel gains the meat.

Dr	Sales account	Cr	Dr	Grand Hotel	Cr
		£ 217		£ 217	

4 Barbara gains the use of her premises . . . and she 'loses' (pays) cash.

Dr	Rent account	Cr	Dr	Cash account	Cr
	£ 75				£ 75

- This is a tricky entry because we are used to talking about 'paying rent'.
- Barbara pays money to a landlord for the use of his building.
- Barbara receives/gains the use of the premises.
- In cases like this, think of the cash entry first and then put in the second entry.

5 Barbara gains the use of her telephone . . . and she loses cash.

Dr	Telephone account	Cr	Dr	Cash account	Cr
	£ 43				£ 43

- Another tricky entry – Barbara receives/gains the use of the telephone.
- Barbara gives the telephone company cash for their service.

If you are uncertain about the telephone account, consider whether Barbara has gained cash or 'lost' cash. You know that Barbara has paid cash to the telephone company so the cash has to be a credit entry (right side). The other entry has to be a debit entry (left side) if we stick to the rules of double-entry. If you cheat at this game you will be found out!

QUESTION 1

Trevor Smith owns and runs a general store. The following transactions took place last week:

1 Trevor's cash sales for the week amount to £1,634.
2 He pays wages for the week £899, paying employees with cash.
3 Trevor takes £180 cash from the business for his own private use.
4 He pays a garage £328 cash for servicing his delivery van.
5 Trevor sells meat and rolls, etc., £65, to the local squash club for a function. The treasurer will pay Trevor next week.

Required Enter the transactions in Trevor Smith's ledger.

If there are a number of transactions that need to be recorded in the same account we do just that – we enter them all in that one account.

WORKED EXAMPLE

Greta Teer owns and runs a newsagents shop. The following transactions took place over the past few days:

1 Cash sales of newspapers amounted to £68.
2 Cash sales of chocolate and sweets amounted to £451.
3 Greta purchased sweets, chocolates, crisps and soft drinks £135 from her wholesaler. She paid cash.
4 She paid £160 cash to her local authority for rates.
5 Greta sold four boxes of crisps for cash £30 to St Agnes' youth club.

Required Enter the transactions in Greta's ledger.

Answer

Dr	Sales account	Cr	Dr	Cash account	Cr
		£		£	£
		68		68	135
		451		451	160
		30		30	

Dr	Purchases account	Cr	Dr	Rates account	Cr
	£			£	
	135			160	

Note

All the transactions involving cash have been entered in one cash account. All the sales transactions have also been entered in one account

QUESTION 2

Ben Chan owns and runs a Chinese take-away. The following transactions are for his business:

1 Ben pays wages £312 in cash.
2 Cash sales amount to £321.
3 Ben pays cash for rent £200.
4 Ben pays £62 cash for rice, potatoes and meat.
5 Ben withdraws cash £250 for holiday spending money.

Required Enter the transactions in Ben's ledger.

It should be obvious that as well as keeping money in the business till, businesses will bank money and will pay many bills by means of cheques. So, as well as having a cash account in the ledger, the business would keep a bank account too.

WORKED EXAMPLE

Sven Drax owns and runs a hotel. He supplies the following information.

1 Sven purchases a freezer for the business, paying £415 by cheque.
2 He purchases for cash £127 worth of fruit and vegetables for the hotel restaurant.
3 Sven purchases petrol £45 for the hotel minibus; he pays cash.
4 He pays £1,500 for a family holiday, paying with a business cheque.
5 He pays £2,178 cash takings into the bank account.

Required Enter the transactions into the hotel ledger.

Answer

Dr	Freezer account	Cr		Dr	Bank account	Cr
	£				£	£
	415				2,178	415
						1,500

Dr	Purchases account	Cr		Dr	Cash account	Cr
	£					£
	127					127
						45

Dr	Motor expenses account	Cr		Dr	Drawings account	Cr
	£				£	
	45				1,500	

Dr	Takings (or sales) account	Cr
		£
		2,178

Note

The freezer is not purchases – it is capital expenditure. There was not (already) an account, so . . . when in doubt open an account. The cheque paid out to the holiday company is drawings – it is not a business expense.

QUESTION 3

Gladys Voisin owns a shop selling games, DVDs, CDs, games and videos. The following transactions have just taken place:

1 Gladys purchases games from her wholesaler £350, paying by cheque.
2 She banks a day's takings £671.
3 Gladys pays her shop insurance £478, paying by cheque.
4 She sells an old display unit for £15 cash.
5 Gladys purchases a DVD player for use in the shop £345. She pays by cheque.

Required Enter the transactions in Gladys's ledger.

> **Credit customers** are people (or businesses) whom we sell goods to; they will pay for their goods at some time in the future. They are goods sold on **credit**.
> Until credit customers pay for the goods they have purchased they will be **debtors**.

> **Credit suppliers** are people (or businesses) whom we purchase goods from; we will settle the debt that we owe at some future date. The goods are purchased on **credit**.
> Until we pay for the goods that we have purchased the credit suppliers will be **creditors**.

All accounts are entered in one book called the ledger. Because the number of accounts could run into many hundreds, it is obviously more convenient to split the ledger into a number of different books.

Can you think of how you might split the ledger to make it more manageable?

We make it more manageable by putting all:

- credit customers' accounts together
- credit suppliers' accounts together
- other accounts in another ledger.

All transactions involving credit customers will be found in the sales ledger (also known as the debtors' ledger).

All transactions with credit suppliers will be found in the purchases ledger (also known as the creditors' ledger).

All other transactions will be found in the general ledger. (For those of you familiar with computerised accounts, the general ledger is often called the nominal ledger in accounting programs.)

Initially you will make mistakes when asked which accounts would appear in which ledger; don't worry about this as we have all made similar mistakes in the past.

The tricky ones are:

- the sales account, which is **not**, I repeat, **not** found in the sales ledger. The sales ledger is reserved for the accounts of credit customers. The sales account would be found in the general ledger
- the purchases account will **not** be found in the purchases ledger. The purchase ledger is reserved for the accounts of credit suppliers only. The purchases account would be found in the general ledger
- we only record credit transactions in the sales ledger and purchase ledger.

If a sale is made for cash it is not entered in the sales ledger. If something is purchased for cash it is not entered in the purchases ledger. These transactions appear in the general ledger.

WORKED EXAMPLE

Jill purchases goods for resale £73, she pays cash.
She sells goods £19 for cash.

Required List the two entries for each transaction that are required in Jill's ledger.

Answer

Debits	Credits
Purchases	Cash
Cash	Sales

When you go to a take-away and order your meal, the proprietor does not open an account for you; he simply takes your money and gives you your meal.
He debits – cash (the sale of your meal would be included in his total sales for the day).
He credits – sales (using the total sales figure for the day).

The splitting of the ledger makes sense. It is sensible that you keep your CDs separate from your socks. You keep your bike parts separate from your jeans, etc.

Ledger accounts may be classified under the following headings:

Personal accounts – these are accounts that record transactions with credit customers and credit suppliers.
Nominal accounts, **real accounts** and **liability accounts** will all be found in the general ledger.
Nominal accounts record expenses, profits, losses and gains.
Real accounts record the acquisition and disposal of fixed assets like land, buildings, equipment and vehicles.
Liability accounts record the acquisition and repayment of loans and overdrafts.

Remember that each account would be in a different ledger according to the classification we have discussed. Each account would be shown on a separate page in the ledger. However, there is not enough space in this book to afford such a luxury, so we will write the accounts on the same page.

QUESTION 4

In which ledger would you expect to find the following accounts? Tick the appropriate box

Account name	Purchases ledger	Sales ledger	General ledger
Tamsin; a credit customer			
Frank; a supplier to be paid next month			
Returns inwards account			
Cash sales account			
Rent account			
Bank account			
Capital account			
Credit sales account			
Drawings account			
Motor expenses account			
Purchases account			

WORKED EXAMPLE

Siobhan Murphy provides the following information for the last few days:

1 Siobhan returns faulty goods £41 to Declan.
2 She purchases a fixed asset £1,450 from Jock on credit.
3 Siobhan sells goods £77 to Fiona, who pays by cheque.
4 She purchases goods for resale £510 from Tom on credit.
5 She purchases goods for resale £65 from Joan for cash.

Required Enter the transactions in Siobhan's ledger (indicate in which ledger each account could be found).

Answer

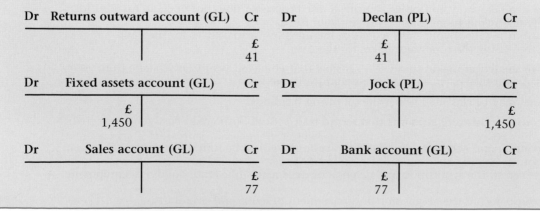

Dr	Returns outward account (GL)	Cr	Dr	Declan (PL)	Cr
		£ 41		£ 41	

Dr	Fixed assets account (GL)	Cr	Dr	Jock (PL)	Cr
	£ 1,450				£ 1,450

Dr	Sales account (GL)	Cr	Dr	Bank account (GL)	Cr
		£ 77		£ 77	

WORKED EXAMPLE *continued*

Dr	Purchases account (GL)	Cr
	£ 510 65	

Dr	Tom (PL)	Cr
		£ 510

Dr	Cash account (GL)	Cr
		£ 65

Note

■ customers and suppliers are accounts in the sales ledger and in the purchases ledger – *but only if the transactions are on credit*
■ accounts that are not personal accounts are found in the general ledger
■ all debits have a corresponding credit
■ all credits have a corresponding debit.

Those readers who have bank accounts will observe that money paid out of the account is entered in the left column (debit) of the bank statement, while moneys received into the account are entered in the right column (credit). This causes problems initially because after what has been said above, this might seem to be the wrong way round. So who is right? Well, the bank and this book are both correct.

You need to remember that the bank statement is written from the point of view of the bank, not you. More details will be given on this later.

QUESTION 5

In the table below, enter the account that should be debited and the account that should be credited.

Transaction	Debit	Credit
Rent paid with cash	Rent account	Cash account
Goods for resale purchased from Knight on credit		
Cash sales		
Wages paid by cheque		
Purchase of fixed asset by cheque		
Carriage inwards paid with cash		
Goods for resale purchased from Day, with cash		
Vehicle service paid by cheque		
Drawings of cash		
Purchase of a fixed asset on credit from Lock		
Carriage outward paid by cheque		

Chapter summary

- All financial transactions are recorded in accounts.
- All accounts are found in the ledger.
- Every debit entry in the ledger must have a corresponding credit entry.
- Every credit entry in the ledger must have a corresponding debit entry.
- The ledger is divided into three parts because it is easier and more convenient to use in this form.
- The purchases ledger contains the accounts of suppliers with credit accounts.
- The sales ledger contains the accounts of customers with credit accounts.
- The general ledger contains nominal, real and liability accounts.

SELF-TEST QUESTIONS

- Complete the sentence 'Every ... needs a corresponding credit'.
- Name the book in which all financial transactions are entered.
- List the three divisions of the book.
- What is the alternative name given to the purchases ledger? What is the alternative name given to the sales ledger?
- Define the term 'account'.
- Explain the meaning of 'personal' accounts.
- Name two 'real' accounts found in the books of account.
- Name two 'nominal' accounts found in the books of account.
- Name two 'liability' accounts.
- Which side of an account is the 'receiving' side?
- Which side of an account is the 'losing' side?

TEST QUESTIONS

QUESTION 6

The following information is given for the business of Derek:

1 Derek purchases goods for resale £48 for cash.
2 He purchases goods for resale £120 from Nita; he pays cash.
3 Derek sells goods to Sadie £11 for cash.
4 He purchases a fixed asset £2,780 for use in the business; he pays cash.
5 Derek sells goods £58 to Doris for cash.

Required Enter the transactions in the ledger accounts.

QUESTION 7

Harriet provides the following information relating to her business:

1 Harriet pays cash wages £349.
2 She sells goods £211 for cash to Albert.
3 Harriet pays her telephone bill £62 with cash.
4 She purchases goods for resale £109 for cash.
5 Harriet draws £210 cash from the business for private use.

Required Enter the transactions in the ledger accounts.

QUESTION 8

The following information relates to the business of Selena, a greengrocer:

1 Selena purchases fruit and vegetables £104 on credit from Docker.
2 She purchases a set of scales £270 on credit from Waites.
3 Selena purchases potatoes £60 for cash from A. Farmer.
4 Her cash sales for the week amounted to £643.
5 Selena sells fruit £58 on credit to the Towers Hotel.

Required Enter the transactions in the ledger accounts.

QUESTION 9

Bhinda owns and runs a garage. The following information relates to her business:

1   Cash petrol sales amount to £1,287.
2   Bhinda purchases a breakdown vehicle £42,500 on credit from W. Rekers.
3   She purchases £3,538 petrol on credit from Esso.
4   Bhinda services the car fleet of I. Hurry £1,473; the amount due will be paid next month.
5   Bhinda purchases a new cash register £2,650 from NCR; she pays by cheque.

Required   Enter the transactions in the ledger accounts. Indicate the ledger in which the account will be found.

QUESTION 10

Raymond is hairdresser. He provides the following information:

1   Raymond purchases new hairdryers for use in his salon £125 on credit from B. Loway.
2   He purchases hair colours and perms £72 from T. Int, paying cash.
3   Raymond purchases cosmetics £212 from B. Lush, paying by cheque.
4   He pays his week's receipts £963 into the business bank account.
5   Raymond pays his business electricity bill £142 by cheque.

Required   Enter the transactions in the ledger accounts. Indicate the ledger in which the account will be found.

QUESTION 11

Arnold owns and runs an electrical goods store. He provides the following information:

1   Sales for the week £3,642 paid into the business bank account.
2   Wages paid in cash £784.
3   Arnold repairs a plasma screen television in Hitters Squash Club £188. The club will settle the bill next month.
4   Arnold purchases spare parts for repairing electrical goods £340 from Dorak Ltd on credit.
5   Telephone bill paid by cheque £166.
6   Repairs to Arnold's family car £320, paid with business cheque.
7   Arnold returns faulty parts £24 to Dorak Ltd.

Required   Enter the transactions in the ledger accounts. Indicate the ledger in which the account will be found.

QUESTION 12

Celia owns and runs a painting and decorating business. The following information relates to the business:

1   Cash receipts for work done £2,653.
2   She purchases paint £157 from B Rush on credit.
3   Celia pays wages £530 cash.
4   Celia pays private telephone bill £79, using business cash.
5   Celia purchases a van £21,750 from Ardale Motors. She will pay for the van next month.
6   She purchases fuel for the van £32; she pays cash.
7   Celia returns paint £18 to B Rush.

Required   Enter the transactions in the ledger accounts. Indicate the ledger in which the account will be found.

QUESTION 13

Bupesh owns and runs a supermarket. The following business transactions have taken place:

1   Bupesh purchases goods for resale £457 from John, paying cash.
2   His cash sales amount to £759.
3   Bupesh purchases goods £265 from Noel on credit.
4   Bupesh receives a cheque £395 for goods sold to Jacqui.
5   He sells goods £511 to Daser Ltd on credit.
6   Bupesh returns faulty goods £43 to Noel.
7   He pays wages £421 by cheque.
8   Daser Ltd returns goods £165.

Required   Enter the transactions in the ledger accounts. Indicate the ledger in which the account will be found.

CHAPTER SEVEN

Books of prime entry

The books of **prime entry** are also known as books of **original entry** and **subsidiary books**. These terms are interchangeable.

- The books of prime entry are used as a convenient way of entering transactions into the double-entry system.
- It is less efficient to make entries as they arise. It is too time consuming and that means it is generally more costly.
- It is better to collect the entries and categorise them into bundles of similar types and then to post from these books in bulk.

For example, when a person is washing up they don't wash one plate, then dry it, then put it away, then come back, wash another plate, dry it and put it away, then wash a fork, dry it and put it away – I am sure that you can see where this is going. It is much better to wash everything in one go, to dry everything in one go, separate the washing-up into plates, cups, knives and forks, and then put them away.

Transactions are listed in the subsidiary books.

Each subsidiary book is a list of similar types of transaction. The items are listed in the book of prime entry until it is worthwhile to post the list to the ledger. Some of this may sound confusing but when you have seen how the books work things will become clear.

All transactions must be entered in one of the books of prime entry before the transaction can be entered in the ledger.

> **Posting** is the term used by accountants for entering transactions into the ledger accounts of the business.

Specification coverage:
AQA Unit 1
OCR Unit 1

By the end of this chapter you should be able to:
- identify and use the six books of prime entry
- understand how financial transactions are entered in the books of prime entry
- post from the books of prime entry to the ledger.

The double-entry system is like a game of football: in order to watch the game, you must first get into the stadium. The only way into the stadium is by presenting a ticket at one of the entrances. You will need a ticket (a source document) to gain access to the double-entry game, through one of the six entrances (the subsidiary books). One entrance to the football stadium is reserved for the players; one entrance to the double-entry game is reserved for a player in the double-entry game (the cash book). So the cash book can be used to get into the stadium and will also play its part in the game.

There are six books of prime entry.

THE PURCHASES DAY BOOK

(Also known as the purchases book or the purchases journal.)

When a purchase invoice is received from a supplier of goods it shows the goods that have been purchased and the price charged. The details are listed in the purchase day book.

The purchase day book is a list of credit purchases made. The source documents are the purchase invoices received.

When it is convenient (this could be daily, weekly or monthly, depending on the volume of purchases made by the business), the list of purchases is totalled and the total is posted to the debit side of the purchases account in the general ledger because the goods have been received.

Each individual supplier's ledger account in the purchase ledger is credited with the value of goods purchased (showing that the supplier has 'given' the goods).

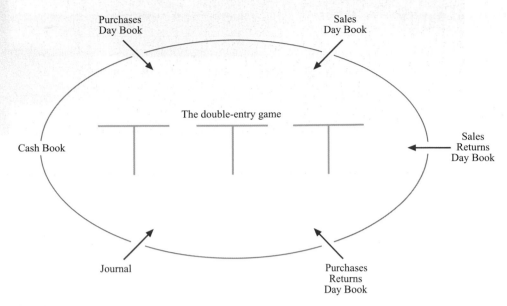

Figure 7.1 The six books of prime entry

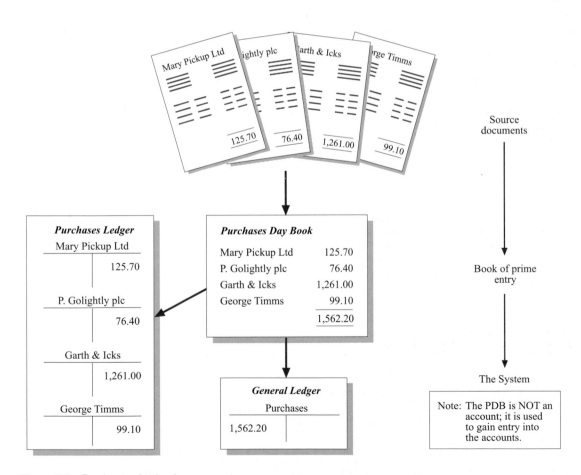

Figure 7.2 Purchases day book

THE SALES DAY BOOK

(Also known as the sales book or the sales journal.)

When goods are sold the supplier sends a sales invoice to the customer. The sales invoice itemises the goods that have been sold and the price of those goods. A copy of this invoice will be retained by the seller.

The copy sales invoice is the source document from which the sales day book is written up.

The sales day book is a list of the copy sales invoices sent to customers.

When it is convenient (this could be daily, weekly or monthly, depending on the volume of sales made by the business), the list is totalled and the total is posted to the credit of the sales account in the general ledger because the goods have been 'given'.

Each individual customer's ledger account in the sales ledger is debited with the value of goods sold to them (indicating that the customer has received the goods).

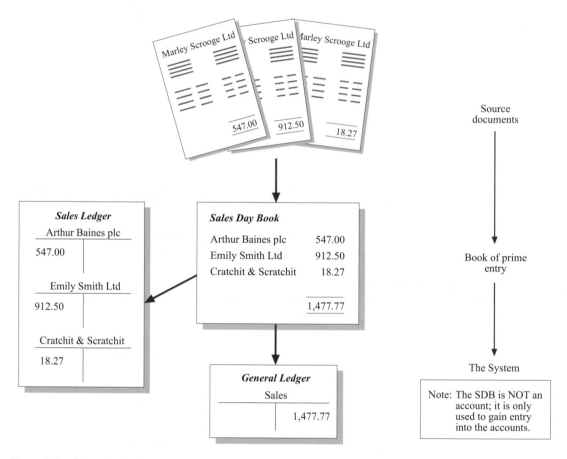

Figure 7.3 Sales day book

THE PURCHASES RETURNS DAY BOOK

(Also known as the purchases returns book or purchases returns journal.)

Sometimes, goods that have been purchased turn out to be faulty; the wrong colour; the wrong size or not useful in some other way. These goods will be returned to the supplier. The supplier in due course will send a credit note.

The credit notes are the source documents from which the purchases returns day book is written up.

The purchases returns day book is a list of all the credit notes received from suppliers.

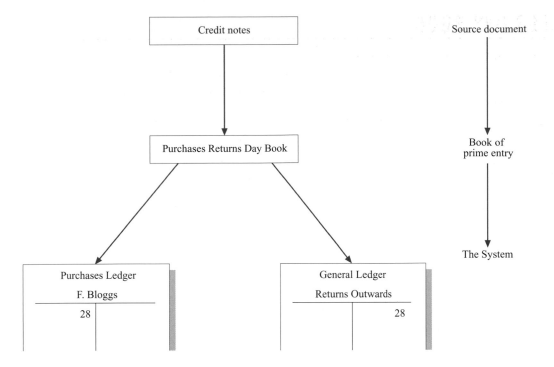

Figure 7.4 Purchases returns day book

When it is convenient, the list is added and the total is posted to the credit of the purchase returns account. This is sometimes known as the returns outward account. (The returns have been sent back to the supplier.)

Each individual entry in the purchase returns day book is then posted to the debit of the respective suppliers account in the purchase ledger. (The suppliers receive the goods.)

THE SALES RETURNS DAY BOOK

(Also known as the sales returns book or sales returns journal.)

Sales that are not acceptable are returned by the customer and a credit note is sent.

A copy of the credit note will be retained and this is the source document from which the sales returns day book is written up.

When convenient, the list is added and the total is posted to the debit of the sales returns account (the goods have been received). The sales returns account is sometimes known as the returns inwards account.

Each individual entry in the sales returns day book is posted to the credit of the customer who returned the goods (they have 'lost' the goods).

THE JOURNAL

(Also known as the journal proper.)

The journal is often a source of confusion for students. Don't worry; its uses are very limited and it is not as difficult as you might assume when you first use it. It is very useful as a revision aid. The journal is also a popular examination topic, favoured by examiners at all levels in accounting.

The journal is used when we cannot comfortably find another book of prime entry to use.

Its layout is different from the day books described above.

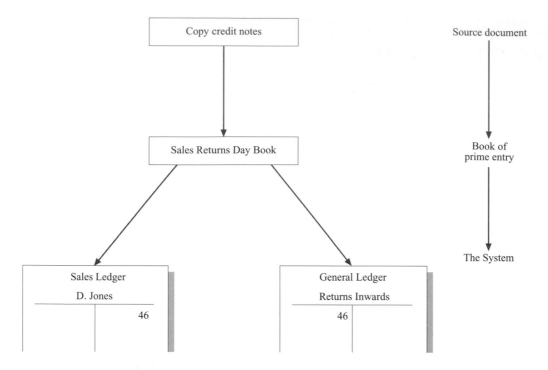

Figure 7.5 Sales returns day book

Note:

In examination questions the 'folio' columns are often omitted.

The journal has six uses:

1 When fixed assets are purchased on a credit basis.
2 When fixed assets are sold on credit.
3 When a business first comes into existence.
4 When a business finally closes.
5 For the correction of errors.
6 For recording inter-ledger transfers.

The source documents used to write up the journal would include:

■ purchase invoices for capital expenditure
■ sales invoices for sales of capital items.

Other source documents will be encountered as we progress with our studies.

WORKED EXAMPLE OF USE 1

On 23 April 20*8 Tina purchased machine xtr/397 costing £12,600 for use in her factory from Dextel and Co, on credit.

Required Prepare the entry in Tina's journal to record the transaction.

Answer

Date	Particulars	Folio	Dr £	Cr £
23 April	Machinery account	GL23*	12,600	
	Dextel Ltd	PL26		12,600

Purchase of Machine xtr/397 on credit from Dextel Ltd.

*Page numbers in the ledgers are for illustrative purposes.

WORKED EXAMPLE OF USE 2

On 6 September 20*8 Hussain sold vehicle P341FTX to Greg's garage for £230. Greg will settle the debt on 31 October 20*8.

Required Prepare the entry in Hussain's journal to record the transaction.

Answer

Date	Particulars	Folio	Debit £	Credit £
6 September	Greg's garage	SL42	230	
	Vehicles account	GL11		230

Sale of vehicle P341FTX to Greg's garage.

WORKED EXAMPLE OF USE 3

Marlene started in business on 1 January 20*8 by paying £14,000 into her business bank account.

Required Prepare the entry in Marlene's journal to record the transaction.

Answer

Date	Particulars	Folio	Debit £	Credit £
1 January	Bank	GL1	14,000	
	Capital account	GL2		14,000

Capital introduced by Marlene.

● EXAMINATION TIP

If you find it difficult to prepare journal entries, try drawing up 'T' accounts as you did in Chapter 6. Then from the accounts draw up the journal.
The journal should be done first as it is the book of prime entry.

WORKED EXAMPLE

On 2 August Jared purchases, on credit, a new lathe for his business (£5,400) from Factre Ltd.

Required Prepare the entries in Jared's journal to record the transaction.

Answer

Imagine you were unsure how to tackle this question. Draw up the 'T' accounts.

Jared gains a lathe

Factre Ltd 'gives' the lathe

Dr	Lathe	Cr	Dr	Factre Ltd	Cr
	£ 5,400				£ 5,400

Which account has been debited? Which account has been credited?

If you can do this, then you can draw up the journal:

Date	Particulars	Folio	Debit £	Credit £
2 August	Machinery account	GL19	5,400	
	Factre Ltd	PL 41		5,400

Purchase of new JY/317 lathe from Factre Ltd.

The final book of prime entry is the cash book.

THE CASH BOOK

This book will be dealt with in more detail in Chapter 10.

It is sufficient to say at this stage that *any* cash (or bank) transactions will be entered in the cash book.

The five other books of prime entry deal only with credit transactions.

The cash book is not only part of our double-entry system, it is also a book of prime entry.

The source documents used to write up the cash book would include:

- cheque book counterfoils
- receipts received from suppliers who have dealt in cash
- copy receipts given to customers
- cash register till rolls.

Other source documents used to write up the cash book will be encountered later.

TRADE DISCOUNT

Trade discount is a reduction in price charged by a supplier to a customer who is in business.

EXAMPLE

Extrav plc sells a range of kitchen fittings to the general public for £1,250.

Stephen is a kitchen designer and fitter. He can purchase the same kitchen fittings from Extrav plc, to fit into one of his customer's kitchens, for £1,000.

Stephen gets a trade discount of £250.

The trade discount expressed as a percentage is 20%.

Trade discount is not recorded in the purchaser's day book.

In Stephen's purchases day book the entry would read:

£

Extrav plc   1,000

Trade discount is not recorded in the seller's books of account either.

WORKED EXAMPLE

The following are the prices of kitchens as charged to the general public by Extrav plc, and the rate of trade discounts allowed to other different retail businesses.

Name of trade customer	Goods	Retail prices charged to the general public	Rate of trade discount
		£	%
G.Harris plc	XZ/439	1,490	25
L Jarvis	XZ/537	630	10
Kat Lean Ltd	VB/552	4,600	50
Max E Mum	NJ/145	6,780	70
O Prune	VB/530	138	30

Required Show the entries as they would appear in the sales day book of Extrav plc.

Answer

Sales day book

	£
G Harris plc	1,117.50
L Jarvis	567.00
Kat Lean	2,300.00
Max E Mum	2,034.00
O Prune	96.60
	6,115.10

Similarly, in the purchases day books of the customers of Extrav plc, the amounts net of the trade discount would be entered.

So in L Jarvis's purchases day book we would find an entry:

Extrav plc   567

Posting to the appropriate ledgers would follow the lines shown earlier in this chapter.

Chapter summary

- All transactions must be entered into a book of prime entry before they can be entered in the double-entry system.
- There are six books of prime entry.
- Five deal with credit transactions:
  – purchases day book
  – sales day book
  – purchases returns day book
  – sales returns day book
  – journal

Chapter summary

- The five are lists from which ledger entries are compiled.
- The cash book deals with all cash and bank transactions and is also part of the double-entry system.
- Trade discount is a reduction in price charged by a supplier to a customer who is in business.

SELF-TEST QUESTIONS

- Give another name for the sales book.
- Give another name for the journal.
- Name the source document used to prepare the purchases day book
- Name the source document used to prepare the sales returns day book.
- Which two ledger accounts are prepared from entries in the sales day book?
- Which two accounts are prepared from entries in the purchases returns day book?
- Give another name for returns inwards.
- Give another name for returns outwards.
- Which book of prime entry is also part of the double-entry system?
- Name one use for the journal.

TEST QUESTIONS

QUESTION 1

The purchases day book of Ghito is shown:

Purchases day book

	£
Andrew	460
Zara	34
Kijah	593
Peter	742
	1,829

Required Prepare the ledger accounts from the entries in the purchases day book.

QUESTION 2

The purchases day book of Reg is shown:

Purchases day book

	£
Collins	599
O'Mally	43
Otis	777
Bradley	75
	1,494

Required Prepare the ledger accounts from the entries in the purchases day book.

QUESTION 3

Bertrand receives the following purchases invoices:

Invoice no.	Supplier's name	Amount of invoice
		£
1	Froot	213
2	Acme	54
3	Dixon	730
4	Gold	107

Required Prepare the appropriate day book and post the entries to the ledger accounts. Indicate the ledger used.

QUESTION 4

Charlotte receives the following purchase invoices:

Invoice no.	Supplier's name	Amount of invoice
		£
5	Garewal	513
6	Shaddon	78
7	Schmidt	920
8	Brax	703

Required Prepare the appropriate day book and post the entries to the ledger accounts. Indicate the ledgers used.

QUESTION 5

The sales day book for Rab is given.

Sales day book

	£
Parker	439
Clive	51
Gray	882
Fitton	29
	1,401

Required Prepare the ledger accounts from the entries in the sales day book.

QUESTION 6

The sales day book for Mandy is given.

Sales day book

	£
Sacks	510
Baggs	409
Perce	67
Walls	111
	1,097

Required Prepare the ledger accounts from the entries in the sales day book

QUESTION 7

Keith has the following copy sales invoices:

Sales invoice no.	Customer name	Amount of invoice
		£
34	Rowan	91
35	Ash	631
36	Holly	76
37	Berry	522

Required Prepare the appropriate day book and post the entries to the ledger accounts. Indicate the ledgers used.

QUESTION 8

Alice has the following copy sales invoices:

Sales invoice no.	Customer name	Amount of invoice
		£
175	Russell	9
176	Cavendish	1,563
177	O'Toole	57
178	Green	63

Required Prepare the appropriate day book and post the entries to the ledger accounts. Indicate the ledgers used.

QUESTION 9

The following purchases returns day book for Gwen is given.

Purchases returns day book

	£
Samson	23
Tardy	54
Suchard	14
	91

Required Prepare the ledger accounts from the purchases returns day book. Indicate the ledgers used.

QUESTION 10

The following purchases returns day book for Jane is given.

Purchases returns day book

	£
Felix	34
Catt	12
Gnort	134
	180

Required Prepare the ledger accounts from the purchases returns day book. Indicate the ledgers used.

QUESTION 11

The following sales returns day book for Harold is given:

Sales returns day book

	£
Randall	38
Hamilton	15
Frame	103
	156

Required Prepare the ledger accounts from the sales returns day book. Indicate the ledgers used.

QUESTION 12

The following sales returns day book for Anders is given:

Sales returns day book

	£
Snood	46
Dores	17
Voisin	39
	102

Required Prepare the ledger accounts from the sales returns day book. Indicate the ledgers used.

QUESTION 13

On 15 June Grant purchased a delivery van for £35,000, on credit from Fogg's Garage.

Required Prepare the journal entries to record this transaction

Remember a narrative is always used.

QUESTION 14

On 7 November 20*8 Phillipa purchased a freezer for her shop for £1,200 from Icecold Ltd. She will pay for the freezer at the end of December 20*8.

Required Prepare the journal entries to record this transaction.

QUESTION 15

On 6 January 20*8 Branch sold a machine used in his business for £200 to Tippers Ltd. Tippers will settle the debt at the end of January 20*8.

Required Prepare the journal entries to record this transaction.

QUESTION 16

On 29 April 20*8 Briggs, a welder, sold an electric generator he had used in his business for £300 on credit to Cox.

Required Prepare the journal entries to record this transaction.

QUESTION 17

Required Complete the table by stating, for each transaction, the book of prime entry to be used; the account to be debited; and the account to be credited.

The first row has been completed for you.

Transaction	Book of prime entry	Account debited	Account credited
Goods sold on credit	Sales day book	Customer	Sales
Fixed asset sold for cash			
Goods for resale purchased on credit			
Cash sales			
Purchase of goods for resale paid cash			
Cheques received from credit customers			
Cash withdrawn for personal use			
Insurance premium paid with cash			
Fixed asset sold payment to be received next month			
Wages paid by cash			

QUESTION 18

Required Complete the table by stating, for each transaction, the book of prime entry to be used; the account to be debited; and the account to be credited.

Transaction	Book of prime entry	Account debited	Account credited
Electricity paid by cheque			
Fixed asset sold on credit			
Purchases made on credit			
Receipts paid into bank			
Credit sale of goods			
Fixed assets purchased on credit			
Goods returned to supplier			
Fixed asset sold for cash			
Goods returned from customer			
Purchases paid for with cash			

QUESTION 19

Required Identify the book of prime entry to be written up from the following source documents:

- invoice received for purchase of goods for resale
- cash register till roll
- copy credit note sent to customer
- invoice received for purchase of new warehouse on credit.

QUESTION 20

Required Identify the book of prime entry to be written up from the following source documents:

- copy sales invoice
- receipt for cash sale of old delivery van
- credit note received from supplier
- cash receipt for purchase of goods for resale.

CHAPTER
EIGHT

The trial balance

We have seen that every time that we make a debit entry into our double-entry system we must also make a credit entry.

If we follow this rule, then the total of all debit entries must equal the sum of all credit entries.

A trial balance is a summary of all the entries in the double-entry system.

It checks that each transaction has been entered once on the debit side of an account and once on the credit side of another account.

A balancing figure is an amount that needs to be included in the debit side or credit side of an account to make the debit side equal to the credit side.

Specification coverage:
AQA Unit 1
OCR Unit 1

By the end of this chapter you should be able to:
- prepare a trial balance
- identify errors not revealed by a trial balance
- prepare and use a suspense account
- calculate the effect that errors will have on gross and net profits.

EXAMPLE

Dr	An account	Cr
£		£
23		45
41		
16		

The debit side of the account adds to £80.
The credit side adds to £45.
To make the account balance we need to insert £35 into the credit side.
The account looks like this:

Dr	An account	Cr
£		£
23		45
41		35
16		
80		80

The account balances.
This process makes it look as though the debit entries were exactly the same amounts as the credit entries – not true!
The debit side was £35 heavier. We need to reflect this when we start the account again.

We carry the balance down.

We start anew with an opening balance of £35.

Dr	An account	Cr
£		£
23		45
41		35
16		
80		80
35		

The rules of our double-entry game say that every time we include a debit entry in the system we must also include a credit entry.

We have done just that. We inserted a credit entry to make the account balance. Our debit entry starts us off again.

WORKED EXAMPLE

The following accounts are given:

Dr	Zog	Cr		Dr	Melvyn	Cr		Dr	Tan	Cr
£		£		£		£		£		£
23		53		12		34		71		90
13		41		25		37		27		38
		8		73				91		

Required Balance the accounts and carry down any balances.

Answer

Dr	Zog	Cr		Dr	Melvyn	Cr		Dr	Tan	Cr
£		£		£		£		£		£
23		53		12		34		71		90
13		41		25		37		27		38
66		8		73		39		91		61
102		102		110		110		189		189
		66		39				61		

When a balance is described as a debit balance or a credit balance, we are describing the balance required to start the account up again; the balance that has been brought down.

In the example above:

- Zog's account has a credit balance of £66
- Melvyn's account has a debit balance of £39
- Tan's account has a debit balance of £61.

QUESTION 1

The following accounts are given:

Dr	Albert	Cr		Dr	Annie	Cr		Dr	Arthur	Cr
£		£		£		£		£		£
14		56		28		9		79		52
34		67		51		7		17		34
61						49		70		

Required Balance the accounts and carry down any balances.

QUESTION 2

The following accounts are given:

Dr	Rent account (GL)	Cr		Dr	Sales account (GL)	Cr		Dr	Tungi (SL)	Cr
£						£		£		£
450						723		46		44
450						218		39		2
450						109				13

Required Balance the accounts and carry down any balances.

We prepare a trial balance by balancing all the ledger accounts and carrying down any outstanding balances on each account.

We then list all the debit balances under a debit column of the trial balance and list each credit balance in a column headed 'credit'.

The debit column is totalled and the credit column is totalled.

The two columns should have the same total.

If we extract a trial balance and the two sides total to the same figure, we can say with some certainty that every debit has a corresponding credit.

If the trial balance totals do not agree, then we can say with some certainty that there are some errors in the double-entry system.

Here are a couple of simple double-entry examples using 'T' accounts, followed by a very simple trial balance.

WORKED EXAMPLE

The following transactions are for Gary's business:

1 Gary purchased goods for resale £153 from Dora on credit.
2 He sold goods £29 to Chris on credit.
3 Gary sold goods for cash £296.
4 He paid motor expenses £68, paying cash

Required Enter the transactions in Gary's ledger. Carry down any balances and check the entries by extracting a trial balance.

Answer

Dr	Purchases account	Cr	Dr	Dora	Cr
	£				£
	153				153

Dr	Sales account	Cr	Dr	Chris	Cr
		£		£	
		29		29	
		296			

Dr	Cash account	Cr	Dr	Motor expenses account	Cr
	£	£		£	
	296	68		68	

Trial balance	£	£	
Purchases	153		If the account shows a debit balance; the trial balance shows a debit balance.
Dora		153	If the account shows a credit balance; the trial balance shows a credit balance.
Sales		325	Sales have credit entries totalling £325; the trial balance shows this balance.
Chris	29		
Cash	228		If the debit side is 'heavier', the trial balance shows the debit balancing figure.
Motor expenses	68		
	478	478	

The trial balance has shown that we have entered our transactions accurately.

WORKED EXAMPLE

The following ledger accounts have been extracted from a ledger.

Dr	Cash account	Cr		Dr	Bank account	Cr
£		£		£		£
42		100		365		534
534		458		912		141
		12				69

Dr	Rent account	Cr		Dr	Wages account	Cr
£				£		
100				458		

Dr	Sales account	Cr		Dr	Purchases account	Cr
		£		£		
		42		141		
		365		69		
		912		12		

Required Balance the accounts. Carry down any balances and extract a trial balance to check the accuracy of the ledger accounts.

Answer

Dr	Cash account	Cr		Dr	Bank account	Dr
£		£		£		£
42		100		365		534
534		458		912		141
		12				69
		_6_				_533_
_576_		_576_		_1,277_		_1,277_
6						533

Dr	Rent account	Cr		Dr	Wages account	Cr
£				£		
100				458		

Dr	Sales account	Cr		Dr	Purchases account	Cr
£		£		£		£
		42		141		
		365		69		
_1,319_		912		_12_		_222_
_1,319_		_1,319_		_222_		_222_
		_1,319_		_222_		

Trial balance

	£	£
Cash	6	
Bank	533	
Rent	100	
Wages	458	
Sales		1,319
Purchases	_222_	
	_1,319_	_1,319_

WORKED EXAMPLE

Sharon owns and runs a clothes shop. The following transactions have taken place:

1 Sharon's cash sales amount to £612.
2 She purchases jeans from Cath, £129 on credit.
3 Sharon sells a shirt and jeans to Ursula, £76 on credit.
4 She pays the shop rent £250 cash.
5 She purchases trainers £345 on credit from Rocky.
6 Sharon pays wages £166 using cash.

Required Enter the transactions in Sharon's ledger.

Carry down any balances.

Extract a trial balance to check the accuracy of your entries.

Answer

Dr	Cash account (GL)	Cr	Dr	Sales account (GL)	Cr
	£	£			£
612		250			612
		166			76

Dr	Purchases account (GL)	Cr	Dr	Cath (PL)	Cr
	£				£
129					129
345					

Dr	Ursula (SL)	Cr	Dr	Rent account (GL)	Cr
	£			£	
76				250	

Dr	Rocky (PL)	Cr	Dr	Wages account (GL)	Cr
		£		£	
		345		166	

Trial balance

	£	£
Cash	196	
Sales		688
Purchases	474	
Cath		129
Ursula	76	
Rent	250	
Rocky		345
Wages	166	
	1,162	1,162

QUESTION 3

The following information is given for Timmy:

1 Timmy sells goods for cash £750.
2 He pays rent £100 cash.
3 Timmy sells goods on credit £48 to Chas.
4 He pays wages £78 cash.

5   Timmy purchases goods for resale £330 on credit from Duncan.
6   He purchases goods for resale £69 from Vera, paying cash.

Required Enter the transactions in Timmy's ledger.

Carry down any balances.

Extract a trial balance to check the accuracy of the entries.

QUESTION 4

Malcolm provides the following information:

1   Malcolm purchases a delivery vehicle £12,650 on credit from Drest Motors.
2   Malcolm purchases goods for resale £542 on credit from S Unset.
3   He purchases fuel for his vehicle £35 cash.
4   He sells goods for cash £212.
5   Malcolm purchases goods for resale £239 on credit from S Unset.
6   He sells goods £360 on credit to Ovis.
7   Malcolm withdraws £50 cash for personal use.
8   He pays insurance premium £100 cash.

Required Enter the transactions in Malcolm's ledger.

Carry down any balances.

Extract a trial balance to check the accuracy of the entries.

The trial balance is made up of the balances extracted from the ledger. It summarises the balances.

If you consider the trial balances that have been prepared so far, you should see that a pattern has started to emerge:

DEBIT BALANCES
- Assets are always debit balances. Examples above are cash balances (an asset); debtors like Ursula (an asset) as she owes money to Sharon.
- Expenses are always debit balances. Examples above are the balance on the rent account; the balance on the wages account; the balance on the purchases account.

CREDIT BALANCES
- Incomes and benefits are always credit balances. The example above is the balance on the sales account.
- Liabilities are always credit balances. The examples above are Cath and Rocky – they are creditors – Sharon owes them money.

A trial balance will show balances thus:

Debit balances	Credit balances
Assets	Liabilities
Expenses	Incomes
	Benefits

QUESTION 5

Wendy owns and runs a card and stationery shop. The following is a list of accounts found in Wendy's ledgers:

Name the ledger in which the account would be found. Place a tick in the appropriate column to show the category into which each item falls.

Indicate whether a balance on the account would appear in the debit or credit column of her trial balance.

EXAMPLE

The following is a list of account headings found in Tricia's ledger.
Place a tick in the appropriate columns to show the category into which each item falls.
Indicate whether a balance on the account would appear in the debit or credit column of her trial balance.

EXAMPLE *continued*

Account Name	Asset	Expense	Liability	Income or benefit	Debit	Credit
Wages						
Premises						
Creditor						
Advertising						
Sales						
Bank overdraft						

Answer

Wages Exp/Dr; Premises Ass/Dr; Creditor Liab/Cr; Advertising Exp/Dr; Sales Inc/Cr; Bank overdraft Liab/Cr.

Account name	Ledger	Asset	Expense	Liability	Income or benefit	Debit	Credit
Motor vehicles							
Rates							
Mortgage							
Carriage inwards							
Premises							
Quentin – a credit customer							
Capital							
Tara – a credit supplier							
Purchases							
Insurance							
Sales							
Carriage outward							

WORKED EXAMPLE

The following balances have been extracted from the ledgers of Lionel on 30 April 20*8.

Buildings at cost £120,000; fixtures and fittings at cost £45,000; van £14,500; motor expenses £4,160; rent £7,000; rates £2,400; insurance £2,100; cash in hand £120; balance at bank £3,670; debtors £850; creditors £1,200; sales £260,000; purchases £140,000; capital £78,600.

WORKED EXAMPLE *continued*

Required Prepare a trial balance at 30 April 20*8 for Lionel.

Answer

Lionel
Trial balance at 30 April 20*8

	Dr £	Cr £
Buildings at cost	120,000	
Fixtures and fittings at cost	45,000	
Van at cost	14,500	
Motor expenses	4,160	
Rent	7,000	
Rates	2,400	
Insurance	2,100	
Cash in hand	120	
Balance at bank	3,670	
Debtors	850	
Creditors		1,200
Sales		260,000
Purchases	140,000	
Capital		78,600
	339,800	339,800

WORKED EXAMPLE

The following balances have been extracted from the ledgers of Leigh on 31 August 20*8:

purchases £87,000; sales £140,000; vehicles at cost £18,000; motor expenses £4,200; rent £8,600; rates £1,500; insurance £2,400; repairs £940; cash £310; bank £4,460; debtors £1,680; creditors £240; drawings £16,500; capital £5,350.

Required Prepare a trial balance at 31 August 20*8 for Leigh.

Answer

Leigh
Trial balance at 31 August 20*8

	£ Dr	£ Cr
Purchases	87,000	
Sales		140,000
Vehicles at cost	18,000	
Motor expenses	4,200	
Rent	8,600	
Rates	1,500	
Insurance	2,400	
Repairs	940	
Cash	310	
Bank	4,460	
Debtors	1,680	
Creditors		240
Drawings	16,500	
Capital		5,350
	145,590	145,590

Do you recognise the trial balance?

It is the 'list' that you used to prepare balance sheets, trading accounts and profit and loss accounts in earlier chapters.

We have divided it into debit balances and credit balances from the ledgers.

Note

- The debit and credit column totals are the same. So we can say with some certainty that whoever did the double-entry bookkeeping probably made a debit entry for every credit entry. ('Probably' means that there could be some missing debit and/or credits of the same total value – these are known as 'compensating errors'. But more of errors later!)
- The debit column of the trial balance contains only assets and expenses; the credit column of the trial balance contains only liabilities and incomes or benefits.

USES OF THE TRIAL BALANCE

The trial balance has only one function and that is: to check the arithmetic accuracy of the double-entry system. However, as you have already seen in earlier chapters, the trial balance can be used as a list from which to prepare the final accounts. It is generally used to prepare the trading account, the profit and loss account and the balance sheet.

LIMITATIONS OF THE TRIAL BALANCE

The trial balance has certain limitations. Even if the trial balance totals do agree, that is no guarantee that there are no mistakes in the system. There are six types of error that will not show in an incorrect trial balance – these will be listed in a moment.

If the totals of a trial balance disagree, you must run through a few checks in order to see that you have not made a simple error:

1 Check that you have added the debit column up correctly and also that you have added the credit column correctly.
2 Check that there are lots more entries in the debit column than there are in the credit column.
   The debit column should only contain assets and expenses. The credit column should only contain liabilities and incomes or benefits.
3 If you cannot find the error, look at the totals. If the debit column is smaller than the credit column total, check that you have not missed a debit balance. If the credit column total is the smaller of the two, check that you have not missed a credit balance.
4 If the error has not been found by going through the three previous points, divide the difference in the totals by two. Then look to see if an asset has been incorrectly placed in the credit column or if a liability has been placed in the debit column, because items in the incorrect column will double the mistake.
5 If you divide the error by 9 and your answer is a whole number, then the error could be what is known as a 'transposition error', for example, £123 entered as £132 or £96 written as £69.

ERRORS THAT ARE NOT REVEALED WHEN EXTRACTING A TRIAL BALANCE

There are six errors that are not revealed by extracting a trial balance:

1 errors of commission
2 complete reversal of entries
3 errors of omission
4 errors of principle
5 errors or original entry
6 compensating errors.

Learn the names of these errors. This is a popular examination topic.

THE TYPES OF ERRORS IN DETAIL

Errors of commission

Errors of commission arise when the correct amount is entered on the correct side of the wrong account.

If £600 rent was paid by cheque and the rates account was debited with £600, this would not be revealed by the trial balance.

Complete reversal of entries

This occurs when the correct figures are used but both entries are entered on the wrong side of the accounts used. For example, if £70 of goods were purchased from P Smith and P Smith was debited with £70, and the purchases account was credited with £70, no error would be revealed.

Errors of omission

These errors occur when a transaction is completely missed from the ledgers. If a purchase invoice was destroyed, there would be no entry in the purchase day book and therefore the purchases account in the general ledger would not contain the transaction and neither would the supplier's account contain the transaction. The debit entry is zero; the credit entry is zero. The debit and credit entries agree.

Errors of principle

These errors occur when a transaction is posted to the incorrect class of account. For example, if a new vehicle was purchased on credit and was inadvertently entered into the motor expenses account, this would not be revealed by the trial balance. Some readers may be confused by the difference between an error of commission and an error of principle.

An error of commission will not affect profits or the validity of the balance sheet.

An error of principle will affect both the profit of the business and will either understate or overstate the entry on the balance sheet.

You may wish to use this rule when trying to decide whether an incorrect posting is an error of commission or an error of principle.

If a vehicle costing £23,500 is posted to the motor expenses account, the profit will be understated by £23,500. The fixed assets shown on the balance will also be understated by £23,500.

Errors of original entry

If a credit sale for £176 was entered in the sales day book as £167, then a debit entry of £167 would be recorded in the customer's account in the sales ledger and a credit entry of £167 would be entered in the sales account in the general ledger. The debit entry is £167; the credit entry is £167. The debit and credit entries agree.

Compensating errors

Compensating errors cancel each other out. If the debit side of an account is totalled incorrectly and is £100 too much, and another totally separate account with credit entries is incorrectly totalled by £100, then no error will be revealed.

WORKED EXAMPLE

Required Identify the types of errors listed below.

1 Vehicle repair paid by cheque £649:

Debit entry	**Credit entry**
Bank account £649	Motor expenses account £649

2 Machine sold for £4,000:

Debit entry	**Credit entry**
Bank account £4,000	Sales account £4,000

3 Goods purchased £29 from Trip & Co. on credit:

Debit entry	**Credit entry**
Purchases account £29	Prit & Co. £29

4 Goods sold £76 on credit to Ricket:

Debit entry	**Credit entry**
Ricket account £67	Sales account £67

Answer

1 Complete reversal of entries.
2 Error of principle.
3 Error of commission.
4 Compensating error (also original entry error).

QUESTION 6

The following errors have been discovered in the ledgers of Howard:

1 Howard had recently purchased shop fittings £3,700 on credit from Minser. The item had been recorded in Howard's journal as:

	Dr	**Cr**
	£	£
Shop fittings	7,300	
Minser		7,300

2 Repairs to his vehicle of £560, paid by cheque, had been entered as a debit in the vehicles account.
3 A purchase invoice for £281 had been destroyed and had not been entered in the purchase day book.
4 A cheque for £33 received from Roter had been entered as a credit in R Oter's account.
5 Repairs carried out on Howard's wife's car of £612 had been entered on the debit side of the business motor expenses account.

Required Identify the types of errors discovered in Howard's ledger.

Although the prime function of a trial balance is to test the accuracy of our double-entry system, we often use a trial balance as a list from which we prepare our final accounts. This saves us much time.

However, if the trial balance fails to balance then we can rest assured that our final accounts will not balance.

When the trial balance fails to balance, the difference between the total of the debit side and the total of the credit side is placed in a temporary account called a 'suspense account'.

If the debit column of the trial balance has a smaller total than the credit column we insert an item 'suspense account' in the debit column in order that the two columns will have the same total. If the total of the credit column of the trial balance is smaller than the total of the debit column then the amount for suspense account would be inserted in the credit column.

We can then prepare a set of draft final accounts, safe in the knowledge that they will balance (provided **we** do not make any errors in their preparation).

EXAMPLE

Lara has extracted a trial balance. The totals of the debit and credit columns do not agree.

	Debit column total	Credit column total
	£	£
	123,456	132,546
Lara inserts a suspense account to make the trial balance balance	9,090	
	132,546	132,546

EXAMPLE

Lawrence has extracted a trial balance from his ledgers. The totals of the debit and credit columns do not agree.

	Debit column total	Credit column total
	£	£
	890,321	889,617
Lawrence inserts a suspense account to make the trial balance balance		704
	890,321	890,321

In the draft final accounts, a suspense account shown as a debit balance in the trial balance will be shown as a current asset on the balance sheet.

If the suspense account has been included as a credit balance in the trial balance, it should be shown as a current liability on the balance sheet.

● EXAMINATION TIP

A word of warning: if you prepare a set of final accounts as an answer to an examination question and those accounts do not balance, run through the checks mentioned earlier. If you do not find the error do not make the balance sheet balance by inserting a suspense item. This wastes time and you are merely drawing attention to the fact that you have made an error in your answer.

How would Lara's suspense account be shown in her final accounts?

Lara's suspense account balance would be shown as a current asset (£9,090) on her draft balance sheet.

How would Lawrence's suspense account be shown in his final accounts?

Lawrence's suspense account balance would be shown as a current liability (£704) on his draft balance sheet.

When the errors that have prevented the trial balance from balancing are found and corrected, the draft accounts are amended and should be correct, according to the information given.

When errors affecting the balancing of the trial balance are found they will be entered in the suspense account (and in another account since we are using a double-entry system).

Casting is a term used by accountants for adding. **Undercast** means that a total is lower than it ought to be. **Overcast** means that a total is greater than it ought to be.

Remember:
- not all errors affect the balancing of the trial balance
- when the corrections are entered in the suspense account, the suspense account balance should be eliminated.

WORKED EXAMPLE

On 31 March 20*8 Vincent's trial balance failed to balance. The debit column total was £20,500 and the credit column was £21,000. The difference was entered in a suspense account.

Since extracting the trial balance the following errors have been found:

1 The purchases account was undercast by £1,000.
2 Goods sold on credit to J. Latimer for £500 were debited to J. Latimer but had not been included in the sales day book.

Required a) Prepare the journal entries to correct the errors.
b) Prepare the suspense account after the corrections have been made.

If journal entries are required, we ask ourselves the following questions:

In the first example:
Which account was debited? Answer: purchases account.
Which account was credited? Answer: suspense account.

In the second example:
Which account was debited? Answer: suspense account.
Which account was credited? Answer: sales account.

Answer
a)

Journal

	Dr	Cr
	£	£
1 Purchases account	1,000	
Suspense account		1,000

Correction of error: Purchase day undercast by £1,000.

| 2 Suspense account | 500 | |
| Sales account | | 500 |

Correction of error: Sale of goods to Latimer not included in sales day book.

b)

Suspense account

	Dr		Cr
	£		£
Trial balance difference	500	Purchases	1,000
Sales account	500		
	1,000		1,000

WORKED EXAMPLE

On 30 November 20*8 Maureen's trial balance failed to agree. The debit column totalled £230,161 and the credit column totalled £189,521. The difference was entered in a suspense account. On further examination of the books of account the following errors were found:

1 Motoring expenses of £1,700 had been entered in the van account.
2 The total of the sales day book for July £16,320 had been posted to the debit side of the purchases account.
3 The total rent received of £4,000 for the year had been entered as a debit entry in the rent payable account.
4 Maureen had withdrawn goods for her own use of £4,700 during the year. These goods had been entered on the debit side of the purchases account.

Required a) Prepare the journal entries to correct the errors.
b) Prepare the suspense account.

Answer
(a)

Journal

	Dr	Cr
	£	£
Motor expenses	1,700	
Van		1,700

Error of principle: Motor expenses included as capital expenditure.

Suspense account	32,640	
Sales		16,320
Purchases		16,320

Posting error: Sales posted incorrectly to purchases account.

Suspense account	8,000	
Rent receivable		4,000
Rent payable		4,000

Posting error: Rent receivable entered incorrectly in the rent payable account.

Drawings	9,400	
Purchases		9,400

Posting error: Drawings entered as purchases.

(b) **[Suspense account]**

	£		£
Sales account	16,320	Trial balance difference	40,640
Purchases account	16,320		
Rent receivable	4,000		
Rent payable	4,000		
	40,640		40,640

Any errors occurring in the double-entry system will generally have an effect on either:

■ the profit and loss account, or
■ the balance sheet.

Errors that affect the component parts of the trading account will affect both:

■ the gross profit, and
■ the net profit.

Errors that affect the component parts of the profit and loss account will affect:

- the net profit. (Any change in net profit will also affect the balance sheet in that net profit affects capital.)

● EXAMINATION TIP

Examination questions frequently ask candidates to correct errors and then to work on a draft net profit to arrive at a corrected net profit for the period.

WORKED EXAMPLE

The following accounts contain errors:
- rates account
- sales account
- wages account
- returns inward account
- Horace's account – a debtor's account.

Required Complete the table showing if there are changes to gross profit and net profit when corrections are made.

Account	Gross profit	Net profit
Rates account		
Sales account		
Wages account		
Returns inward account		
Horace's account		

Answer

Account	Gross profit	Net profit
Rates account	No change	Change
Sales account	Change	Change
Wages account	No change	Change
Returns inward account	Change	Change
Horace's account	No change	No change

QUESTION 7

The following accounts contain errors:

- rent account
- mortgage account
- insurance account
- drawings account
- advertising account
- returns outward
- carriage outward
- purchases account.

Required Complete the table showing changes to gross profit and net profit when corrections are made.

Account	Gross profit	Net profit
Rent account		
Mortgage account		
Insurance account		
Drawings account		
Advertising account		
Returns outward account		
Carriage outward account		
Purchases account		

After any errors are discovered:

- the journal should be used to effect the changes
- the ledger accounts should be corrected
- gross profit should be adjusted
- net profit should be adjusted, and
- changes to balance sheet items should be made.

WORKED EXAMPLE

The trial balance of Gordon Brannen failed to balance on 31 March 20*8. The difference was entered in a suspense account. A set of draft final accounts was prepared before the errors were discovered. The draft net profit was £27,864.

The following errors were discovered:

1 The purchase day book had been overcast by £100.
2 A payment made to M Dixon £121 had been posted to the incorrect side of her account.
3 Fixtures purchased for £2340 had been entered in the purchase day book.
4 Goods sold on credit to B Hoyle £97 had been completely omitted from the books of account.
5 An insurance payment for £430 had been correctly entered in the cash book but had not been entered in the insurance account.

Required (a) Prepare journal entries to correct the errors.
(b) Prepare a suspense account after the errors have been corrected.
(c) Prepare a statement showing the corrected net profit.

Answer

(a)

Journal

	Dr	Cr
	£	£
Suspense	100	
Purchases		100
Correction of error: Purchase day book overcast by £100.		
Dixon	242	
Suspense		242
Payment of £121 posted to the incorrect side of Dixon's account.		
Fixtures	2340	
Purchases		2340
Fixtures incorrectly entered in purchases account.		
B Hoyle	97	
Sales		97
Sale of goods to Hoyle omitted from ledgers.		

Insurance   430
  Suspense   430
Insurance premium omitted from insurance account.

(b)   **Suspense account**

	£		£
Purchases	100	Dixon	242
*Trial balance difference	<u>572</u>	Insurance	<u>430</u>
	672		672

Note that the amount of the difference on the trial balance * was not given in the question.
It must be assumed to be the amount necessary to make the suspense account balance, since all the errors have been corrected.

(c) Statement of corrected net profit

	£
Profit as per draft accounts	27,864
1 Decrease in purchases	100
3 Decrease in purchases	2,340
4 Increase in sales	97
5 Increase in insurance	(430)
Corrected net profit	29,971

Error 2 does not affect the net profit. It would, however, affect the total of creditors which appears on the balance sheet. It would reduce current liabilities.

● EXAMINATION TIP

If a transaction has no effect, tell the examiner this. If you don't say, the examiner does not know whether you have omitted the transaction because this is the correct treatment or because you do not know what the effect will be.

When correcting a draft net profit, remember that:

- any expense account that is debited in the journal will reduce draft net profit
- any expense account that is credited in the journal will increase draft net profit.

Notes to the answer
- Always use headings. They often carry marks; don't throw these marks away!
- Always give a precise narrative to each journal entry.
- You may have to calculate the trial balance difference to enter in the suspense account.
- Identify any items you have not used in the statement of adjusted profit. If you don't, an examiner does not know whether you have missed the transaction out deliberately because you do not know how to treat the item.

Chapter summary

- A trial balance is extracted from the three ledgers.
- It is a summarised version of all the accounts extracted from the three ledgers.
- The debit column of a trial balance lists assets and expenses.
- The credit column of a trial balance lists liabilities and incomes and benefits.
- A trial balance checks the arithmetical accuracy of the double-entry bookkeeping system.
- If the trial balance balances it is not a guarantee that the system is free of errors.
- There are six types of error that will not be disclosed by extracting a trial balance.

- The trial balance can also be used as a useful list from which to prepare the final accounts of the business.
- A suspense account is used to make the debit column total agree with the credit column total if the trial balance does not balance.
- When errors are rectified the suspense account should 'disappear'.

SELF-TEST QUESTIONS

- The debit side of an account totals £242; the credit side totals £200. What is the balance on the account?
- Generally, which side of a trial balance will have the most entries?
- Liabilities are shown on the...........side of a trial balance. Fill in the gap.
- Incomes are shown on the............side of a trial balance. Fill in the gap.
- From which ledger are the figures used in a trial balance extracted?
- In which ledger would you expect to find the account of Gerald, a supplier of goods on credit?
- In which ledger would you expect to find the returns inwards account?
- The trial balance balances so there are no mistakes in the double-entry system. True or false?
- What is the main use of a trial balance?
- What is an error of commission?
- What does the mnemonic CROPOC stand for?
- The debit column of a trial balance totals £230,150 and the credit column totals £230,000. What amount will be entered in a suspense account?
- What does the term 'overcast' mean?
- Would an error in the carriage inwards account affect gross profit or net profit?
- Would an expense account credited in the journal increase or decrease net profit?

TEST QUESTIONS

QUESTION 8

The following information is given for Boris Klien at 31 July 20*8:

capital at 1 August 20*7 £2,387; motor vehicle £18,000; machinery £21,000; premises £75,000; wages £23,471; rent £8,500; rates £1,342; purchases £68,577; sales £202,767; returns inwards £312; returns outwards £928; stock 1 August £4,968; debtors £14,307; creditors £8,942; bank balance £4,547; mortgage £25,000.

Required Prepare a trial balance at 31 July 20*8.

QUESTION 9

The following information is given for Sue Lycett at 31 December 20*8:

Trial balance at 31 August 20*8

	Dr	Cr
	£	£
Capital	45,578	
Vehicles at cost	43,500	
Office equipment at cost	17,600	
Debtors		4,656
Creditors	2,873	
Stock 1 September 20*7	4,502	
Purchases	56,221	
Sales		132,448
Wages	34,662	
Motor expenses	3,189	

Rent and rates	4,692	
Insurances		1,634
Advertising	2,654	
General expenses	4,654	
Carriage inwards	543	
Carriage outwards		511
Returns inwards		1,985
Returns outwards	588	
Bank balance		346
Cash in hand	138	
	221,394	141,580

Required Redraft the trial balance, making any corrections deemed necessary.

QUESTION 10

The following information is available for Malcolm Troqueer:

Trial balance at 31 January 20*8

	Dr	Cr
	£	£
Capital	7,486	
Premises at cost	60,000	
Office equipment at cost	12,000	
Delivery vehicle at cost		8,000
Mortgage on premises	30,000	
HP debt on vehicle		2,000
Purchases		83,904
Sales		181,657
Wages	34,000	
General expenses		16,471
Debtors	9,384	
Creditors	7,168	
Bank overdraft	1,477	
Cash in hand	236	
Stock 1 February 20*7		5,793
Suspense	136,074	
	297,825	297,825

Required Redraft the trial balance, making any corrections deemed necessary.

QUESTION 11

The following information is available:

1   Rent account has been overcast £300.
    Wages account has been undercast £150.
    Sales account has been overcast £150.
2   Returns inwards £219 has been debited to sales account.
3   Purchase of delivery vehicle £19,650 has been debited to motor expenses.
4   Purchase of one ball point pen 17 pence has not been included in the books of account because it is such a trivial amount.

Required Identify the types of errors described.

QUESTION 12

The following information is available:

1   Business motor expenses for the week £82 has been entered in the cash book as £28.
2   Capital introduced by the proprietor £4,000 has been entered in the sales account.
3   A credit sale to Danny £49 has been credited to Dani's account.
4   The cost of an advertisement to sell the motorbike of the proprietor's son £28 has been included in the advertising account.

Required Identify the types of errors described.

QUESTION 13

After extracting a trial balance, Ralph discovered the following errors in his double-entry system:

1 Rent £200 has been entered in the rates account.
2 The wages account has been undercast by £400.
3 Payment made to Tom £146 entered in cash book but not in Tom's account.
4 Payment for insurance £273 debited in cash book and credited to insurance account.

a) Prepare journal entries showing the corrections necessary to correct the errors.
b) Prepare a suspense account to correct the errors showing the original trial balance difference.
c) State which side of the trial balance was the larger before the discovery of the errors.

QUESTION 14

After extracting a trial balance Jeanne discovered the following errors:

1 Bank charges £149 have not been entered in any books of account.
2 The sales day book has been undercast by £1,100.
3 A car service £550 on Jeanne's private car has been included in motor expenses.
4 Carriage inwards £48 has been included in the carriage outwards account.

Required a) Prepare journal entries showing the entries necessary to correct the errors.
b) Prepare a suspense account to correct the errors showing the original trial balance difference.
c) State which side of the trial balance was the larger before the discovery of the errors.

QUESTION 15

The following errors have been discovered in the books of Monirul. He has already prepared a draft trading and profit and loss account. These have revealed a gross profit of £48,712 and a net profit of £13,467.

1 Purchases £321 from Beatrice have been debited to her account.
2 The sales returns day book has been undercast by £100.
3 Purchases on credit £1,461 have been omitted from the general ledger.
4 The sales day book has been overcast £1,010.

Required a) Prepare journal entries necessary to correct the errors.
b) Prepare a suspense account to correct the errors showing the original trial balance difference.
c) State which side of the trial balance was the larger before the discovery of the errors.
d) Prepare a statement showing the gross profit after correcting the errors.
e) Prepare a statement showing the net profit after correcting the errors.

QUESTION 16

The following errors have been discovered in the books of Jenni. She has already prepared a draft trading and profit and loss account. These have revealed a gross profit of £107,648 and a net profit of £23,614.

1 A cheque £217 paid to G Ray has been debited to Gray.
2 Carriage inwards £126 has been debited to carriage outwards.
3 A rent payment of £572 has been credited to the rent payable account as £752.
4 Jenni's drawings £432 have been included in wages as £342.
5 Wages account has been overcast by £1,200.

Required a) Prepare journal entries necessary to correct the errors.
b) Prepare a suspense account to correct the errors, showing the original trial balance difference.
c) State which side of the trial balance was the larger before the discovery of the errors.
d) Prepare a statement showing the gross profit after correcting the errors.
e) Prepare a statement showing the net profit after correcting the errors.

CHAPTER
NINE

The ledger accounts in detail

Up to now we have used 'T' accounts to record the two sides of a transaction. This is fine and it will give us the information that we require. However, it would be more useful if the 'T' accounts gave us more details of each transaction.

- It would be useful to know when the transaction took place.
- It would also be useful to be able to follow the whole transaction through to its completion, especially when a problem occurs in the system.

These problems are rectified by simple means.

Each entry should be preceded by:

- the **date** of the transaction
- a **description** stating where the corresponding entry can be located
- the appropriate **folio number** of the 'other' entry.

An entry in a ledger account may look like this:

Dr			An account		Cr
		GL		£	
7 April	Sales	17		217	

The transaction took place on 7 April. The 'opposite' entry, i.e. the credit entry, is in the sales account and the credit entry can be found on page 17 of the general ledger.

Dr		Another account			Cr
			GL	£	
	12 Sept	Purchases	28	416	

The transaction took place on 12 September. The debit entry is in the purchases account which is on page 28 of the general ledger.

> **● EXAMINATION TIP**
>
> If you are ever asked to prepare a ledger account then it must have all the details to score all of the marks. However, when you are working things out you may use 'T' accounts because this is faster and just as accurate. Many accountants and teachers use 'T' accounts to solve tricky problems and for general workings.

> **REVISION TIP**
>
> Try jotting down your workings using 'T' accounts. When you gain confidence in their use you will find that you can use them as a revision tool and for solving problems.

The information shown in ledger accounts is derived from one of the books of prime entry.

Specification coverage:
AQA Unit 1
OCR Unit 1

By the end of this chapter you should be able to:
- write up a ledger account in detail.

WORKED EXAMPLE

The following transactions took place during the first week of October.

1 1 October Purchased goods for resale on credit from Arkimed plc £120.
2 1 October Sold goods on credit to Morris & Co £600.
3 2 October Purchased vehicle on credit from Pooley Motors plc £17,400.
4 4 October Sold goods on credit to Nelson plc £315.
5 4 October Purchased goods for resale on credit from Bain & Co £450.
6 4 October Purchased goods for resale on credit from Darth & Son £170.
7 7 October Sold goods on credit to Olivia Ltd £1,340.
8 7 October Returned damaged goods £38 to Arkimed plc.
9 7 October Purchased goods for resale on credit from Charlene £320.

Required a) Identify the source document that has been used in each case to write up the book of prime entry.
b) Write up the books of prime entry.
c) Show the entries as they appear in each ledger account.

Answer

(a) Purchase invoices   Copy sales invoices   Credit note
    Transactions 1,3,5,6,9.   Transactions 2,4,7.   Transaction 8.

(b)

	Purchase day book		£		Sales day book		£
1 Oct	Arkimed plc	PL 1	120	1 Oct	Morris plc	SL 1	600
4 Oct	Bain & Co	PL 2	450	4 Oct	Nelson plc	SL 2	315
4 Oct	Darth & Son	PL 3	170	7 Oct	Olivia Ltd	SL 3	1,340
7 Oct	Charlene	PL 4	320				2,255
			1,060				

	Purchase returns day book		£		Journal		£
7 Oct	Arkimed	PL 1	38	2 Oct	Vehicles	GL 4	17,400
					Pooley Motors plc	PL 5	17,400
					Purchase of vehicle from Pooley Motors plc.		

(c)
Purchases ledger

Dr				Arkimed plc			Cr
7 Oct	Returns outward	PRDB 1	38	1 Oct	Purchases	PDB 1	120

Dr				Bain &Co			Cr
				4 Oct	Purchases	PDB 1	450

Dr				Darth & Son			Cr
				4 Oct	Purchases	PDB 1	170

Dr				Charlene			Cr
				4 Oct	Purchases	PDB 1	320

Dr				Pooley Motors plc			Cr
				2 Oct	Vehicles	J 1	17 400

Sales ledger

Dr				Morris plc			Cr
1 Oct	Sales	SDB 1	600				

Dr				Nelson plc			Cr
4 Oct	Sales	SDB 1	315				

Dr		Olivia Ltd		Cr
7 Oct	Sales	SDB 1 1,340		

General ledger

Dr		Purchases account		Cr
7 Oct	Sundry creditors	PDB 1 1,060		

Dr		Sales account		Cr
		7 Oct Sundry debtors SDB 1		2,255

Dr	Returns outward account		Cr
	7 Oct Sundry creditors PRDB 1		38

Dr	Vehicles account		Cr
2 Oct Pooley Motors plc	J1 17,400		

How can we check the accuracy of our bookkeeping entries?

We can check the (arithmetic) accuracy of the entries in the double-entry system by extracting a trial balance.

The trial balance extracted from the ledgers above shows:

	Dr	Cr
	£	£
Creditors		
Arkimed		82
Bain & Co		450
Darth & Son		170
Charlene		320
Pooley Motors plc		17,400
Debtors		
Morris plc	600	
Nelson plc	315	
Olivia Ltd	1,340	
Purchases	1,060	
Sales		2,255
Returns outward		38
Vehicle	17,400	
	20,715	20,715

We can say that the bookkeeping entries are arithmetically correct.

The cash book is a book of prime entry. It contains the business cash account and the business bank account. We will consider the cash book in much more detail later.

The following example uses the cash book as a book of prime entry.

WORKED EXAMPLE

The following transactions took place during December:

1 1 December paid rent using cash £250.
2 2 December paid rates by cheque £110.
3 6 December paid wages using cash £1,782.
4 13 December paid wages using cash £1,780.
5 17 December paid insurance premium by cheque £240.
6 20 December paid wages using cash £1,780.
7 27 December paid wages using cash £1,781.
8 31 December paid rent by cheque £250.

WORKED EXAMPLE *continued*

Required a) Enter the transactions in a book of prime entry.
             b) Show the necessary ledger accounts.

Answer

a)

Cash book

Dr   **Cash account**   **Cr**

1 Dec	Rent	GL 1	250
6 Dec	Wages	GL 4	1,782
13 Dec	Wages	GL 4	1,780
20 Dec	Wages	GL 4	1,780
27 Dec	Wages	GL 4	1,781

Dr   **Bank account**   **Cr**

2 Dec	Rates	GL 2	110
17 Dec	Insurance	GL 3	240
31 Dec	Rent	GL 1	250

b)

General ledger

Dr   **Rent account**   **Cr**

1 Dec	Cash	CB 1	250
31 Dec	Bank	CB 1	250

Dr   **Rates account**   **Cr**

2 Dec	Bank	CB 1	110

Dr   **Insurance account**   **Cr**

17 Dec	Bank	CB 1	240

Dr   **Wages**   **Cr**

6 Dec	Cash	CB 1	1,782
13 Dec	Cash	CB 1	1,780
20 Dec	Cash	CB 1	1,780
27 Dec	Cash	CB 1	1,781

Entering transactions in the books of prime entry and then the ledgers is not a difficult task; it just takes patience and the ability to enter transactions twice – once on the debit side of an account and once on the credit side of another account. Remember: practice makes perfect!

Chapter summary

- Ledger accounts must show date, details of 'opposite' entry, folio details and amount of transaction.
- 'T' accounts must only be used for revision purposes or as part of workings.
- All transactions must be entered in a book of prime entry before being posted to a ledger.

SELF-TEST QUESTIONS

- Identify the four pieces of information you would expect to find on the debit side of every account.
- Identify the four pieces of information you would expect to find on the credit side of every account.
- When would you use 'T' accounts?
- Which source documents would you use to write up the sales day book?

- Which source document would you use to write up the purchase returns day book?
- Which type of account would you expect to find in the purchases ledger?
- Which type of account would you expect to find in the sales ledger?
- Name a personal ledger.

TEST QUESTIONS

QUESTION 1

Explain which book of prime entry would be used to enter the following transactions:

1 Goods for resale purchased on credit from Dast.
2 Goods returned to Berks.
3 Purchase of office equipment from Cronin for cash.
4 Goods sold to Perks on credit.
5 Cash sales.

QUESTION 2

Which book of prime entry would be used to enter the following transactions?

1 Goods returned by Marshall, a customer.
2 Purchase of computer for use in the office on credit from Offo Ltd.
3 Goods sold to Barker on credit.
4 Goods for resale purchased for cash from Tinto.
5 Petrol purchased from Clive Road Garage for cash.
6 Purchase of office equipment from Desks & Co for cash.

QUESTION 3

The following transaction took place during March 20*8:

March		£
2	Sold goods on credit to Fallon	217
6	Purchased goods on credit from Westby	179
19	Purchased goods on credit from Rawstron	731
23	Sold goods on credit to Slee	52
24	Sold goods on credit to Earley	770
31	Purchased goods on credit from Coulson	229

Required a) Enter the transactions in the appropriate books of prime entry.
b) Show the necessary entries in the ledgers.

QUESTION 4

The following credit transactions took place during August 20*8:

August		£
4	Purchased goods for resale from Dillon	551
6	Purchased goods for resale from Black	901
11	Sold goods to Adder	510
23	Purchased goods from Breem	56
30	Sold goods to Goody	190
31	Sold goods to O'Shea	77

Required a) Enter the transactions in the appropriate books of prime entry.
b) Show the necessary entries in the ledgers.

QUESTION 5

The following credit transactions took place during February 20*8:

February		£
1	Sold goods to Davidson	59
5	Purchased goods from Sellars	911
6	Purchased goods from Garewal	187
7	Purchased goods from Chan	67
15	Sold goods to Nixon	563
23	Goods returned by Davidson	19
27	Goods returned to Sellars	45

| 28 | Sold goods to Nismo | 518 |
| 28 | Goods returned to Garewal | 12 |

Required a) Enter the transactions in the appropriate books of prime entry.
b) Show the necessary entries in the ledgers.

QUESTION 6

The following credit transactions took place during April 20*8:

April		£
1	Sold goods to Marks	458
3	Sold goods to Henry	121
4	Goods retuned by Marks	59
7	Purchased goods from Binns	72
8	Sold goods to Shaw	923
9	Purchased goods from Baxter	777
21	Purchased goods from Spencer	43
25	Goods returned by Henry	21
28	Sold goods to Marks	631
29	Goods returned to Binns	55

Required a) Enter the transactions in the appropriate books of prime entry.
b) Show the necessary entries in the ledgers

QUESTION 7

The following credit transactions took place during October 20*8:

October		£
3	Sold goods to Clement	456
5	Purchased delivery van from Austen Motors	23,580
8	Sold goods to Lycett	53
12	Purchased goods from Crosby	598
13	Goods returned by Clements	34
14	Sold goods to Clements	437
21	Purchased goods from Cox	674
22	Purchased goods from Patel	771
29	Purchased goods from Freer	50
30	Goods returned to Crosby	140

Required a) Enter the transactions in the appropriate books of prime entry.
b) Show the necessary entries in the ledgers.

QUESTION 8

The following credit transactions took place during December 20*8:

December		£
4	Purchased goods from Taylor	632
5	Sold goods to Butcher	562
8	Purchased shop fittings from Archer	7,600
11	Sold goods to Gravinski	87
14	Returned goods to Taylor	135
15	Sold goods to Bush	908
18	Goods returned by Butcher	99
20	Purchased goods from Lim	412
29	Goods sold to McDuff	138
30	Purchased goods from Taylor	44

Required a) Enter the transaction in the appropriate books of prime entry.
b) Show the necessary entries in the ledgers.

QUESTION 9

Jim Kelly owns a clothes shop. The following transactions took place during June 20*8:

June		£
1	Goods sold on credit to Thomas	97
4	Goods purchased on credit from Tunk Ltd	573
7	Display units purchased on credit from Sheep Ltd	3,750
8	Cash sales for the week	752

12	Goods returned by Thomas	97
14	Goods purchased on credit from Tupp	880
15	Cash sales for week	893
22	Cash sales for week	439
23	Goods sold to Shah on credit	254
27	Goods returned to Tupp	108
29	Cash sales for week	1,065
30	Goods purchased from Rult on credit	349

Required   a) Enter the transactions in the appropriate books of prime entry.
             b) Show the necessary entries in the ledgers.

QUESTION 10

Rebecca owns a garage. The following transaction took place during March 20*8:

March		£
2	Goods purchased on credit from Spanners plc	452
4	Credit sales to Drodlet	290
6	Goods purchased for cash from Lygett	740
9	Credit sales to Drodlet	540
11	Purchase of hydraulic jack from Upps Ltd on credit	5,250
12	Cash sales to Corston	230
16	Goods returned to Spanners plc	27
19	Goods returned by Drodlet	53
23	Goods purchased on credit from Fox	993
27	Cash sale to Bishop	450
28	Goods returned to Lygett	18
30	Goods purchased on credit from Fadley	651
31	Goods sold on credit to Mundy	511

Required   a) Enter the transactions in the appropriate books of prime entry.
             b) Show the necessary entries in the ledgers.

CHAPTER
TEN

The two-column cash book

We have looked in some detail at the five books of prime entry used to gain entry into the double-entry system.

The sixth and final book of prime entry is the cash book. The other five books were concerned with **credit** transactions. The cash book records **all** transactions concerning **money**.

Money can be in the form of cash, cheques and credit and debit card transactions.

In a previous chapter we used a cash account and a bank account. You may have noticed that those accounts were used very frequently and as a result became very full with entries. Generally in business these accounts are used more frequently than any other accounts. This means that is sensible to remove these two accounts from the general ledger and keep them apart from the other accounts.

The cash and bank accounts are kept separately in one book – the cash book.

Because it is such an important and sensitive area of the business, all cash and cheque transactions are usually the responsibility of one senior or well-qualified person – the cashier.

The accounts in the cash book work on double-entry principles like all other accounts:

- the debit (or receiving) side is found on the left
- the credit (or giving) side is on the right.

The only difference in the layout of the cash book is that the debit entries are distanced from the credit entries by extra columns and information, and that the debit entries, generally, take up the whole of the left page, while the credit entries take up the whole of the right page.

The layout is the same on both sides of the cash book.

Specification coverage:
AQA Unit 1
OCR Unit 1

By the end of this chapter you should be able to:
- write up a two-column cash book
- make entries involving cash and cheques received
- make entries involving cash and cheque payments
- make contra entries in the cash book.

EXAMPLE

The debit side of the cash book looks like this:

Cash book					
Date	Particulars	Folio	Cash	Bank	

The credit side of the cash book looks like this:

Cash book					
	Date	Particulars	Folio	Cash	Bank

EXAMPLE *continued*

The whole cash book looks like this:

Cash book									
Date (1)	Particulars (2)	Folio (3)	Cash (4)	Bank (5)	Date (6)	Particulars (7)	Folio (8)	Cash (9)	Bank (10)

The columns are used in the same way that the ledger columns were used:

(1) and (6) give the date on which the transaction occurred.
(2) and (7) identify the account where the corresponding entry can be found.
(3) and (8) show the page of the ledger where the corresponding entry can be found.
(4) all cash received is entered in this column.
(5) all monies paid into the business bank account are recorded in this column.
(9) all cash payments made are recorded in this column.
(10) all payments made by cheque are recorded in this column.

WORKED EXAMPLE

Joe Flint maintains a two-column cash book. The following transactions have taken place:

1 September Joe paid R Serth £34 cash
2 September he paid T Horse £167 cash
5 September he paid V Dole £78 cash.

Required Enter the transactions in Joe's cash book.

Answer

Cash book									
Date	Particulars	Folio	Cash	Bank	Date	Particulars	Folio	Cash	Bank
					1 Sept	R.Serth	PL9	34	
					2 Sept	T.Horse	PL6	167	
					5 Sept	V.Dole	PL2	78	

WORKED EXAMPLE

Fred Baggs maintains a two-column cash book. The following transactions have taken place:

3 February Fred paid rent £400 by cheque
7 February he paid Gary £67 by cheque
9 February he paid wages £832 by cheque.

Required Enter the transactions in Fred's cash book.

Answer

Cash book									
Date	Particulars	Folio	Cash	Bank	Date	Particulars	Folio	Cash	Bank
					3 Feb	Rent	GL8		400
					7 Feb	Gary	PL9		67
					9 Feb	Wages	GL15		832

WORKED EXAMPLE

Rageh maintains a two-column cash book. The following transactions have taken place:

4 May Cash received from Nigel £213
5 May Cash received from Harry £92
9 May Cash received from Hilary £729.

Required Enter the transactions in Rageh's cash book.

Answer

Cash book

Date	Particulars	Folio	Cash	Bank	Date	Particulars	Folio	Cash	Bank
4 May	Nigel	SL12	213						
5 May	Harry	SL 7	92						
9 May	Hilary	SL 8	729						

WORKED EXAMPLE

Bertha maintains a two-column cash book. The following transactions have taken place:

 2 January Cheque received from Steve £249
 3 January Cash sales banked £851
11 January Cheque received from Mustaf £29.

Required Enter the transactions in Bertha's cash book.

Answer

Cash book

Date	Particulars	Folio	Cash	Bank	Date	Particulars	Folio	Cash	Bank
2 Jan	Steve	SL5		249					
3 Jan	Cash sales	GL23		851					
11 Jan	Mustaf	SL7		29					

WORKED EXAMPLE

Garibaldi maintains a two-column cash book. The following transactions have taken place:

 2 April Cash received from Xavier, a customer, £458
 4 April Motor repairs £530 paid by cash
 6 April Cash received from Milly, a customer £77
 7 April Rent £210 paid by cash
 9 April Insurance premium £156 paid by cash
12 April Cash sales £743.

Required Enter the transactions in Garibaldi's cash book.

WORKED EXAMPLE *continued*

Answer

Cash book

Date	Particulars	Folio	Cash	Bank	Date	Particulars	Folio	Cash	Bank
2 Apr	Xavier	SL 4	458		4 Apr	Motor expenses	GL23	530	
6 Apr	Milly	SL 13	77		7 Apr	Rent	GL 8	210	
12 Apr	Cash sales	GL 2	743		9 Apr	Insurance	GL11	156	

WORKED EXAMPLE

Hertz maintains a two-column cash book. The following transactions have taken place:

   3 October Price, a supplier, was paid £350 by cheque
   6 October Hertz received a cheque for £450, an overpayment of rent
   9 October Takings paid into bank £2,187
11 October Bliff, a customer, paid by cheque £639
12 October Cheque received from Box £93, paid into the bank
17 October Rates £219 paid by cheque.

Required Enter the transactions in Hertz's cash book.

Answer

Cash book

Date	Particulars	Folio	Cash	Bank	Date	Particulars	Folio	Cash	Bank
6 Oct	Rent	GL 6		450	3 Oct	Price	PL4		350
9 Oct	Sales	GL17		2187	11 Oct	Bliff	SL23		639
12 Oct	Box	PL14		93	17 Oct	Rates	GL7		219

It is now simply a matter of putting cash payments and cash receipts in the same book as cheque payments and monies paid into the bank.

WORKED EXAMPLE

Matthew maintains a two-column cash book. The following transactions have taken place:

   1 November Cheque from Norman, a customer, £288 paid into bank
   2 November Motor expenses paid by cheque £311
   5 November Matthew draws a cheque for private use £150
10 November Cash takings £2,390
15 November Motor fuel purchased with cash £42
21 November Cheque paid into bank for rates rebate £273
29 November Paid wages in cash £1,309
30 November Takings £5,630, paid directly into bank.

Required Enter the transactions in Matthew's cash book.

Answer

Cash book

Date	Particulars	Folio	Cash	Bank	Date	Particulars	Folio	Cash	Bank
1 Nov	Norman	SL 4		288	2 Nov	Motor expenses	GL 12		311
10 Nov	Sales	GL9	2390		5 Nov	Drawings	GL23		150
21 Nov	Rates	GL11		273	15 Nov	Motor expenses	GL12	42	
30 Nov	Sales	GL9		5630	29 Nov	Wages	GL7	1309	

QUESTION 1

Miller maintains a two-column cash book. The following **cash** transactions have taken place:

1 February	Cash received from Cling, a customer, £176
3 February	Cash paid to cleaner £94
5 February	Cash takings £522
6 February	Motor fuel purchased for cash £51
7 February	Cash received from Laker £83
8 February	Wages paid in cash £317.

Required Enter the transactions in the cash book.

QUESTION 2

Pratesh maintains a two-column cash book. The following **cash** transactions have taken place:

1 May	Cash received from Knight, a customer, £102
2 May	Cash takings £760
5 May	Stationery purchased £75
6 May	Cash received from McGough £54
7 May	Brunton, a supplier, paid £68
8 May	Part-time worker paid £49.

Required Enter the transactions in the cash book.

QUESTION 3

Allen maintains a two-column cash book. The following transactions have taken place using the business **bank account**:

1 July	Insurance premium paid by cheque £548
4 July	Wages paid by cheque £752
6 July	Cheque received from Hanks £138
7 July	Allen withdraws money for personal use by cheque £150
8 July	Cash sales banked £2,693
9 July	Cheque received from Kann £198.

Required Enter the transactions in the cash book.

QUESTION 4

Glaze maintains a two-column cash book. The following transactions have taken place:

1 April	Received rates refund by cheque £450
2 April	Cash sales £2,490
2 April	Rent paid by cheque £650
3 April	Cash sales paid directly into the bank £787
4 April	Paid wages in cash £236
4 April	Received loan £12,000, paid directly into bank
4 April	Purchased motor van paid cheque £9,800
6 April	Paid Trew, a supplier, cash £23.

Required Enter the transactions in the cash book.

The source documents used to write up the cash book are:

■ Debit side:
  – copy receipts
  – till rolls
  – paying in book counterfoils.
■ Credit side
  – receipts
  – cheque book counterfoils.

A further source of information to be used to write up the cash book is the bank statements sent out by the bank showing details of the business's transactions – but more of this source later.

Cash in hand is the term used to describe the amount of cash held by a business at any one time. The cash in hand in a shop would be found in the tills. In a larger business it might be found in the safe.

At the end of an appropriate length of time, the cash book should be balanced. (The time when balancing takes place will generally depend on the size of the business and the number of transactions that are included in the cash book.) Both of the balances in the cash book should be verified.

■ How could you verify the cash balance brought down?
■ How could you verify the bank balance brought down?

The balance brought down in the cash column should agree with the cash in hand at that date.

The bank balance in the cash book can be verified by reference to the bank statement.

The cash and bank columns of the cash book are balanced in the same way that ledger accounts are balanced.

The balances are brought down to start the 'new' time period.

Remember the cash balance will always be brought down as a debit. The bank balance brought down could be either a debit or a credit balance.

WORKED EXAMPLE

The cash book of Grey is shown.

Cash book

Date	Particulars	Folio	Cash	Bank	Date	Particulars	Folio	Cash	Bank
1 Nov	Reid	SL6		1439	4 Nov	Wages	GL4		428
6 Nov	Sales	GL9	1,270		7 Nov	Hunt	PL6	73	
8 Nov	Gong	SL23		451	11 Nov	Rent	GL6		600
14Nov	Potts	SL14		349	16 Nov	Trig	PL16	38	

Required Balance the cash and bank columns of the cash book on 16 November and carry any balances down.

Answer

Cash book

Date	Particulars	Folio	Cash	Bank	Date	Particulars	Folio	Cash	Bank
1 Nov	Reid	SL6		1,439	4 Nov	Wages	GL4		428
6 Nov	Sales	GL6	1,270		7 Nov	Hunt	PL6	73	
8 Nov	Gong	SL23		451	11 Nov	Rent	GL6		600
14 Nov	Potts	SL14		349	16 Nov	Trig	PL16	38	
					16 Nov	*Balances*	c/d	1,159	1,211
			1,270	2,239				1,270	2,239
17 Nov	Balances b/d		1,159	1,211					

Note: Make sure that all four totals are on the same line. Balance the cash columns first; then balance the bank columns; don't try to do them both at the same time.

● EXAMINATION TIP

Always bring balances down; if you don't you will lose at least one mark in an examination

QUESTION 5

The cash book of Rowe is shown.

Cash book

Date	Particulars	Folio	Cash	Bank	Date	Particulars	Folio	Cash	Bank
2 Jan	Hatters	SL17	238		9 Jan	Postages	GL21	45	
5 Jan	Cash sales	GL7	1,458		11 Jan	Blagg	PL 25		347
9 Jan	Ffunders	SL34		2,376	14 Jan	Wages	GL6	905	
15 Jan	Rodder	SL10		349	16 Jan	Defroux	PL13		312

Required Balance the cash and bank columns of the cash book on 16 January and carry any balances down.

A transaction that appears on both the debit and credit sides of the double-entry system is called a **contra entry**. Contra entries have no effect on the wellbeing of the business.

Clearly, it is unsafe to keep large amounts of cash and cheques on the business premises for prolonged periods of time. The cashier will arrange for the monies received to be taken to the bank and deposited when the amount in the till or safe warrants it.

EXAMPLE

The following is an extract from the cash book of Grant:

Cash book

Date	Particulars	Folio	Cash	Bank	Date	Particulars	Folio	Cash	Bank
4 Jul	Cash sales	GL32	4,397		5 Jul	Purchases	GL7	48	
4 Jul	Bradley	SL51	74						

Grant has more than £4,000 cash on his premises – this represents a security risk. He pays £4,000 into the business bank account on 5 July.

Talk yourself through this transaction:

Grant takes £4,000 from the till … the cash column loses £4,000.

Date	Particulars	Folio	Cash	Bank
5 July	Bank	C	4,000	

Note
- The date of the transaction.
- The particulars stating where the 'opposite' entry is to be found (in the bank column)
- 'C' is for 'contra', showing that Grant's business is neither better nor worse off because of the transaction.
- £4,000 in the cash column shows that cash has been 'lost'.

Grant takes the money to the bank and the bank receives the money.

Date	Particulars	Folio	Cash	Bank
5 July	Cash	C		4,000

Note
- The date of the transaction.
- The particulars stating where the opposite entry is to be found (in the cash column).
- 'C' is for 'contra', showing that Grant's business is neither better nor worse off because of the transaction.
- £4,000 in the bank column shows that money has been received into the bank account.

The effect on the business is the same as the effect on your finances that would occur if you removed a five pound note from one pocket and put it in another pocket.

Another common contra entry in the cash book is the withdrawal of cash from the bank for use in the business. This transaction often occurs when cash wages need to be paid and the business has insufficient cash in the safe to make up the necessary wage packets.

(Because of security measures, many larger businesses now pay wages and salaries directly into staff bank accounts, so that large amounts of cash do not need to be transported from the bank and then kept on the business's premises.)

EXAMPLE

The following is an extract from the cash book of Dan:

Cash book									
Date	Particulars	Folio	Cash	Bank	Date	Particulars	Folio	Cash	Bank
12 Aug	Robson	SL32		4,574	11 Aug	Machinery	GL6		2,350
16 Aug	Nkomo	SL79		5,490					

Wages amounting to £4,529 have to be paid in cash on 18 August. Dan withdraws this sum from the bank on 17 August.

If we talk ourselves through the process the entries become clear:

Dan goes to the bank and withdraws £4,529.

Date	Particulars	Folio	Cash	Bank
17 Aug	Cash	C		4,529

He returns to his business premises and puts the cash in the safe.

Date	Particulars	Folio	Cash	Bank
17 Aug	Bank	C	4,529	

QUESTION 6

On 17 December Phil draws £27,300 from the business bank account to pay the wage bill due on 20 December.

On 23 December he pays £4,768 cash receipts into the bank account.

Required Show the entries necessary to complete both transactions.

Date	Particulars	Folio	Cash	Bank	Date	Particulars	Folio	Cash	Bank
17 Dec					17 Dec				
23 Dec					23 Dec				

Many larger businesses now keep a cheque payments book and a cash receipts and lodgement book. This is certainly the case where the bulk of transactions are conducted through the bank account.

Chapter summary

- The cash book is a book of prime entry and is part of the double-entry system.
- All transactions that involve cash are entered in the cash book.
- All cash transactions are entered in the cash columns.
- All transactions involving cheques are entered in the bank columns.
- Contra items have no effect on the worth of the business.
- Any balance shown in the cash column must be a debit balance.
- Balances shown in the bank column could be either a debit or a credit balance.

SELF-TEST QUESTIONS

- Draw out the headings used in a two-column cash book.
- What does the word 'contra' mean?
- Complete the sentence: 'The cash book is not only a book of prime entry it is also part of the …………….. …………………system.'
- In which column would a cash sale be entered?
- In which column would a cheque for the payment of rates be entered?
- Complete the sentence: 'Money taken from the safe and deposited in the bank would be………….in the cash column of the cash book and be …………….in the bank column.' (Enter 'debit' or 'credit'.)
- Which book of prime entry would you use to record a sale of goods on credit?
- Name two source documents used to write up the cash book.
- Is it possible to have a credit balance in the cash column of the cash book?
- Is it possible to have a credit balance in the bank column of the cash book?
- Complete the sentence: 'Money withdrawn from the bank for use in the business would be ………. in the cash column of the cash book and be………….in the bank column.' (Enter 'debit' or 'credit'.)

QUESTION 7

The following transactions relate to the business of Martin:

1 May	Cash sales £349
2 May	Electricity bill by cash £163
3 May	Received cheque £561 from Ed, a customer
6 May	Cash sales £670
6 May	Cash paid into the bank £500
7 May	Paid wages by cheque £471
8 May	Purchased stationery £112 by cash.

Required a) Enter the transactions in the cash book.
b) Balance the cash book on 7 May.

QUESTION 8

The following transactions relate to the business of Silver:

3 October	Cheque received £540 from Benedict
4 October	Cash sales £469
7 October	Cash received £591 from Frout
8 October	Telephone bill paid £261 by cheque
8 October	Gas bill paid £171 cash
8 October	Cash paid into bank £750
9 October	Cheque received £347 from Neal.

Required a) Enter the transactions in the cash book.
b) Balance the cash book on 9 October.

QUESTION 9

The following transactions relate to the business of Hunter:

2 April	Cash sales £1,792
3 April	Cash paid into bank £1,500;
4 April	Cheque received from Burgess £286
6 April	Rent paid by cheque £240
7 April	Insurance premium £110 paid by cash
8 April	Cheque paid for repairs £892
8 April	Cash sales £135.

Required a) Enter the transactions into the cash book.
b) Balance the cash book on 8 April.

QUESTION 10

The following transactions relate to the business of Lamb:

3 November	Cash sales £452
5 November	Cash withdrawn by Lamb for private use £125
6 November	Cash sales £2,380
6 November	Cash paid into bank £2,500
8 November	Wages paid by cheque £1,432
9 November	Cheque paid to Ripon, a supplier, £475
10 November	Cash paid for cleaning materials £28.

Required a) Enter the transactions in the cash book.
b) Balance the cash book on 10 November.

QUESTION 11

The following transactions relate to the business of Golightly:

2 January	Cash sales paid directly into bank £3,487
3 January	Cash received from Thompson, a customer, £172
3 January	Motor expenses paid by cheque £345
5 January	Rates paid by cheque £210
6 January	Cash sales £1,372
7 January	Cash paid into bank £1,000
9 January	Motor fuel purchased £48 cash.

Required a) Enter the transactions in the cash book.
b) Balance the cash book on 9 January.

QUESTION 12

The following transaction relate to the business of Dublin:

3 May	Cash sales £4,268
3 May	Cash paid into bank £4,000
5 May	Rates paid by cheque £245
6 May	Cheque received from Marks, a customer, £2,120
7 May	£2,467 withdrawn from the bank for use in the business
8 May	Wages paid £2,467 cash.

Required a) Enter the transactions in the cash book.
b) Balance the cash book on 8 May.

QUESTION 13

The following transactions relate to the business of York:

19 October   Cash sales £2,380
20 October   Stationery purchased £120 cash
21 October   Motor fuel purchased £38 cash
21 October   £1,950 cash paid into bank
22 October   Cash sales paid directly into bank £2,785
23 October   Cheque paid cash to Todd, a supplier, £490
24 October   Cash withdrawn from bank £2,500
25 October   Wages paid £1,988 cash.

Required   a) Enter the transactions in the cash book.
              b) Balance the cash book on 25 October.

QUESTION 14

The following transactions relate to the business of Robin:

23 May   Cash sales £2,887
24 May   Telephone bill paid £176 cash
24 May   Vehicle repair paid £483 by cheque
25 May   Wages paid £1,784 cash
27 May   Cash sales £2,590
28 May   Cheque received from Retop Ltd £674
29 May   Cash paid into bank £2,000
30 May   Robin withdrew £275 cash from bank for personal use.

Required   a) Enter the transactions in the cash book.
              b) Balance the cash book on 30 May.

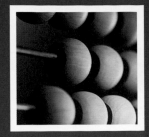

CHAPTER
ELEVEN

The three-column cash book

DISCOUNTS

There are two types of discount available to businesses:

1   Trade discount is a reduction in the price of goods charged by a manufacturer or distributor to a retailer. Trade discount is not recorded in the double-entry books of account.

> ### EXAMPLE
>
> Six beds having a retail price of £800 each are sold by a manufacturer to a retailer at a trade discount of 40%.
>
> The retailer records purchases of £2,880 (six × £480) (£800 per bed less £320 trade discount). The manufacturer records sales of £2,880 also.

2   Cash discount is a reduction in the price charged for goods when a credit customer settles their debt within a time stipulated by the supplier. Cash discounts are available to encourage a debtor to settle a debt promptly.

> ### EXAMPLE
>
> A customer owes £100.
>
> A retailer may indicate that if the debt is settled before the month-end a cash discount of 5% will be allowed.
>
> The debtor pays before the month-end so only £95 needs to be paid – £100 less £5 cash discount.
>
> However, both the receipt of the money and the discount are recorded by the retailer and the customer.

Specification coverage:
AQA Unit 1
OCR Unit 1

By the end of this chapter you should be able to:
- write up a three-column cash book
- distinguish between trade discount and cash discount
- account for VAT in the cash book
- account for VAT in the petty cash book.

To record cash discounts:

WORKED EXAMPLE

On 1 August Sahera has three debtors. Her settlement terms allow a cash discount of 5% to customers who settle their debts before the end of August.

Debtor	Amount owed	Date of payment by cheque
Geoff	£2,800	23 August
Edward	£80	17 September
Fiona	£360	29 August

Required Prepare the ledger accounts and record the settling of the debts due. (For illustrative purposes only, Sahera does not keep a cash book.)

Answer

Sales ledger

Dr   **Geoff**   **Cr**

23 Aug Bank		GL1	2660.00
23 Aug Discount. Allowed		GL 2	140.00

Dr   **Edward**   **Cr**

17 Sept Bank	GL1	80.00

Dr   **Fiona**   **Cr**

29 Aug Bank	GL1	342.00
29 Aug Discount allowed	GL2	18.00

General ledger

Dr   **Bank account**   **Cr**

23 Aug	Geoff	SL1	2660.00	
29 Aug	Fiona	SL3	342.00	
17 Sept	Edward	SL2	80.00	

Dr   **Discount allowed account**   **Cr**

| 23 Aug | Geoff | SL1 | 140.00 | |
| 29 Aug | Fiona | SL3 | 18.00 | |

So you can see that discount allowed is credited to the customer's account, thus reducing the amount to be paid in settlement. It is debited to the discount allowed account in the general ledger.

WORKED EXAMPLE

Sahera has three creditors on 1 August. (Again, for illustrative purposes only, Sahera does not keep a cash book.

Supplier	Amount owed	Cash discount available if payment made before 31 August %
Arbuckle & Co	£400	2
BTQ plc	£7,400	5
Carot Ltd	£200	3

Sahera settled the amounts she owed by cheque on 26 August.

Required Prepare the ledger accounts in Sahera's books of account, recording the payments made by Sahera.

Answer

Dr				Arbuckle & Co		Cr
26 Aug	Bank	GL3	392.00			
26 Aug	Discount received	GL4	8.00			

Dr				BTQ plc		Cr
26 Aug	Bank	GL3	7030.00			
26 Aug	Discount received	GL4	370.00			

Dr				Carot Ltd		Cr
26 Aug	Bank	GL3	194.00			
26 Aug	Discount received	GL4	6.00			

General ledger

Dr	Bank account				Cr
		26 Aug	Arbuckle & Co	PL1	392.00
		26 Aug	BTQ plc	PL2	7030.00
		26 Aug	Carot Ltd	PL3	194.00

Dr	Discount received account				Cr
		26 Aug	Arbuckle & Co	PL1	8.00
		26 Aug	BTQ plc	PL2	370.00
		26 Aug	Carot Ltd	PL3	6.00

You can see that discount received is debited to the supplier's account, thus reducing the amount that Sahera has to pay in settlement. The discounts are credited to the discount received account in the general ledger.

To summarise:

- Discount allowed is debited to the discount allowed account in the general ledger and is credited to the customer's account in the sales ledger.
- Discount received is credited to the discount received account in the general ledger and is debited to the supplier's account in the purchase ledger.

Memorandum columns record information that is not part of the double-entry system.

To write up the discount accounts in the general ledger in the way outlined above means that all the accounts in the sales ledger must be scrutinised and all the accounts in the purchases ledger must also be examined and lists must be made of all the discounts allowed and discounts received in order to post them to the general ledger.

This could be a mammoth task. We simplify our work by adding an extra column to those already found in the cash book.

We have already used a 'two-column' cash book (cash columns and bank columns). The principles used still hold good. We introduce a third column on the debit and credit for discounts so that we now have a three-column cash book. The three-column cash book headings look like this:

Date	Particulars	Folio	Discount	Cash	Bank	Date	Particulars	Folio	Discount	Cash	Bank

The discount columns are memorandum columns; they record the discounts but are not part of the double-entry system. This is a much more efficient way of collecting the information necessary to write up the discount accounts in the general ledger, rather than examining every account in the sales ledger and every account in the purchases ledger.

Note that we will now dispense with the folio columns in most examples and questions. Folios are very rarely required in examination answers.

The entries to record the above transactions in Sahera's cash book would look like this:

EXAMPLE

Cash book

Date	Particulars	Discount	Cash	Bank	Date	Particulars	Discount	Cash	Bank
23 Aug	Geoff	140.00		2,660.00	6 Aug	Arbuckle & Co	8.00		392.00
29 Aug	Fiona	18.00		342.00	26 Aug	BTQ plc	370.00		7,030.00
17 Sept	Edward			80.00	26 Aug	Carot Ltd	6.00		194.00
17 Sept	Balance c/d			4,534.00					
		158.00		7,616.00			384.00		7,616.00
					18 Sept	Balance b/d			4,534.00

The cash and bank columns in the cash book are balanced as they were in the two-column version of the cash book.

The discount columns are totalled. They are *not* compared and balanced since there is no connection between the two columns. One column refers to customer's accounts; the other column refers to supplier's accounts.

The discount columns are MEMORANDUM columns only – they are not part of the double-entry system.

The totals of the discount columns are then posted to the respective discount allowed and discount received accounts in the general ledger.

The purchase ledger accounts and the sales ledger accounts are the same as previously shown. However, the discount accounts would look like this:

EXAMPLE

General ledger

Dr		Discount allowed account		Cr
		17 Sept	Sundry debtors	158.00

Dr		General ledger Discount received account		Cr
		17 Sept	Sundry creditors	384.00

Note

The totals are used; the individual discounts are not shown. Notice also that two separate accounts are used.

Chapter summary

- Trade discount is not recorded in the books of account.
- Cash discount is a reward for prompt payment.
- Cash discount allowed is credited in the debtor's account and debited to the discount allowed account in the general ledger.
- Cash discount received is debited to the creditor's account and credited to the discount received account in the general ledger.
- To save time, both types of cash discount are listed in the cash book. The totals of the two columns are posted separately to the two discount accounts in the general ledger.
- The discount columns in the cash book are memorandum columns only – they are not part of the double-entry system.

SELF-TEST QUESTIONS

- Explain the term 'cash discount'.
- Explain the term 'trade discount'.
- Discount .... is debited to the discount .... account in the general ledger. (Fill the gaps.)
- Discount .... is credited to the discount ....account in the general ledger (Fill the gaps.)
- On which side of the cash book would you find the discount allowed column?
- On which side of the cash book would you find the discount received column?
- Which columns of the cash book are balanced off regularly?
- Which columns of the cash book are not balanced off?
- What is meant by the term 'memorandum column'?
- Under what circumstances would you write 'C' for contra against transactions in the cash book?

TEST QUESTIONS

QUESTION 1

Tom Cunningham had cash in hand £217 and a balance at bank £1,132 at 1 February. The following transactions took place during February:

1 February	Cash sales £912.
1 February	Paid Mowlem £834 by cheque.
2 February	Received cheque from McAllister £138.
3 February	Cash sales £468.
4 February	Received cheque from Tyson £1,172.
4 February	Paid Laker £137 by cheque.
4 February	Purchased goods for cash £126.
5 February	Purchased goods for cash £488.
5 February	Paid £750 cash into the bank account.

Required a) Prepare Tom's cash book for the period 1 February to 5 February.
b) Post the entries in the cash book to the appropriate ledger accounts

QUESTION 2

B Branden had cash in hand £861 and a balance at bank £1,307 at 1 November. The following transactions took place during November:

3 November	Purchased goods for cash £677.
3 November	Paid A Capp £317 by cheque.
4 November	Cash sales £709.
5 November	Cash sales £487.
6 November	Paid C Nesta £288 by cheque.
7 November	Paid wages £836 by cheque.
7 November	Cash sales £369.
7 November	Paid T Richards £412 by cheque.
8 November	Received cheque £279 from J. Bond.
8 November	Received cheque £97 from L Earl.
8 November	Paid £1,000 cash into the bank account.

Required a) Prepare Branden's cash book for the period 1 November to 8 November.
b) Post the entries in the cash book to the appropriate ledger accounts.

QUESTION 3

Sven David had cash in hand £88 and a balance at bank £376 on 1 May.

The following transactions took place during May:

1 May	Cheque received from Gholar £600; he has deducted £30 cash discount.
2 May	Purchased goods for cash £308.
3 May	Purchased goods for cash £613.
3 May	Cash sales £845.
3 May	Cheque received from Tempest £210; she has deducted £12 cash. discount
4 May	Cheque received from Trevor £120; he has deducted £8 cash discount.
6 May	Paid Breem £40 by cheque.
7 May	Cash sales £466.
7 May	Paid £250 cash into the bank account.

Required a) Prepare Sven's cash book for the period 1 May to 7 May.
b) Post the entries in the cash book to the appropriate ledger accounts.

QUESTION 4

Roy Becker had cash in hand £281 and a balance at bank £834 on 6 December.

The following transactions took place in December:

6 December	Cheque received from Healy £765 in settlement of his debt of £800.
7 December	Cash sales £3,276.
7 December	Purchased goods for cash £234.
8 December	Cheque received from Callaghan £480; she has deducted £30 cash discount.
8 December	Goods purchased for cash £801.
8 December	Cheque received from Wilson £26.
9 December	Paid Heath £712 by cheque after deducting £38 cash discount.
10 December	Goods purchased for cash £523.
11 December	Cash sales £930.
12 December	Paid Bassi £750 by cheque after deducting £40 cash discount.
12 December	Paid £2,500 cash into the bank account.

Required a) Prepare Roy's cash book for the period 6 December to 12 December.
b) Post the entries in the cash book to the appropriate ledger accounts.

QUESTION 5

Arthur Mow had cash in hand £237 and a bank overdraft of £2,875 on 16 October.

The following transactions took place the following week:

17 October	Cash sales £1,658.
18 October	Paid £1,500 cash into the bank account.
19 October	Withdrew cash £3,500 from bank to provide cash for wage payments.
19 October	Paid wages by cash £3,562.
19 October	Paid Foggerty £345 by cheque in settlement of £350 debt.
20 October	Received cheques from:

Briggs £657 in settlement of debt of £670
Nelson £812; cash discount allowed £13
Mandosa £65 in settlement of debt of £68.

22 October   Paid electricity bill £563 by cheque.
23 October   Cash sales £2,319.
23 October   Paid £2,500 cash into bank account.

Required a) Prepare Arthur's cash book for the week ended 23 October.
         b) Post the entries in the cash book to the appropriate ledger accounts.

QUESTION 6

Bjorn Tyke had cash in hand £407 and a bank overdraft of £238 on 1 August.

The following transactions took place during the first week in August:

2 August   Cash purchases £137.
2 August   Paid Harrison by cheque to settle a debt of £300. Harrison allowed Tyke 4% cash discount.
3 August   Cash sales £1,601.
3 August   Cash purchases £718.
3 August   Cheque received from Parker £156; he had deducted £4 cash discount.
3 August   Debt of £700 owed to Neal settled. Neal allowed 1% cash discount.
5 August   Cheque received from Nicholson £570; she has deducted £30 cash discount.
5 August   Cash sales £1,671
6 August   Cheque paid to R. Smith Ltd £18,500 for purchase of delivery van on 31 July.
6 August   Paid motor expenses £116 in cash.
6 August   Paid £2,500 cash into the bank account.

Required a) Prepare Bjorn's cash book for the period 1 August to 7 August.
         b) the entries in the cash book to the appropriate ledger accounts.

CHAPTER
TWELVE

Bank reconciliations

We have seen that the whole double-entry system can be checked by extracting a trial balance.

Remember that even if the trial balance does balance, it does not necessarily mean that there are no errors in the double-entry system.

All you can be sure of is that the double-entry system is arithmetically correct.

Can you remember the six types of errors that are not revealed by extracting a trial balance? Remember CROPOC? If not, refer back to page 74.

Altogether we use four checks to verify the accuracy of the system.

Three we do at frequent intervals throughout the year; the fourth, the trial balance, is generally prepared at the year-end, although a trial balance could be extracted every day to see if the system is arithmetically correct.

Let us first look at the two checks that are used to verify the entries in the cash book.

Specification coverage:
AQA Unit 1

By the end of this chapter you should be able to:
- update the bank columns of a cash book
- identify unpresented cheques
- identify lodgements not yet credited
- prepare a bank reconciliation statement.

CHECKING THE ACCURACY OF THE CASH BALANCE SHOWN IN THE CASH BOOK

We check the cash balance shown in the cash columns of the cash book very frequently. (We cannot be any more precise than this because it would be impossible to say exactly how often the cash would be checked in any particular business.) Some businesses, like the corner shop, would perhaps only check the cash balances on a weekly basis, whereas very large organisations may check the cash balances much more frequently.

How often would you check the cash balances in your tills if you were the owner of a shop? It might depend on how much cash goes through each till. It might depend on how many staff have access to the tills and how trustworthy those members of staff are.

CHECKING THE CASH

We add all the money that is in the till and check it against the till roll total. The two should be the same. Checking the cash is done fairly frequently, because if there is a discrepancy it is much easier to remember what might have caused any difference. For example, money may have been taken from the till to pay the window cleaner and no note has been made of the payment. It is much easier to remember this immediately after the event than, say, some four months later.

The cash in the till should not only agree with the till roll total but also should agree with the total of the cash columns in the cash book kept by the business.

This is the first check and most frequent check undertaken by businesses. It is fairly straightforward and very easy to do.

CHECKING THE ACCURACY OF TRANSACTIONS RECORDED IN THE BANK COLUMNS OF THE CASH BOOK

This often gives students a few problems.

> The **drawer** is the person (or business) using the cheque for payment.

> The **payee** is the person to whom the cheque is made payable.

How are the bank columns written up?

The bulk of banking transactions are undertaken by the bank on instructions given by the managers of the business. The instructions to undertake transactions involving the use of the banking system are given to the bank by:

1 cheque – cheques are simply instructions given to the bank to take money from an account and give the money to someone else
2 paying-in slip – these slips record the amount of cash and cheques paid into the business account.

When any bank transaction is undertaken, two records are kept of the transaction:

One is recorded by the business in the cash book. The other record is kept by the bank. The two records kept are taken from different parts of the source document.

When money is paid into the high street bank the person paying in the money will fill in a slip showing the numbers and amounts of each type of coin and note deposited, plus a list of all the cheques that are being paid in. They fill in a counterfoil which duplicates this information. The money and cheques are handed to the bank cashier, who checks the amounts for accuracy and then stamps the paying in slip and the duplicate (counterfoil or stub). From this counterfoil, the debit entries are made in the cash book so this is one of the source documents used to write up the cash book.

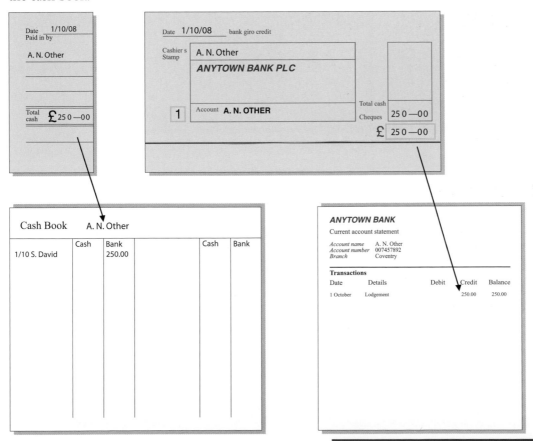

The bank uses the actual paying in slip to show the money and cheques that have been deposited in the business bank account. These entries will appear as credit entries on the business bank statement, which is a copy of the bank's records.

When payment is made by cheque, the cheque is filled out with the payee's name, the date and the amount in both words and figures, and then the drawer signs the cheque and sends it to the creditor (the person who has been owed the money). The cheque counterfoil is used as the source document to write up the credit bank column in our cash book.

The bank uses the cheque that has been sent to the payee (the creditor) to enter withdrawals from the business account. These withdrawals will be shown on the debit side of the bank statement.

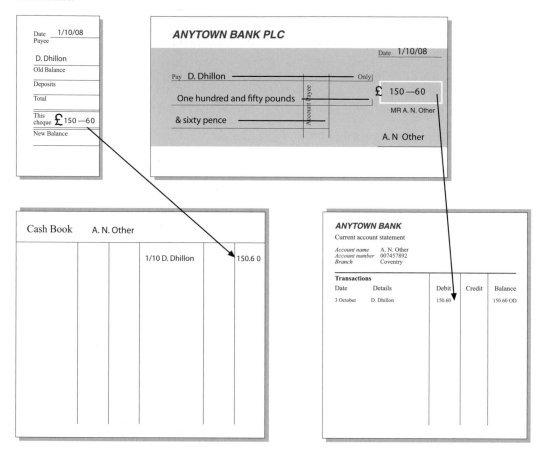

Note

The third column on the bank statement shows a running balance figure.

A statement will be sent on a frequent basis, usually at the end of every month, but in the case of very large businesses the bank statement may be sent to the business on a weekly basis.

Standing orders are payments made automatically by a bank on behalf of customers. They are set amounts and may be paid weekly, monthly or annually.

Direct debits are payments made by the bank on behalf of customers. The authority to withdraw money from the account is given to the payee. The amounts withdrawn from the account are generally variable.

Bank charges are made by banks to cover the costs of maintaining the drawer's account.

Interest on overdrafts is the interest charged by banks when an account is overdrawn.

Credit transfers are amounts paid into an account directly through the banking system instead of by issuing a cheque.

Dishonoured cheques are cheques that have not gone through the drawer's bank account. Often this may be because the drawer has insufficient funds in their account to honour (pay) the cheque.

● EXAMINATION TIP

Learn these definitions. They are frequently asked for in examinations. They are frequently answered poorly!

The bank statement and the cash book should be identical since the cash book is prepared from the counterfoils which are duplicates of the original documents from which the bank draws up its bank statement.

Can you think of any reasons why these two should not be identical?

- The counterfoil might not actually agree with the cheque. The cheque might show '£110' but the cheque counterfoil could show '£101', so our cash book will show '£101' and the bank statement will show '£110'. Which amount is correct? The bank will have taken £110 out of the account so this is the correct amount and our counterfoil and cash book should be changed.
- The counterfoil might not have been filled in at all. The amount shown in the bank statement should be entered in the cash book.
- The bank may have made payments from the account on a standing order and the payment from the account has, for the moment, been overlooked by the drawer and not yet included in the business cash book. The amounts should be entered as a payment in the credit bank column of the cash book.
- The bank may have made payment from the account by direct debit and the payment from the account has been overlooked by the drawer. The amount should be entered as a payment in the credit bank column of the cash book.
- The bank may have taken money from the account as bank charges and this amount has not yet been included in the business cash book. The amount should be included as a payment in the credit bank column of the cash book.
- The bank may have made an interest charge for a period when the bank statement shows a debit balance (i.e. the account has been overdrawn). The amount of interest charged should be entered as a payment in the credit bank column of the cash book.
- The bank may have received deposits on behalf of the business directly through the banking system. Any credit transfers should be entered as receipts by debiting the bank column in the cash book.
- When a cheque is received the cheque will be banked. It is entered in the debit bank column of the cash book. If, subsequently, the cheque is dishonoured this fact will be shown on the bank statement. (This is referred to colloquially as a cheque that has bounced.) The trader cannot adjust her bank account until the bank informs the trader. If it is not also shown in the cash book the dishonoured cheque should be entered as a payment in the credit bank column of the cash book.
- The trader can make the following errors:
  - addition errors in either bank column of the cash book
  - entering the incorrect amount from the cheque and paying in counterfoils
  - entering the correct amount on the incorrect side of the cash book.
- The bank could make the following errors:
  - entering a withdrawal that should have been debited to the account of someone else
  - entering a deposit that should have been credited to the account of someone else.

Note

It is highly unlikely that addition errors will take place in bank statements since they are computer generated.

QUESTION 1

The following transactions have taken place:

1 A cheque paid to Watkins for £200.
2 The total of cash sales for the day £1,730.
3 A payment by cheque to Smith for £200, less 5% cash discount.
4 £3,430 cash sales paid into the business bank account.
5 Payment of £435 cash to a supplier.
6 £2,000 cash withdrawn from the bank for business use.

Required Explain how each transaction should be treated in the cash book

Lodgements are payments made into the bank account.

We have seen how entries using the banking system are recorded in the cash book.

Cheques received are shown in the debit bank column of the cash book.

Cheques paid to suppliers of goods and services are shown in the credit bank columns of the cash book.

QUESTION 2

Required Explain:

(a) The type of transactions that would increase the bank balance.

(b) The type of transactions that would decrease the bank balance.

The amounts withdrawn from the bank account by cheque should appear as identical amounts on the credit bank columns of the cash book and the debit columns of the bank statement.

Amounts paid in should appear as identical amounts in the debit bank columns of the cash book and the credit columns of the bank statement.

We have already listed reasons why the cash book kept by a business and the record kept by the bank may be different. If we correct the differences all should be well.

Why is there a need to prepare a bank reconciliation statement?

We need to check that:

- all transactions using banking facilities have been recorded
- all transactions have been recorded accurately by both the business and the bank
- all transactions have gone through the bank account kept at the bank.

Clearing a cheque refers to the passage of a cheque through the banking system. It involves the transfer of money from one account to another. This can take a few days if the accounts are held at different banks.

When a trader pays a supplier by cheque this should be entered in the credit bank column of the cashbook (using the counterfoil as the source document) on the same date that the cheque was written. However, the bank will not show the cheque on the bank statement until several days later – this could be as much as a week later (days in the post plus days in the clearing system).

When the trader pays money into the business bank account, it will be immediately recorded in the trader's bank column in his/her cash book. However, the bank will not credit it to the trader's bank account until the cheque is cleared.

Note: The bank statement is prepared from the actual cheques and paying in slips received by the bank. If an error is made on the counterfoil two different amounts will be recorded by the bank and by the trader.

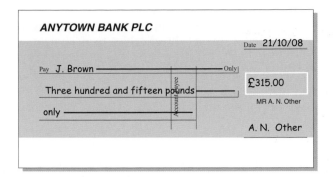

Which is correct?

The bank will respond to their instructions which are to remove £315 from the account and pay it to someone else.

After all the necessary adjustments have been made, the cash book should contain exactly the same information as the bank statement.

Or should it?

Well, it could, but in real life the likelihood of this happening is fairly remote because of the reasons outlined below.

Some cheques paid out by the trader and entered in the cash book will still be in the postal system, in the payee's office or in the bank clearing system. These cheques have yet to be presented at the trader's bank – they are called '**unpresented cheques**'.

Some deposits made by the trader on the day the bank statement is produced by the bank may not yet be recorded on the statement. These items are called '**lodgements not yet credited by the bank**'.

So we have to reconcile (bring together) the two different amounts. This is done in the bank reconciliation statement. The statement is set out thus:

EXAMPLE

Bank reconciliation at … (the date when the reconciliation is taking place).

Balance at bank as per cash book

Add unpresented cheques

Less lodgements not yet credited by the bank

Balance at bank as per bank statement.

● EXAMINATION TIP

Learn the layout for a bank reconciliation statement. It is a popular examination topic.

PROCEDURE USED IN PREPARING A BANK RECONCILIATION STATEMENT

1 Balance the cash book. Remember, only the cash and bank columns are balanced. The discount columns are totalled.
2 Compare the bank columns of the cash book with the bank statement.
Tick all the entries shown in the cash book and their corresponding entries in the bank statement.

3   Bring the cash book up to date by:
    a) entering payments made by the bank, but not yet entered in the cash book, in the credit
        bank column of the cash book (standing orders, direct debits, bank charges, fees and
        interest and dishonoured cheques).
    b) entering amounts received by the bank, but not entered in the cash book, in the debit
        bank column of the cash book.
4   Correct any errors discovered in the bank columns of the cash book.
5   If the bank statement contains errors inform the bank, make a note of the error and ask the
    bank for an adjusted bank statement balance.
6   Prepare the bank reconciliation statement:

    Bank Reconciliation Statement as at   .... (date)
    Balance as per cash book
    Add unpresented cheques
    Less lodgements not yet credited by the bank
    Balance at bank as per the bank statement   .... (date)

Note

The adjusted balance shown in the bank columns of the cash book is the balance to be shown in:

a) the trial balance and
b) the balance sheet.

Remember to post all the items entered in the cash book adjustments to the appropriate
accounts.

WORKED EXAMPLE

The bank columns of P. Court's cash book shows the following details:

Dr		Bank £			Cheque	Bank £	Cr
1 April	Balance b/d	486.87	3 April	H Poster	341	34.22	
7 April	H Rowe	345.51	4 April	T Hannah	342	72.91	
10 April	F Thon	56.32	17 April	C Dale	343	310.00	
23 April	M Singh	178.54	22 April	D Collins	344	130.08	
30 April	J Cust	12.55	24 April	N Bedi	345	54.01	
			30 April	R Eddie	346	145.37	
			30 April	Balance c/d		333.20	
		1,079.79				1,079.79	
1 May	Balance b/d	333.20					

She received her bank statement on 3 May.

Date	Details	Debit £	Credit £	Balance £
1 April	Balance			486.87
7 April	Lodgement		345.51	832.38
9 April	342	72.91		759.47
10 April	341	34.22		725.25
	Lodgement		56.32	781.57
15 April	Direct debit (Insurance)	45.66		735 91
17 April	Credit transfer (M Cox)		61.00	796.91
23 April	Lodgement		178.54	975.45
29 April	344	130.08		845.37
	345	54.01		791.36
30 April	Bank charges	6.43		784.93

Required a) Make any necessary adjustments to P Court's cash book.
            b) Prepare a bank reconciliation statement at 30 April.

WORKED EXAMPLE *continued*

Answer

Workings:

Tick all the items that appear both in Court's cash book and her bank statement.

The item that remains unticked in the debit bank column of the cash book is:

> Cust £12.55

The items that remain unticked in the credit bank column of the cash book are:

> Dale   £310.00
>
> Eddie   £145.37

The item that remains unticked in the credit column of the bank statement is:

> Cox £61.00

The items that remain unticked in the debit column of the bank statement are:

> Direct Debit for insurance   £45.66
>
> Bank charges   £6.43

It is important that Court's cash book is updated. The cash book is a vital part of her double-entry records so it should be correct and contain all the transactions relating to the business.

The three transactions remaining unticked on the bank statement have taken place. They remain unticked because she has not yet recorded them.

The first task is to record them in the cash book.

In real life the cash book would simply be extended for a few lines to enable the entries to be made.

a)

Dr		Cash book				Cr
		Bank				**Bank**
		£				£
1 May	Balance b/d	333.20	15 April	Insurance		45.66
17 April	M. Cox	61.00	30 April	Bank charges		6.43
			30 April	Balance c/d		<u>342.11</u>
		<u>394.20</u>				<u>394.20</u>
1 May	Balance b/d	342.11				

The balance shown is the balance to be entered on Court's trial balance. It is also the balance to be shown as a current asset on her balance sheet.

We should not forget to complete the double-entry for these transactions (although it is purely for illustrative purposes, as the question did not ask for this):

Dr	Cox (SL)	Cr
	17 April Bank 61.00	

Dr Insurance account (GL)	Cr	Dr Bank charges account (GL)	Cr
15 April Bank 45.66		30 April Bank 6.43	

● EXAMINATION TIP

Do not give the examiner more than he asks for. You will not score extra marks. You will penalise yourself by taking more time to answer the question.

WORKED EXAMPLE *continued*

b) Bank reconciliation statement at 30 April

	£	£
Balance at bank as per the cash book		342.11
Add unpresented cheques		
Dale	310.00	
Eddie	145.37	455.37
		797.48
Less lodgements not yet credited		
Cust		12.55
Balance at bank as per bank statement		784.93

We have reconciled the bank balance shown in the cash book with that shown in the bank statement.

We can say with certainty that the transactions recorded in bank columns of the cash book are accurate.

WORKED EXAMPLE

The bank columns of D. Dhillon's cash book are shown.

Dr			Cash book				Cr
1 Oct	Balance b/d	127.63	2 Oct	M Vaughan	673	272.61
7 Oct	D Paster	367.42	4 Oct	C Chan	674	81.13
15 Oct	T Henley	84.56	11 Oct	M Vere	675	364.42
15 Oct	B Tain	97.42	27 Oct	D Perth	676	182.09
31 Oct	M Sond	216.84	29 Oct	N Lister	677	12.13
31 Oct	Balance c/d	18.51				
		912.38				912.38
			1 Nov	Balance b/d		18.51

He received his bank statement on 4 November.

ANYTOWN BANK PLC

Current account statement

Account name   D. DHILLON
Account number 007457892
Branch   Coventry

Transactions

Date	Details	Debit	Credit	Balance
1 October	Balance			127.63
3 October	Lodgement		367.42	495.05
7 October	674	81.31		413.74
	Lodgement		84.56	498.30
10 October	Lodgement		97.42	595.72
15 October	675	364.42		231.30
16 October	673	272.61		41.31 OD
31 October	Credit transfer G. Jackson		41.99	0.68
	Stdg order Loan repmt	150.00		149.32 OD
	Dishonoured cheque	12.48		161.80 OD
	Bank charges	27.56		189.36 OD

WORKED EXAMPLE *continued*

a) Make any adjustments to Dhillon's cash book.

b) Prepare a bank reconciliation statement at 31 October.

Answer

a)

Dr		£	Cash book		Cr £
31 Oct	Credit transfer G. Jackson	41.99	31 Oct	Balance b/d	18.51
			4 Oct	Correction – C. Chan	0.18
			31 Oct	s/o Loan repayment	150.00
			31 Oct	Dishonoured cheque	12.48
31 Oct	Balance c/d	166.74	31 Oct	Bank charges	27.56
		208.73			208.73
			31 Oct	Balance b/d	166.74

Note

The amount paid to Chan has been increased – the bank has paid him £81.31 so the cash book has to record the payment.

Note that the dishonoured cheque has been credited in the cash book.

Notice also that the opening balance is a credit balance on the bank statement, indicating that Dhillon has money in the bank. At the end of October a debit balance is shown on the bank statement, indicating that Dhillon is overdrawn.

b)

D Dhillon
Bank reconciliation at 31 October

	£	£	
Balance at bank as per cash book		166.74 OD	
Add unpresented cheques			
D. Perth	182.09		
N. Lister	12.13	194.22	(this positive amount
		27.48	added to a negative
			amount gives this
			positive result)
Less lodgements not yet credited			
M. Sond		216.84	(this amount deducted
			gives a negative result
Balance at bank as per bank statement		189.36 OD	

Once more we can say that all the transactions recorded in the bank columns of the cash book have been recorded accurately.

Chapter summary

- Bank reconciliations are used to check the accuracy of transactions recorded in the bank columns of the cash book.
- It is a two-stage operation – the cash book is updated first, then the actual reconciliation is prepared by adjusting the balance shown in the cash book for unpresented cheques and lodgements not yet credited in the bank statement.

SELF-TEST QUESTIONS

- Why would a trader prepare a bank reconciliation statement?
- How often is a bank reconciliation statement prepared?
- Explain the term 'drawer'.
- What is a standing order?
- What is the difference between a standing order and a direct debit?
- What is meant by the term 'overdrawn'?
- Why are credit transfers often missing from the bank columns of the cash book?
- Fill in the gaps:

Bank reconciliation statement.........................31 March 20*8

	£
Balance at bank as per cash book	210
.........unpresented cheques	156
	.....
..........lodgements not yet credited	99
Balance at bank as per bank statement	.....

TEST QUESTIONS

QUESTION 3

The bank columns of Philip Robb's cash book are as follows:

Dr			Cash book		Cr
		£			£
1 July	Balance b/d	320	2 July	Stone	86	126
17 July	AVT Ltd	630	5 July	Baines	87	417
24 July	B. Rush	420	19 July	Brown	88	326
			31 July	Edge	89	312
			31 July	Balance c/d		189
		1,370				1,370
1 Aug	Balance b/d	189				

Philip receives his bank statement on 5 August:

ANYTOWN BANK PLC

Current account statement

Account name	P. ROBB
Account number	943436192
Branch	Sheffield

Transactions

Date	Details	Debit	Credit	Balance
1 July	Balance			320
5 July	86	126		194
17 July	Lodgement		630	824
23 July	88	326		498
24 July	Lodgement		420	918
28 July	87	417		501

Required Prepare a bank reconciliation statement at 31 July.

QUESTION 4

The bank columns of Tim Robson's cash book are as follows:

Dr — **Cash book** — **Cr**

		£				£
2 Apr	Balance b/d	721	3 Apr	T. Galloway	314	291
10 Apr	S. Tay	560	12 Apr	G. Ayre	315	438
27 Apr	R. Stock	186	14 Apr	M. Beam	316	17
			23 Apr	H. Misty	317	146
			29 Apr	T. Beck	318	132
			30 Apr	Balance c/d		443
		1,467				1,467
1 May	Balance b/d	443				

Tim Robson received his bank statement on 3 May.

ANYTOWN BANK PLC

Current account statement

Account name T. ROBSON
Account number 205104012
Branch Reading

Transactions

Date	Details	Debit	Credit	Balance
1 April	Balance b/d			721
8 April	314	291		430
19 April	Lodgement		560	990
26 April	317	146		844
26 April	316	17		827
27 April	Lodgement		186	1,013

Required Prepare a bank reconciliation statement at 30 April.

QUESTION 5

The bank columns of Lucy Hill's cash book are as follows:

Dr — **Cash book** — **Cr**

		£				£
2 Nov	Balance b/d	261	4 Nov	P. Charles	77	211
10 Nov	A. Zargreb	384	8 Nov	S. Fence	78	14
27 Nov	V. Campbell	29	12 Nov	C. Mutt	79	137
			17 Nov	T. Parker	80	58
			23 Nov	G. Bowden	81	169
			30 Nov	Balance c/d		85
		674				674
1 Dec	Balance b/d	85				

Lucy received her bank statement on 4 December.

ANYTOWN BANK PLC

Current account statement

Account name   L. HILL
Account number   396106600
Branch   Oxford

Transactions

Date	Details	Debit	Credit	Balance
2 Nov	Balance b/d			261
9 Nov	77	211		50
10 Nov	Lodgement		384	434
21 Nov	80	58		376
23 Nov	79	137		239
28 Nov	81	169		70
29 Nov	78	14		56

Required Prepare a bank reconciliation statement at 30 November.

QUESTION 6

The bank columns of Rebecca Florin's cash book are as follows:

Dr			Cash book			Cr
		£				£
1 Mar	Balance b/d	1287	5 Mar	M Waters	414	97
21 Mar	P Dobie	716	9 Mar	S Gonzalez	415	238
31 Mar	J Porage	128	14 Mar	C Batt	416	41
			14 Mar	D Bundle	417	562
			17 Mar	L French	418	125
			31 Mar	Balance c/d		1,068
		2,131				2,131
1 April	Balance b/d	1,068				

Rebecca received her bank statement on 2 April.

ANYTOWN BANK PLC

Current account statement

Account name   R. FLORIN
Account number   566193640
Branch   Manchester

Transactions

Date	Details	Debit	Credit	Balance
1 March	Balance			1,287
10 March	414	97		1,190
13 March	415	238		952
20 March	416	41		911
29 March	Lodgement		716	1,627
29 March	417	562		1,065
30 March	418	125		940

Required Prepare a bank reconciliation statement at 31 March.

QUESTION 7

The bank columns of Lily Baxter's cash book are as follows:

Dr				£					Cr £
1 Jan	Balance b/d			93	4 Jan	B George	612		236
15 Jan	H Young			1438	6 Jan	T Gorman	613		541
29 Jan	G Bralter			412	7 Jan	T Heath	614		82
					11 Jan	D Tan	615		176
					29 Jan	P Vent	616		456
					30 Jan	Balance c/d			452
				1,943					1,943
1 Feb	Balance b/d			452					

Lily received her bank statement on 2 February,

ANYTOWN BANK PLC

Current account statement

Account name   L. BAXTER
Account number 451341201
Branch   Liverpool

Transactions

Date	Details	Debit	Credit	Balance
1 Jan	Balance			93
10 Jan	612	236		143 OD
12 Jan	614	82		225 OD
15 Jan	Lodgement		1,438	1,213
19 Jan	613	541		672
20 Jan	615	176		496

Required Prepare a bank reconciliation statement at 31 January.

QUESTION 8

The bank columns of Leslie Vine's cash book are as follows:

Dr				£					Cr £
1 June	Balance b/d			734	2 June	T Royal	931		261
8 June	P Time			368	4 June	T Hassan	932		147
16 June	V Sass			541	11 June	R Peal	933		298
30 June	T Chinois			432	11 June	W Rooney	934		75
					12 June	Z Nex	935		611
					15 June	O Preston	936		181
					30 June	Balance c/d			502
				2,075					2,075
1 July	Balance b/d			502					

Leslie received his bank statement on 4 July.

```
ANYTOWN BANK PLC

Current account statement

Account name     L. VINE
Account number   731834149
Branch           Stockport

Transactions
Date        Details          Debit    Credit   Balance

1 June      Balance                            734
8 June      931              261               473
8 June      Lodgement                 368      841
15 June     934              75                766
16 June     935              611               155
16 June     Lodgement                 541      696
22 June     932              147               549
```

Prepare a bank reconciliation statement at 30 June.

QUESTION 9

The bank columns of Vera Dawson's cash book are as follows:

Dr		£				Cr £
			1 Jan	Balance b/d		267.42
3 Jan	N. Orbert	446.27	3 Jan	O. Lever	127	38.56
7 Jan	S. Brown	290.42	4 Jan	B. Render	128	129.81
16 Jan	J. Smythe	312.46	8 Jan	C. Dunn	129	1,264.36
31 Jan	T. Recks	530.22	12 Jan	P. Green	130	8.40
31 Jan	Balance c/d	146.44	18 Jan	G. Wright	131	17.26
		1,725.81				1,725.81
			1 Feb	Balance b/d		146.44

Vera received her bank statement on 4 February.

```
ANYTOWN BANK PLC

Current account statement

Account name     V. DAWSON
Account number   674832198
Branch           Bristol

Transactions
Date       Details                Debit      Credit   Balance

1 Jan      Balance                                    267.42 OD
3 Jan      Lodgement                         446.27   178.85
5 Jan      127                    38.56               140.29
7 Jan      Lodgement                         290.42   430.71
15 Jan     Direct debit
           Electricity            246.38              184.33
16 Jan     Lodgement                         312.46   496.79
18 Jan     129                    1,264.36            767.57 OD
21 Jan     130                    8.40                775.97 OD
31 Jan     Bank charges           12.52               788.49 OD
31 Jan     Interest on overdraft  26.78               815.27 OD
```

Make any adjustments to Vera Dawson's cash book.

Prepare a bank reconciliation statement at 31 January.

QUESTION 10

The bank columns of Matthew Carter are as follows:

Dr		£				Cr £
1 Oct	Balance b/d	127.63	2 Oct	M Vaughan	673	272.61
3 Oct	D Parker	367.42	4 Oct	C Chan	674	81.13
7 Oct	T Henley	84.56	11 Oct	M Vere	675	364.42
15 Oct	B Tain	97.42	27 Oct	D Perth	676	182.09
31 Oct	M Sand	216.84	29 Oct	N Lister	677	12.13
31 Oct	Balance c/d	18.51				
		912.38				912.38
			1 Nov	Balance b/d		18.51

Cash book

ANYTOWN BANK PLC

Current account statement

Account name   M. CARTER
Account number 457839018
Branch   Ipswich

Transactions

Date	Details	Debit	Credit	Balance
1 Oct	Balance			127.63
3 Oct	Lodgement		367.42	495.05
6 Oct	Standing order			
	—loan repayment	150.00		345.05
7 Oct	Lodgement		84.56	429.61
8 Oct	674	81.31		348.30
10 Oct	673	273.61		74.69
15 Oct	Lodgement		97.42	172.11
17 Oct	675	364.42		192.31 OD
31 Oct	Bank charges	12.48		204.79 OD
	Bank overdraft interest	27.57		232.36 OD

Required (a) Make any necessary adjustments to Matthew's cash book.
(b) Prepare a bank reconciliation statement at 31 October.

QUESTION 11

On 30 April 20*8 Pat Nicholson received her bank statement. It showed a credit balance of £858. The bank columns of her cash book showed a debit balance of £180.

On the same date it was found that:

■ a cheque lodged in the bank £200 had not been entered in the cash book
■ a cheque lodged in the bank £460 had been entered in the cash book as £640
■ a credit transfer £165 had not been entered in the cash book
■ cheques amounting to £493 had not been presented to the bank.

Required a) Make any necessary adjustments to Pat's cash book.
b) Prepare a bank reconciliation statement at 30 April 20*8.

QUESTION 12

On 31 August 20*8 Bernard Drouin received his bank statement. It showed a credit balance of £210. The bank columns of his cash book showed a debit balance of £170.

On the same date it was found that:

■ a cheque paid into the bank account £109 had not been entered in the cash book
■ a standing order for insurance £245 had not been entered in the cash book
■ cheques amounting to £348 had not been presented to the bank
■ lodgements amounting to £172 had not yet been credited by the bank.

Required a) Make any necessary adjustments to Bernard's cash book.

b) Prepare a bank reconciliation statement at 31 August 20*8.

QUESTION 13

On 31 March 20*8 the cash book of Nancy Best showed a bank overdraft of £590.

On the same date it was found that:

- cheques amounting to £938 had not been presented at the bank for payment
- a standing order for loan interest £83 had not been entered in the cash book
- a direct debit for water rates £31 had not been entered in the cash book
- a credit transfer from Thelma Rodders for £66 had not been entered in the cash book
- lodgements £206 had not yet been credited to Nancy's account by the bank.

Required a) Make any necessary adjustments to Nancy's cash book.

b) Prepare a bank reconciliation statement at 31 March 20*8 showing clearly the balance at bank as per Nancy's bank statement.

QUESTION 14

On 31 December 20*8 Tracy Beddow's cash book showed a debit balance of £374.

On the same date it was found that:

- cheques amounting to £236 had not been presented at the bank for payment
- a direct debit for electricity £99 had not been entered in the cash book
- bank overdraft interest £103 had not been entered in the cash book
- bank charges £86 had not been entered in the cash book
- a standing order £46 for a trade magazine had not been entered in the cash book
- a cheque received from Traster Ltd for £85 had been entered in the cash book as £58
- lodgements amounting to £487 had not yet been credited to Tracy's account by the bank.

Required a) Make any necessary adjustments to Tracy's cash book.

b) Prepare a bank reconciliation statement at 31 December 20*8 showing clearly the balance at bank as per Tracy's bank statement.

CHAPTER
THIRTEEN

Control accounts

We have already seen that the arithmetical accuracy of the whole double-entry book keeping system is checked by extracting a trial balance. Although in theory there is only one book used to record all double-entry transactions, the ledger is actually divided into three.

QUESTION 1

Required Name the three ledgers.

QUESTION 2

Some of the accounts in Theresa's ledger are listed:

- sales account
- purchases account
- the account of Abdul, a credit customer
- the account of Bart, a credit supplier
- sales returns account
- purchase returns account
- the account of Chel, a credit supplier
- cash sales account
- the account of Dodd, a credit customer
- carriage inwards account.

Required Identify the ledger in which the accounts would be found.

The bulk of all entries in the double-entry system are in the personal ledgers:

- the sales ledger
- the purchases ledger.

Because there are so many entries in these two ledgers, there is great potential for errors to be made. Control accounts are used to check the accuracy of the entries made in both the sales ledger and the purchase ledger.

Each month a control account is prepared for each ledger. In this way, errors can be identified as being in one particular ledger in the month that they have occurred.

The control account summarises all the individual entries that have been made in the sales ledgers and the purchase ledgers in any particular month. Any entry in any sales ledger or purchases ledger account will be duplicated in the control account.

If a business has a vast number of credit customers it may divide the sales ledger according to geographical areas, customers of particular sales persons, alphabetically, etc. The sales day book would reflect any divisions of the sales ledger.

> **Memorandum accounts** record financial information in account form but they are not part of the double-entry system.

Some businesses use control accounts as part of their double-entry system. They maintain personal credit customers' accounts in detail as memorandum accounts. These memorandum accounts are used:

- to send out monthly statements
- for credit control purposes, i.e. identifying bad debts and potential doubtful debtors.

Specification coverage:
AQA Unit 1
OCR Unit 2

By the end of this chapter you should be able to:
- check the accuracy of entries in the sales ledger
- check the accuracy of entries in the purchase ledger
- explain how debit balances can occur in the purchase ledger
- Explain how credit balances can occur in the sales ledger.

Businesses may also maintain personal credit suppliers' accounts in detail as memorandum accounts. These memorandum accounts are used:

■ to check monthly statements received
■ for credit control purposes.

Other businesses use the detailed sales and purchase ledger accounts as part of their double-entry system. They maintain control accounts as memorandum accounts.

> **○ EXAMINATION TIP**
>
> For the purposes of examination technique, the construction of control accounts is the same whether or not they are maintained as part of the double-entry system or as memorandum accounts.

> **Schedule of debtors** is a list of debtors' balances extracted from the sales ledger.

> **Schedule of creditors** is a list of creditors' balances extracted from the purchases ledger.

PREPARATION OF SALES LEDGER CONTROL ACCOUNTS

The sales ledger control account is a replica in total of all the entries made in the individual sales ledger accounts. Here is a simple illustration:

WORKED EXAMPLE

Sales ledger

Dr	Clogg		Cr	Dr	Saddler		Cr
		£				£	
		£				£	£
1 May Sales	50	9 May Cash	48	7 May Sales	60	12 May Returns inward	29
		9 May Disc Alld	2			14 May Bank	20
	50		50			14 May Bal c/d	11
					60		60
				15 May Bal b/d	11		

Required Prepare a sales ledger control account at 15 May for the ledger shown.

Answer

Dr		Sales ledger control account			Cr
		£			£
1 May	Sales	50	9 May	Cash	48
7 May	Sales	60	9 May	Discount allowed	2
			12 May	Returns inward	29
			14 May	Bank	20
			14 May	Balance c/d	11
		110			110
15 May	Balance b/d	11			

The control account is an exact replica of all the ledger accounts. If you can remember this you should not get the items required in preparing the control account on the wrong side. (This, of course, assumes that you understand on which side each of the entries appears in an individual account!)

The most common error that students make when answering an examination question is to reverse the control account.

In reality we cannot look at every individual account in the sales ledger and copy them into the sales ledger control account. Nor can we add each of the different categories of entries together – it would be too time consuming. We can, however, get the necessary figures in total by using the books of prime entry.

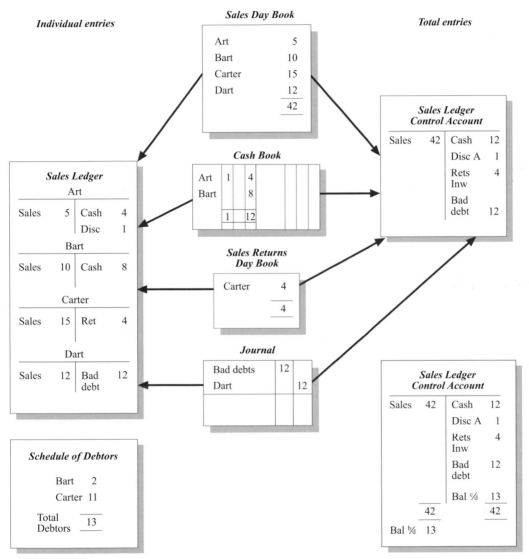

Figure 13.1 The sales ledger control account

WORKED EXAMPLE

Petra started business in May 20*8. She provides the following totals from her books of prime entry on 31 May 20*8:

credit sales £7,300; cash sales £2,100; sales returns £420; monies received from debtors £5,400.

A schedule of debtors extracted from Petra's sales ledger totals £1,480.

Required Prepare a sales ledger control account for May 20*8 for Petra.

Answer

Dr			Sales ledger control account			Cr		
			£				£	
31 May	Sales		7,300	31 May	Returns inward	420		
				31 May	Cash	5,400		
				31 May	Balance c/d	1,480		*figure included to make control account balance*
			7,300			7,300		
1 June	Balance b/d		1,480					

The debtors at the end of May, according to the control account, should be £1,480. This figure should agree with the total of balances listed on the schedule of debtors – it does, so we can say that the sales ledger is arithmetically correct for the month of May 20*8.

Note

- The £2100 cash sales should not be included – these do not appear in the sales ledger as the sales ledger is reserved only for credit customers.
- The £1,480 debit balance should also be brought down on the sales ledger control account.

WORKED EXAMPLE

At the end of her second month of trading Petra provides you with the following information which she has extracted from her books of prime entry on 30 June 20*8:

credit sales £9,400; cash sales £2,750; monies received from debtors £6,200; discount allowed to credit customers £610; sales returns £240. (Bring forward the debtor's balance from the May sales ledger control account.)

Required Prepare a sales ledger control account for June 20*8.

Answer

Dr		Sales ledger control account				Cr
		£				£
1 June	Balance b/d	1,480	30 June	Cash		6,200
30 June	Sales	9,400	30 June	Discount allowed		610
			30 June	Returns inward		240
			30 June	Balance c/d		3,830
		10,880				10,880
1 July	Balance b/d	3,830				

QUESTION 3

Petra provides the following information, which has been extracted from her books of prime entry on 31 July 20*8:

	£
Credit sales	9,600
Cash sales	2,350
Monies received from debtors	7,200
Discount allowed	910
Returns inward	340
Returns outward	400

She is also able to provide the following information:

Debtors 1 July 20*8	3,830
Schedule of debtor's total 31 July 20*8	4,980

Note

- Returns <u>in</u>wards are goods that have been returned by credit customers and have been received <u>into</u> Petra's business.
- Returns <u>out</u>wards are goods that have been returned and have gone <u>out</u> of Petra's business.

Required Prepare a sales ledger control account for the month of July 20*8.

QUESTION 4

Petra provides the following information, which has been extracted from her books of prime entry on 31 August 20*8:

	£
Credit sales	10,100
Cash sales	2,450
Monies received from debtors	7,400
Discount allowed	870
Dishonoured cheque	360
Returns inward	600
Returns outward	550

She is also able to provide the following information:

	£
Debtors 1 August 20*8	4,980
Schedule of debtor's total 31 August 20*8	4,870

The dishonoured cheque for £360 was originally part of the monies received and, because it has now been 'returned', should be entered on the debit side of the control account.

Required a) Prepare a sales ledger control account for the month of August 20*8.
b) Explain what the control account reveals.

● EXAMINATION TIP

Do not forget to bring balances down — if you fail to do this it will cost you valuable marks.

PREPARATION OF PURCHASE LEDGER CONTROL ACCOUNTS

The purchase ledger control account is a replica of all the entries made in the individual purchase ledger accounts. Here is a simple illustration:

EXAMPLE

Dr		Saleem		Cr		Dr		Toshak		Cr	
			£		£				£		£
13 July Cash		347		1 July Purchases	350	19 July Cash		20		7 July Purchase	125
Discount received		3				24 July R'turns					
		350			350	outward		18			
						31 July Bal c/d		87			125
								125		1 Aug Balance b/d	87

Dr		Purchase ledger control account			Cr
			£		£
13 July	Cash		347	1 July Purchases	350
13 July	Discount received		3	7 July Purchases	125
19 July	Cash		20		
24 July	Returns outward		18		
31 July	Balance c/d		87		
			475		475
				1 Aug Balance b/d	87

Once again, this simple but effective illustration relies on the fact that you must understand what an individual account in the purchase ledger looks like.

We cannot look at every individual account in the purchase ledger and total them.

We use totals that can be found in the books of prime entry.

WORKED EXAMPLE

EXAMPLE 1

Yip started in business in February 20*8. He provides the following totals from his books of prime entry on 29 February 20*8:

credit purchases £9,430; cash purchases £1,790; purchase returns £105; monies paid by Yip to creditors £8,100; a schedule of creditors extracted from the purchase ledger on 29 February 20*8 totals £1,225.

Required Prepare a purchase ledger control account for February 20*8.

Answer

Dr		Purchase ledger control account			Cr
			£		£
29 February	Returns outward		105	29 February Purchases	9,430
29 February	Cash		8,100		
29 February	Bal c/d		1,225		
			9,430		9,430
				1 March Balance b/d	1,225

According to the control account the creditors at the end of February should amount to £1,225. This agrees with Yip's schedule of creditors, so we can say that his purchase ledger is arithmetically correct.

Cash purchases were not included because they do not appear in the purchase ledger – the ledger is only used to record Yip's transactions with his credit suppliers.

WORKED EXAMPLE *continued*

EXAMPLE 2

Yip provides you with the following information which has been extracted from his books of prime entry for March 20*8, his second month of trading:

credit purchases £8,600; cash purchases £2,930; monies paid by Yip to creditors £6,800; discount received from creditors £460; purchase returns £120.

(Bring forward the creditor's balance from the February purchase ledger control account.)

Required Prepare a purchase ledger control account for March 20*8.

Answer

Dr			Purchase ledger control account			Cr
		£				£
31 March	Cash	6,800	1 March	Balance b/d		1,225
31 March	Discount received	460	31 March	Purchases		8,600
31 March	Returns outward	120				
31 March	Balance c/d	2,445				
		9,825				9,825
			1 April	Balance b/d		2,445

QUESTION 5

Yip provides the following information from his books of prime entry for April 20*8:

	£
Credit purchases	9,200
Cash purchases	3,150
Monies paid to creditors by Yip	9,300
Discount received	700
Returns inward	610
Returns outward	150

He is also able to provide the following information:

	£
Creditors 1 April 20*8	2,445
Schedule of creditors total 30 April 20*8	1,495

Required Prepare a purchase ledger control account for the month of April 20*8.

QUESTION 6

Yip provides the following information from his books of prime entry for May 20*8:

	£
Credit purchases	9,350
Cash purchases	4,075
Monies paid to creditors by Yip	7,900
Discount received	460
Returns inward	670
Returns outward	170

He is also able to provide the following information:

	£
Creditors 1 May 20*8	1,495
Schedule of creditors total 31 May 20*8	2,335

Required a) Prepare a purchase ledger control account for May 20*8.
b) Explain what the control account reveals.

CREDIT BALANCES IN THE SALES LEDGER

Usually, any closing balance in the account of an individual credit customer will be a debit. However, it is possible that an individual debtor account may end with a credit balance. How can this happen?

WORKED EXAMPLE

EXAMPLE 1

Petra sells £720 goods to Claude on 3 October.

On 23 October Claude sends Petra a cheque for £720.

On 29 October Claude returns £30 of goods which have proved to be faulty.

Required Prepare the account of Claude as it would appear in Petra's sales ledger at 31 October 20*8.

Answer

The question asks for the account so it must be produced in detail, not as a 'T' account.

Dr		Claude			Cr
		£			£
3 October	Sales	720	23 October	Bank	720
			29 October	Returns inward	30

You can see that at 31 October there is a credit balance in Claude's account, although this account is contained in Petra's sales ledger (debtors ledger).

In Petra's list of outstanding balances in the sales ledger at 31 October 20*8 she will have to show this balance on Claude's account as a creditor. It will also feature in the sales ledger control account for October as a creditor.

Do not deduct this amount from Petra's total debtors. It must be included in a trial balance at 31 October 20*8 and a balance sheet prepared at 31 October 20*8 with other creditors.

EXAMPLE 2

Toddy is a regular customer of Petra. He has paid £50 on the 24th of each month to Petra by standing order since 24 May 20*8. On 6 September Petra sells £230 of goods to Toddy.

Required Prepare the account of Toddy as it would appear in Petra's sales ledger at 30 September 20*8.

Answer

Dr		Toddy			Cr
		£			£
6 September	Sales	230	24 May	Bank	50
			24 June	Bank	50
			24 July	Bank	50
			24 August	Bank	50
30 September	Balance c/d	20	24 September	Bank	50
		250			250
			1 October	Balance b/d	20

In Petra's list of outstanding balances in her sales ledger at 30 September the balance standing on Toddy's account will be shown as a credit of £20 – he is a creditor at that date – and this should be shown accordingly on a trial balance extracted on 30 September or any balance sheet prepared at 30 September.

A credit balance could also appear in a debtor's account if the customer had made an over-payment or was allowed additional cash or trade discount after the account had been settled.

DEBIT BALANCES IN THE PURCHASE LEDGER

Similar circumstances could result in debit balances appearing on the list of balances extracted from a purchase ledger.

Debit balances would appear in the purchase ledger if a trader:

- settled his account with a supplier and then returned faulty goods
- pays a fixed amount each month which in total exceeds the amount of purchases made
- was allowed additional discount after settling his/her account
- had over-paid an outstanding balance.

Any credit balances in the sales ledger at a month end will be shown as credit balances in the sales ledger control account for that month.

Any debit balances in the purchase ledger at a month end will be shown as debit balances in the purchase ledger control account for that month.

WORKED EXAMPLE

Harvey provides the following information from his books of prime entry at 31 July 20*8:

Credit sales for July	6,930
Monies received from debtors during month	5,100
Discount allowed	450
Returns inward	180

He provides the following additional information:

Debit balances appearing in the sales ledger at 1 July 20*8	2,100
Credit balances appearing in the sales ledger at 1 July 20*8	30
Creditor appearing in sales ledger schedule of debtor's total at 31 July 20*8	90

Required Prepare the sales ledger control account for July 20*8.

Answer

Dr			Sales ledger control account			Cr
		£				£
1 July	Balance b/d	2,100	1 July	Balance b/d		30
31 July	Sales	6,930	31 July	Cash		5,100
			31 July	Discount allowed		450
			31 July	Returns inward		180
31 July	Balance c/d *(given)*	90	31 July	Balance c/d *(missing figure)*	3,360
		9,120				9,120
1 August	Balance b/d	3,360	1 August	Balance b/d		90

CONTRA ENTRIES

WORKED EXAMPLE

Contra entries are sometimes called 'set offs'.

A business may well be both a customer of and a supplier to another business. For example, B Neal had supplied Hoole with fabrics valued at £4,300 on credit. Neal purchased £700 curtains for his business on credit from Hoole.

This would appear in Neal's books of account as follows:

Sales ledger			Purchase ledger		
Dr	Hoole	Cr	Dr	Hoole	Cr
Sales	4,300			Purchases	700

It would not seem sensible for Neal to send £700 to Hoole while demanding that Hoole pay £4,300. The usual procedure in cases like this is to transfer the smaller amount from one ledger to the other. The entries are:

Sales ledger

Dr		Hoole		Cr
		Transfer from purchases ledger		700

Purchases ledger

Dr		Hoole		Cr
Transfer to sales ledger	700			

This will close one account (in the purchases ledger) and reduce the balance owed by Hoole (in the sales ledger). The accounts now look like this:

Sales ledger

Dr		Hoole		Cr
Sales	4,300	Transfer to purchases ledger		700

Purchases ledger

Dr		Hoole		Cr
Transfer from sales ledger	700	Purchases		700

All transactions should be recorded in a book of prime entry. Entries involving transfers should be entered in the journal:

Journal

		Dr	Cr
Hoole	PL 26	700	
Hoole	SL 15		700

Transfer of credit balance in Hoole's account in purchases ledger to Hoole's account in sales ledger.

All entries in the personal ledgers must also be shown in the control accounts.

There will be an entry on the credit side of Neal's sales ledger control account.

There will also be an entry on the debit side of Neal's purchases ledger control account, reflecting the entries in the two personal ledgers.

WORKED EXAMPLE

EXAMPLE 1

In Rodney's books, Ernie has a debit balance of £100 in Rodney's sales ledger and a credit balance of £30 in Rodney's purchases ledger.

Required Show the contra entries (set offs) as they would appear in both Rodney's sales ledger control account and his purchases ledger control account.

Answer

Dr	Rodney sales ledger control account		Cr
	Transfer from purchases ledger		30

Dr	Rodney purchases ledger control account		Cr
Transfer to sales ledger	30		

EXAMPLE 2

In Derek's books, Eric has a debit balance of £710 in Derek's sales ledger and a credit balance of £1,400 in Derek's purchases ledger.

Required Show how the contra (set offs) would appear in both Derek's sales ledger control account and his purchases ledger control account.

Answer

Dr	Sales ledger control account		Cr
	Transfer to purchases ledger		710

Dr	Purchases ledger control account		Cr
Transfer from sales ledger	710		

Note:

It does not matter whether the debit balance or the credit balance is greater when showing the contra in the control accounts:

- the sales ledger control account is always credited, and
- the purchases ledger control account is always debited.

In the personal ledgers the smaller balance is the balance that is transferred.

WORKED EXAMPLE

Damien provides the following information taken from his books at 30 November 20*8:

Sales ledger balances 1 November £6,340; purchase ledger balances 1 November £3,960; credit sales for November £140,100; credit purchases for November £64,300; monies received from debtors for November £139,570; monies paid to creditors in November £63,030; discounts allowed £350; discounts received £180; returns inwards £900; returns outward £600; transfers from sales ledger to purchases ledger £440.

Required a) Prepare a sales ledger control account showing the closing balance of outstanding debtors at 30 November 20*8.
b) Prepare a purchases ledger control account showing the closing balance of outstanding creditors at 30 November 20*8.

WORKED EXAMPLE *continued*

Answer

Dr			Sales ledger control account		Cr
1 November	Balance b/d	6,340	30 November	Cash	139,570
30 November	Sales	140,100	30 November	Discount allowed	350
			30 November	Returns inward	900
			30 November	Transfer to purchases ledger	440
			30 November	Balance c/d	5,180
		146,440			146,440
1 December	Balance b/d	5,180			

Dr			Purchases ledger control account		Cr
30 November	Cash	63,030	1 November	Balance b/d	3,960
30 November	Discount received	180	30 November	Purchases	64,300
30 November	Returns outward	600			
30 November	Transfer from sales ledger	440			
30 November	Balance c/d	4,010			
		68,260			68,260
1 December	Balance b/d	4,010			

Provision for doubtful debts (see Chapter 17) is not included in a sales ledger control account.

The provision is not entered in specific individual debtor's accounts.

Only transactions that appear in the ledger accounts appear in the control accounts. Therefore, if the provision does not appear in a personal ledger account . . . it will not appear in the control account.

REVISION TIP

Practise preparing individual accounts from the sales ledger and the purchases ledger – control accounts are similar but use larger amounts of money.

ADVANTAGES OF USING CONTROL ACCOUNTS

1 They act as a check on the accuracy of all the postings made to the personal ledgers and this checks the reliability of the ledger accounts.
2 They enable some errors in the ledgers to be located quickly.
3 If the trial balance does not balance, the control accounts may indicate which personal ledger(s) contain the error(s).
4 Total amounts owed by debtors and total amounts owing to creditors can be ascertained quickly, enabling a trial balance and/or a balance sheet to be prepared quickly.
5 They may be used to give responsibility to staff by making them responsible for sections of the ledger.
6 They may be used as a check of the honesty of staff. The control account should be prepared by a member of staff who is not involved in the maintenance of the ledger being checked.

LIMITATIONS OF USING CONTROL ACCOUNTS

The main **limitation of using control accounts** as a means of verifying the accuracy of the personal ledgers rests on the fact that not all errors in the ledgers will be revealed by the preparation of a control account.

Within the ledger there could be:

■ compensating errors, plus errors of:
■ omission
■ commission
■ original entry and
■ reversal errors.

The details of how these errors could arise can be found in Chapter 8 'The trial balance'.

Chapter summary

- Control accounts help find errors in the two personal ledgers quickly.
- A control account will be prepared for each personal ledger each month.
- Any transaction that is entered in the sales ledger will appear in the sales ledger control account.
- Any transaction that is entered in the purchase ledger will be entered in the purchase ledger control account.
- Provision for doubtful debts does not appear in the sales ledger control account.
- Transfers from one ledger to another are entered in both control accounts.
- These set offs are credited to the sales ledger control account and debited to the purchase ledger control account.

SELF-TEST QUESTIONS

- Why might a business keep control accounts?
- How often will a business prepare control accounts?
- In which control account would you find returns inwards?
- In which control account would you find bad debts?
- In which control account would you expect to find provision for doubtful debts?
- Identify one advantage of using control accounts.
- Explain how you could find a debit balance in the purchase ledger.
- Explain how you could find a credit balance in the sales ledger.
- 'Set offs' are always found on the .... side of the sales ledger control account and on the .... side of the purchase ledger control account.
- What type of business would never have a sales ledger control account?

QUESTION 7

The following information relates to the purchase ledger of Tricia Clott for the month of October 20*8:

	£
Total creditors on 1 October 20*8	3,741
Credit purchases	10,452
Cash paid to creditors	9,779
Discounts received	1,230

Required Prepare a purchases ledger control account for the month of October 20*8.

QUESTION 8

The following information relates to the creditors' ledger of Phillip Tyke for the month of February 20*8:

	£
Total creditors on 1 February 20*8	6,813
Credit purchases	18,734
Total cash purchases	2,451
Cash paid to creditors	19,003
Discounts received	872

Required Prepare a creditors' ledger control account for the month of February 20*8.

QUESTION 9

The following information relates to the sales ledger of Frew Niell for the month of December 20*8:

	£
Total debtors on 1 December 20*8	1,006
Credit sales	5,408
Cash received from debtors	4,921
Discounts allowed	561

Required Prepare a sales ledger control account for the month of December 20*8.

QUESTION 10

The following information relates to the debtors' ledger of Martin Daley for the month of July 20*8:

	£
Total debtors on 1 July 20*8	4,110
Credit sales	16,882
Cash received from debtors	18,530
Discounts allowed	1,451

Required Prepare a debtors' ledger control account for the month of July 20*8.

QUESTION 11

The following information is given for May 20*8 for Greg Trout:

	£
Total creditors on 1 May 20*8	22,556
Credit purchases	117,004
Cash purchases	4,662
Cash paid to creditors	109,621
Discounts received	3,551
Discounts allowed	3,239
Returns outwards	1,572
Returns inwards	1,422

Required Prepare a purchases ledger control account for the month of May 20*8.

QUESTION 12

The following information is given for September 20*8 for Ted Brester:

	£
Total creditors on 1 September 20*8	2,921
Credit purchases	6,443
Cash purchases	2,091
Cash paid to creditors	4,220
Discounts received	622
Discounts allowed	428
Returns outwards	1,261
Returns inwards	720

Required Prepare a purchases ledger control account for the month of September 20*8.

QUESTION 13

Claire Droy supplies the following information for August 20*8:

	£
Total debtors on 1 August 20*8	456
Credit sales	10,674
Cash sales	4,441
Cash received from debtors	8,634
Discounts received	3,001
Discounts allowed	1,329
Returns outwards	358
Returns inwards	566

Required Prepare a sales ledger control account for the month of August 20*8.

QUESTION 14

Dick Dresden supplies the following information for March 20*8:

	£
Total debtors on 1 March 20*8	5,127
Credit sales	11,439
Cash sales	3,771
Cash received from debtors	9,528
Discounts received	1,994
Discounts allowed	2,331

| Returns outwards | 731 |
| Returns inwards | 841 |

Required Prepare a debtors' ledger control account for the month of March 20*8.

QUESTION 15

Xiu Jin supplies the following information for October 20*8:

	£
Credit balances in purchase ledger on 1 October 20*8	3,551
Debit balances in purchase ledger on 1 October 20*8	37
Credit purchases	15,338
Cash purchases	4,119
Cash paid to creditors	12,440
Discounts received	1,084
Discounts allowed	936
Returns outwards	32
Returns inwards	631
Debit balances in purchases ledger on 31 October 20*8	154

Required Prepare a purchases ledger control account for the month of October 20*8.

QUESTION 16

Melodie Clyde supplies the following information for November 20*8:

	£
Debit balances in debtors' ledger on 1 November 20*8	5,308
Credit balances in debtors' ledger on 1 November 20*8	650
Credit purchases	5,773
Cash purchases	3,411
Credit sales	11,453
Cash sales	2,766
Cash paid to creditors	4,720
Cash received from debtors	9,539
Discounts received	393
Discounts allowed	197
Returns outwards	671
Returns inwards	777
Credit balances in debtors' ledger on 30 November 20*8	240

Required Prepare a debtors' ledger control account for the month of November 20*8.

QUESTION 17

Rory McDuff supplies the following information for the month of December 20*8:

	£
Debit balances in sales ledger on 1 December 20*8	7,449
Debit balances in purchases ledger on 1 December 20*8	342
Credit balances in sales ledger on 1 December 20*8	247
Credit balances in purchases ledger on 1 December 20*8	4,552
Credit sales	43,650
Credit purchases	20,005
Cash sales	8,643
Cash purchases	4,571
Cash received from credit customers	39,754
Cash paid to credit suppliers	19,003
Discounts received	251
Discounts allowed	166
Returns outwards	543
Returns inwards	510
Transfers from sales ledger to purchase ledger	300
Provision for doubtful debts on 31 December 20*8	150
Debit balances in purchases ledger on 31 December 20*8	45
Credit balances in sales ledger on 31 December 20*8	188

Required a) Prepare a sales ledger control account for the month of December 20*8.
b) Prepare a purchases ledger control account for the month of December 20*8.

QUESTION 18

Ifor Jones supplies the following information for the month of February 20*8:

	£
Debit balances in sales ledger on 1 February 20*8	18,539
Debit balances in purchases ledger on 1 February 20*8	341
Credit balances in sales ledger on 1 February 20*8	450
Credit balances in purchases ledger on 1 February 20*8	9,557
Credit sales	123,921
Credit purchases	47,509
Cash sales	34,652
Cash purchases	18,674
Cash received from credit customers	112,659
Cash paid to credit suppliers	45,620
Discounts received	762
Discounts allowed	673
Returns outwards	1,290
Returns inwards	732
Transfers to purchases ledger from sales ledger	489
Provision for doubtful debts on 29 February 20*8	340
Debit balances in purchases ledger on 29 February 20*8	65
Credit balances in sales ledger on 29 February 20*8	138

Required a) Prepare a sales ledger control account for the month of February 20*8.
b) Prepare a purchases ledger control account for the month of February 20*8.

CHAPTER
FOURTEEN

Accruals and pre-payments

So far in our studies we have assumed that money spent and money received exactly matched the time period under review. For example, we have assumed that:

■ rent paid in February was for the use of premises in February
■ wages paid in July was payment for work done in July
■ the figures shown in the trial balance prepared at 31 December 20*8 showed all the incomes and all the expenses for the year ended 31 December 20*8; nothing more and nothing less.

When calculating profits, accountants are interested in accounting for the resources that the business has used during the financial year to generate the revenue receipts for that same year.

The accruals concept recognises the difference between the actual payment of cash and the legal obligation to pay cash.

Specification coverage:
AQA Unit 1
OCR Unit 1

By the end of this chapter you should be able to:
■ explain the accruals concept
■ make appropriate entries for accruals and pre-payments in the final accounts.

EXAMPLE

Larry runs a small newsagent's shop. He has signed a tenancy agreement with his landlord stating that he can use the shop for the next five years on payment of a rental of £6,000 per annum, payable quarterly in advance on 1 January, 1 April, 1 July and 1 October.

At 31 December 20*8, Larry's financial year-end, Larry has only paid his landlord £4,500 (i.e. he still owes the rent that was due to be paid on 1 October).

The amount shown on Larry's profit and loss account for rent is £6,000 since Larry has had the use of a resource (the shop) worth £6,000 to help him generate his profits.

When preparing a trading and profit and loss account a trader must include all items of expenditure paid and payable.

The accruals concept also recognises the distinction between the receipt of cash and legal right to receive cash. This may sound a little strange at first but it will soon become clear.

So from now on, when we prepare a set of final accounts we shall include all the items that apply to the accounting period under consideration.

Some expenses listed in the trial balance are always paid in advance, for example:

■ insurance has to be paid in advance
■ business rates are paid in advance.

Other expenses listed on the trial balance might not be paid up to date, for example:

■ part of Larry's rent payable had not been paid
■ wages earned for work already done may not be due to be paid until next month.

DEALING WITH ACCRUED EXPENSES

> **Trade creditors** are amounts owed to the suppliers of goods for resale.

> **Trade debtors** are amounts owed by credit customers who have not yet settled their account.

An extract from Larry's trial balance at 31 December 20*8 would show:

	Dr £	Cr £
Rent payable	4,500	

When we prepare the profit and loss account for the year ended 31 December 20*8, the entries shown above would show:

Profit and loss account extract for the year ended 31 December 20*8

	Dr £	Cr £
Gross profit		....
Less expenses		
Rent payable	6,000	

But this cannot be totally correct. Larry has increased his debit entries by £1,500 with no corresponding increase in his credit entries.

He needs to include an extra credit in his final accounts – rent payable owed at the year-end.

In the balance sheet prepared at the year-end, trade creditors represent amounts owed to suppliers who have supplied goods but who have not yet been paid.

Since the rent payable is owed at the balance sheet date this too must be a creditor.

Larry has used his premises and not yet paid for their use. Rent payable must be shown as a current liability along with the trade creditors.

Note

- The balance sheet has not been credited.
- The balance sheet is not part of the double-entry system; it is merely a sheet showing balances outstanding at the end of the financial year.
- The outstanding rent is included in current liabilities with other credit balances (e.g. the trade creditors).

The balance sheet at 31 December 20*8 would show:

Current liabilities
Accrued expenses (rent)   1500

QUESTION 1

The following items are shown on a trial balance extracted on 30 June 20*8:

	£
Wages	43,000
Motor expenses	8,600
Telephone	2,400
Advertising	1,800
Heating and lighting expenses	2,000

At the financial year-end the following amounts remained outstanding and unpaid:

	£
Wages	872
Motor expenses	750
Telephone	280
Advertising	560
Heating and lighting	391

Required Complete the table below, showing the amounts to be included as an expense in the profit and loss account for the year ended 30 June 20*8 and the amount to be shown as a current liability in the balance sheet as at 30 June 20*8.

Answer

Expense	Profit and loss entry	Current liability
Wages		
Motor expenses		
Telephone		
Advertising		
Heating and lighting		

DEALING WITH PREPAID EXPENSES

Sometimes a business will pay for services before they actually receive the service. For example, insurance has to be paid for before cover is provided. Local authority business rates are also due to be paid before the period for which they are due.

Since we are accounting for resources used in the period covered by the final accounts, any amounts paid in advance must be disregarded.

WORKED EXAMPLE

An extract from Larry's trial balance at 31 December 20*8 shows:

	£
Insurance	2,300
Business rates	1,200

Insurance paid for January 20*9 amounts to £100.

Business rates paid for the three months ending 31 March 20*9 amounts to £300.

Required Prepare a profit and loss extract for the year ended 31 December 20*8 showing the entries for insurance and business rates.

Answer

Larry
Profit and loss account extract for the year ended 31 December 20*8

	£	
Gross profit		....
Less expenses		
Insurance	2,200	
Business rates	900	

Larry does not include the £100 paid for *next year's insurance cover,* nor the £300 for *next year's rates bill.*

He only includes the payments made to acquire the resources that have been used to run his business this year.

But it cannot be right to reduce the two expenses without corresponding entries.

We can reduce debits by increasing credits (check this out – it is correct).

In effect, Larry has credited insurance with £100; he has credited business rates with £300. He needs to include two extra debits – two extra debtors.

An extract from Larry's balance sheet at 31 December 20*8 will show:

	£
Current assets	
Amounts prepaid – insurance	100
– business rates	300

QUESTION 2

The following items appear in a trial balance extracted on 31 August 20*8:

Rent	7,500
General expenses	5,412
Insurance	1,872
Salaries	45,670
Rates	1,750

The following additional information is available at 31 August 20*8:

Amounts owing	Rent	500
	General expenses	521
	Salaries	729
Amounts paid for the year ending 31 August 20*9		
	Insurance	341
	Rates	812

Required Complete the table. Indicate the amount to be included in the profit and loss account for the year ended 31 August 20*8 and the amount to be shown on the balance sheet at 31 August 20*8.

Answer

Expense	Profit and loss account entry	Current asset	Current liability
Rent			
General expenses			
Insurance			
Salaries			
Rates			

DEALING WITH OUTSTANDING REVENUES

When revenue has been earned during a financial year, but has not yet been paid, the revenue due must be included in the final accounts.

EXAMPLE

Larry sublets the rooms above his shop to Dan for a rental of £50 per week. At

31 December Dan owes two weeks' rent. Larry's profit and loss account would show a full year's rental income of £2,600, even though he has only actually received £2,500 from Dan.

When preparing a trading and profit and loss account a trader must include all items of revenue received or receivable for the time period under review.

QUESTION 3

Malcolm's gross profit for the year ended 30 November 20*8 is £72,385. Malcolm works on a commission basis for Hijah Ltd. He earns 10% commission on all goods sold. Sales of goods received from Hijah Ltd for the year ended 30 November 20*8 were £87,750. Malcolm has received commission amounting to £7,000 in the year ended 30 November 20*8.

Required Fill in the missing amounts in his final accounts.

Answer

Malcolm
Profit and loss account extract for the year ended 30 November 20*8

	£
Gross profit	72,385
Commission receivable	....

Balance sheet extract at 30 November 20*8

Current assets	£
Commission receivable owing	....

QUESTION 4

Gilly's gross profit for the year ended 31 December 20*8 is £123,902. Gilly sublets part of her premises at an annual rental of £3,900. At the financial year-end 31 December 20*8, Gilly's tenant owes £225 for three weeks' unpaid rent.

Fill in the missing amounts in her final accounts.

Answer

Gilly
Profit and loss account extract for the year ended 31 December 20*8

	£
Gross profit	123,902
Rent receivable	....

Balance sheet extract at 31 December 20*8

Current assets	£
Rent receivable owing	....

Sometimes commission receivable and rent receivable may be paid in advance. The amounts relating to *next year* will not be included in *this year's* final accounts.

WORKED EXAMPLE

Horace works on commission for Henri. Horace has earned £5,320 commission for the year ended 31 January 20*8. At 31 January 20*8 Horace has received commission payments of £6,000.

Required State:

a) the amount to be entered in Horace's profit and loss account for the year ended 31 January 20*8
b) the amount to be shown in the balance sheet at 31 January 20*8.

Answer

The amount to be shown in the profit and loss account is £5,320. This should be shown as an addition to the gross profit.

£680 is shown under current liabilities in the balance sheet (Horace owes Henri £680 at the end of the year).

Amounts owed for expenses by a business at the financial year-end are usually totalled and entered in the balance sheet as a current liability. The total is known as one of the following:

- accruals
- accrued expenses
- expense creditors
- expenses owing.

Amounts paid in advance for expenses by the business at the financial year-end are usually totalled and entered in the balance sheet as a current asset. The total is known as one of the following:

- prepayments
- prepaid expenses
- payments in advance.

Amounts owed to a business for commission receivable and rent receivable are usually shown with prepayments as accrued income.

Amounts received in advance for commission receivable and rent receivable are usually shown with accruals.

Chapter summary

- We account for resources used during a financial year, not money paid to acquire resources.
- The accruals concept recognises the difference between the actual payment of cash and the legal obligation to pay cash. Accruals are current liabilities. Prepayments are current assets.
- The concept also recognises the distinction between the actual receipt of cash and the legal right to receive cash. Cash received before it is due is a current liability. Cash owed to us but not yet paid is a current asset.

SELF-TEST QUESTIONS

- The accruals concept is sometimes known as the .... concept.
- Define an accrual.
- Identify two other terms used to describe an accrual in a balance sheet.
- Define a prepayment.
- Identify two other terms used to describe a prepayment in a balance sheet.
- The amount of an expense on the trial balance is always entered in the profit and loss account. True or false?
- A prepayment is a current asset. True or false?
- An accrued expense is a current asset. True or false?

- Money paid for the next financial year's rent is a current asset. True or false?
- Money received from a tenant for next year's rent is a current asset. True or false?

TEST QUESTIONS

QUESTION 5

Ben Trent provides the following trial balance extracted from his books of account on 31 March 20*8, after his first year of trading:

	Dr £	Cr £
Sales		123,563
Purchases	44,832	
Rent	5,600	
Rates	2,340	
Wages	47,892	
Motor expenses	2,357	
General expenses	7,459	
Capital		26,061
Drawings	14,670	
Trade debtors	8,564	
Trade creditors		5,430
Bank balance	1,340	
Equipment at cost	8,000	
Delivery van at cost	12,000	
	155,054	155,054

Additional information at 31 March 20*8:

stock was valued at £8,459; accrued wages amount to £874.

Required Prepare:

a) a trading and profit and loss account for the year ended 31 March 20*8
b) a balance sheet at 31 March 20*8.

QUESTION 6

Lottie Chum provides the following trial balance extracted from her books of account on 31 October 20*8, after her first year of trading.

	Dr £	Cr £
Capital		92,112
Drawings	17,500	
Purchases	67,431	
Sales		165,997
Motor expenses	5,700	
Wages	84,532	
Heating and lighting	4,632	
Rates	1,280	
General expenses	8,349	
Premises at cost	45,000	
Equipment at cost	18,000	
Van at cost	6,500	
Trade debtors	4,673	
Trade creditors		5,342
Bank overdraft		376
Cash in hand	230	
	263,827	263,827

Additional information at 31 October 20*8:

stock was valued at £11,096; heating and lighting owing amounted to £329.

Required Prepare:

a) a trading and profit and loss account for the year ended 31 October 20*8
b) a balance sheet at 31 October 20*8.

QUESTION 7

Toby Moore provides the following trial balance extracted from his books of account on 31 July 20*8.

	Dr £	Cr £
Stock 1 August 20*7	8,756	
Sales		134,908
Purchases	54,731	
Returns inwards	453	
Returns outwards		612
Drawings	25,000	
Capital		76,810
Wages	34,770	
Motor expenses	1,443	
Insurance	880	
General expenses	4,119	
Premises at cost	65,000	
Machinery at cost	16,000	
Vehicle at cost	7,400	
Trade debtors	811	
Trade creditors		2,678
Bank overdraft		4,637
Cash in hand	282	
	219,645	219,645

Additional information at 31 July 20*8:

stock was valued at £9,315; insurance has been prepaid £58.

Required Prepare:

a) a trading and profit and loss account for the year ended 31 July 20*8
b) a balance sheet at 31 July 20*8.

QUESTION 8

Natasha Bedi provides the following trial balance extracted from her books of account on 31 January 20*8:

	Dr £	Cr £
Purchases	112,754	
Sales		232,987
Returns inwards	458	
Returns outwards		2,610
Stock 1 February 20*7	8,503	
Capital		82,911
Long-term loan		50,000
Drawings	34,675	
Wages	73,097	
Rates	2,540	
Telephone	670	
Motor expenses	7,904	
General expenses	12,554	
Trade debtors	23,564	
Trade creditors		9,432
Bank balance	4,672	
Cash in hand	549	
Premises at cost	54,000	
Office equipment at cost	23,500	
Delivery vehicle at cost	18,500	
	377,940	377,940

Additional information at 31 January 20*8:

stock was valued at £10,564; rates paid in advance £320.

Required Prepare:

a) a trading and profit and loss account for the year ended 31 January 20*8
b) a balance sheet at 31 January 20*8.

QUESTION 9

Seok Chin provides the following trial balance extracted from her books of account on 30 April 20*8:

	Dr £	Cr £
Long-term loan		120,000
Capital		72,318
Drawings	26,500	
Premises at cost	80,000	
Equipment at cost	23,000	
Vehicles at cost	84,000	
Purchases	238,056	
Sales		407,843
Returns inwards	1,453	
Returns outwards		573
Carriage outwards	1,323	
Rates	1,660	
Wages	73,009	
Motor expenses	32,540	
Telephone	3,760	
General expenses	8,116	
Stock 1 May 20*7	23,510	
Trade debtors	34,534	
Trade creditors		23,665
Bank overdraft		7,439
Cash in hand	377	
	631,838	631,838

Additional information at 30 April 20*8:

stock was valued at £26,449; wages owing amounted to £2,007; rates have been prepaid £342.

Required Prepare:

a) a trading and profit and loss account for the year ended 30 April 20*8
b) a balance sheet at 30 April 20*8.

QUESTION 10

Sol Jensen provides the following trial balance extracted from his books of account on 31 December 20*8:

	Dr £	Cr £
Sales		211,901
Purchases	116,754	
Returns inwards	453	
Returns outwards		509
Stock 1 January 20*8	20,064	
Carriage inwards	2,431	
Carriage outwards	1,342	
Wages	78,549	
Drawings	24,650	
Rent and rates	4,352	
Advertising	2,649	
Loan interest	1,250	
Insurance	4,380	
Office expenses	5,672	
General expenses	12,879	
Premises at cost	72,500	
Office equipment at cost	24,000	
Debtors	18,901	
Creditors		8,005
Bank balance	345	
Cash in hand	476	
Capital		126,232
Long-term bank loan		45,000
	391,647	391,647

Additional information at 31 December 20*8:

stock was valued at £18,593; loan interest owing £250; office expenses owing £329; rates paid in advance £183; insurance paid in advance £465.

Required Prepare:

a) a trading and profit and loss account for the year ended 31 December 20*8
b) a balance sheet at 31 December 20*8.

QUESTION 11

Julie Wreak provides the following trial balance extracted from her books of account on 31 May 20*8:

	Dr £	Cr £
Capital		95,894
Long-term loan		250,000
Premises at cost	240,000	
Lorry at cost	45,000	
Office equipment at cost	17,000	
Drawings	34,700	
Purchases	239,075	
Sales		407,563
Returns inwards	1,554	
Returns outwards		658
Carriage inwards	347	
Carriage outwards	1,453	
Wages	84,342	
Motor expenses	34,527	
Stationery	3,642	
Rent receivable		2,300
Rates	2,480	
Insurance	4,673	
Loan interest	2,400	
Bank overdraft		2,457
Cash in hand	754	
Stock 1 June 20*7	36,734	
Trade debtors	28,976	
Trade creditors		18,785
	777,657	777,657

Additional information at 31 May 20*8:

stock was valued at £34,897; wages amounting to £6,238 had not been paid; £600 loan interest remains unpaid; the tenant owes £700 rent receivable; £562 insurance has been paid for the year ending 31 May 20*9; rates paid in advance amounts to £135.

Required Prepare:

a) a trading and profit and loss account for the year ended 31 May 20*8
b) a balance sheet at 31 May 20*8.

QUESTION 12

Tonya Gook provides the following trial balance extracted from her books of account on 30 November 20*8:

	Dr £	Cr £
Capital		53,660
Drawings	32,784	
Equipment at cost	28,000	
Vehicle at cost	22,000	
Purchases	79,842	
Sales		196,432
Returns inwards	571	
Returns outwards		615
Carriage inwards	460	
Carriage outwards	1,386	
Stock 1 December 20*7	7,968	
General expenses	3,968	
Wages	79,870	
Rent payable	5,600	
Insurances	1,610	
Advertising	3,330	
Motor expenses	22,361	
Electricity charges	2,467	
Rates	2,590	
Long-term loan		45,000
Loan interest payable	3,500	
Rent receivable		2,815
Commission receivable		4,800
Trade creditors		11,370
Trade debtors	14,628	
Bank	1,725	
Cash in hand	32	
	314,692	314,692

Additional information at 30 November 20*8:

stock was valued at £6,236; accrued wages £368; advertising owing amounted to £267; commission receivable paid in advance was £150; insurance has been prepaid £142; rates have been prepaid £240; rent receivable owing amounted to £85.

Required Prepare:

a) a trading and profit and loss account for the year ended 30 November 20*8
b) a balance sheet at 30 November 20*8

CHAPTER
FIFTEEN

Closing down the double-entry system

We have already seen how the double-entry system works. The system relies on the basic principle: 'Every debit must have a corresponding credit.'

Can you remember the three checks that we use throughout the year to verify the accuracy of parts of the double-entry system?

- Count the cash in hand and compare it to the balance shown in the cash column of the cash book.
- Prepare a bank reconciliation statement to check the accuracy of the entries made in the bank columns of the cash book.
- Prepare control accounts to check the accuracy of the transactions recorded in the purchases and sales ledgers.

The fourth and final check that we undertake before preparing the final accounts is to prepare a trial balance.

We have seen that we consistently check the whole double-entry system by extracting a trial balance.

This means that when we prepare the 'final accounts' we know that they will balance (providing we do not make fundamental errors in their preparation).

Real accounts are general ledger accounts in which purchase and sale of fixed assets and cash and bank transactions are recorded. Real accounts include land and premises, machinery, vehicles, cash and bank.

Nominal accounts are general ledger accounts that record incomes and expenses such as purchases, sales, wages, rent, motor expenses, etc.

Specification coverage:
AQA Unit 1
OCR Unit 1

By the end of this chapter you should be able to:
- close the nominal accounts in the general ledger
- prepare detailed trading and profit and loss accounts
- make entries in the stock account
- value stock using the lower of cost or net realisable value.

WORKED EXAMPLE

The following transactions took place during the year ended 31 August 20*8. All transactions were paid by cheque.

26 September 20*7 purchase of vehicle £17,500; 30 September 20*7 payment for rent £700; 11 October 20*7 purchase of vehicle £16,900; 17 October 20*7 paid for advertising £120; 1 November 20*7 paid wages £13,200; 23 November 20*7 paid for advertising £2,600; 31 December 20*7 paid rent £700; 1 February 20*8 paid wages £13,700; 31 March 20*8 paid rent £700; 31 March 20*8 paid rates £1,300; 1 May 20*8 paid wages £12,900; 17 June 20*8 paid advertising £340; 30 June 20*8 paid rent £700; 1 August 20*8 paid wages £14,600.

Required Prepare the wages, rent, rates, advertising and vehicles accounts for the year ended 31 August 20*8.

WORKED EXAMPLE *continued*

Answer

Dr	Vehicles account	Cr
26 Sept Bank 17,500		
11 Oct Bank 16,900		

Dr	Rent account	Cr
30 Sept Bank 700		
31 Dec Bank 700		
31 Mar Bank 700		
30 June Bank 700		

Dr	Advertising account	Cr
17 Oct Bank 120		
23 Nov Bank 2,600		
17 June Bank 340		

Dr	Wages account	Cr
1 Nov Bank 13,200		
1 Feb Bank 13,700		
1 May Bank 12,900		
1 Aug Bank 14,600		

Dr	Rates account	Cr
31 Mar Bank 1,300		

The credit entries corresponding to all the debit entries shown would appear in the bank account.

The arithmetical accuracy of the double-entry system is checked by extracting a trial balance at the end of each financial year, before preparing a trading account, a profit and loss account and a balance sheet.

If the totals of each column in the trial balance are the same we can prepare our final accounts safe in the knowledge that they should balance; if our final accounts do not balance then the error must lie in our preparation.

Remember that there could be errors in the double-entry system that would not be revealed by extracting a trial balance (CROPOC!).

Up to now we have used the trial balance not only to check the arithmetical accuracy of our double-entry system; we have also used it as a list of information from which we can prepare our final accounts. We will continue to use our trial balance for both these purposes.

At the end of each financial year we need to close down any accounts that we have finished with for the year in question. Not all accounts will be closed down.

Some accounts contain information that is relevant to the business's activity in the future. In fact, we only close down the nominal accounts in the general ledger since the information they contain will be used to calculate the year's profits. The real accounts will remain to carry their information through into the following year.

A **private ledger** contains accounts of a sensitive nature that the owner of a business does not wish others to see.

How are the nominal accounts closed?

The nominal accounts are closed by transferring the balances on each account to two further accounts found in the general ledger. The two further accounts are:

■ the trading account
■ the profit and loss account.

Yes, they are accounts and they ought to be in the general ledger. In reality, though, they are rarely kept in the general ledger. The information contained in both accounts is of a sensitive nature and so they will be kept separate from the rest of the general ledger in a private ledger.

A private ledger is part of the general ledger that is kept apart for obvious reasons.

Can you think of other accounts that the owner of a business might wish to keep in a private ledger? You may have thought of the drawings account or the loan account, etc.

EXAMPLE

The accounts shown in the worked example above would be closed as follows.

The nominal accounts are transferred to the trading account or the profit and loss account. The transfers will close the accounts for the year in question and will leave them clear to start a fresh new year.

The accounts shown in the worked example will be used to illustrate this point:

Dr	Vehicles account		Cr
26 Sept	Bank	17,500	
11 Oct	Bank	16,900	

Dr		Rent account		Cr
30 Sept	Bank	700		
31 Dec	Bank	700		
31 Mar	Bank	700		
30 June	Bank	700	31 Aug P&La/c	2,800
		2,800		2,800

Dr	Advertising account		Cr
17 Oct	Bank	120	31 Aug P&La/c 3,060
23 Nov	Bank	2,600	3,060
17 Jun	Bank	340	
		3,060	

Dr		Wages account		Cr
1 Nov	Bank	13,200		
1 Feb	Bank	13,700		
1 May	Bank	12,900		
1 Aug	Bank	14,600	31 Aug P&La/c	54,400
		54,400		54,400

Dr	Rates account		Cr
31 Mar Bank	1,300	31 Aug P&La/c	1,300
	1,300		1,300

Dr		Bank account		Cr
		26 Sep	Veh	17,500
		30 Sep	Rent	700
		11 Oct	Veh	16,900
		17 Oct	Adv	120
		1 Nov	Wages	1,200
		23 Nov	Adv	2,600
		31 Dec	Rent	700
		1 Feb	Wages	13,700
		31 Mar	Rates	1,300
		31 Mar	Rent	700
		1 May	Wages	12,900
		30 Jun	Rent	700
		1 Aug	Wages	14,600

Profit and loss account for the year ending 31 August 20*8

Rent	2,800	
Advertising	3,060	
Wages	54,400	
Rates	1,300	

Notice that credit entries are made using double-entry principles; each credit in a nominal account is matched by a debit in the profit and loss account.

Note that the vehicle account and the bank account stay open since we will use these accounts next year.

Note

The purchases, sales, purchase returns and sales returns accounts will be closed using the same technique, but the balances on those accounts are transferred to the trading account.

Not only does the closing of the nominal accounts provide us with information to enable us to calculate the profits made by the business, it also enables us to have a fresh start in the general ledger nominal accounts next year. Imagine if we did not tidy out these accounts on an annual basis; some accounts would have hundreds of thousands of entries after twenty years or so!

The rule is that all accounts providing us with information that is relevant to one financial year

are closed down at the end of that year – the other accounts remain in the books as balances to start up the system again next year. All these balances are shown on the sheet for balances – the balance sheet on the final day of the financial year.

The profit and loss account is also balanced off and closed down. We can then prepare the next year's profit and loss account in a year's time.

WORKED EXAMPLE

The following trial balance has been extracted from the books of Patel, a trader, after his first year of trading:

Trial balance at 31 December 20*8

	£	£
Purchases	41,600	
Sales		103,110
Land and buildings at cost	60,000	
Furniture and fittings at cost	7,000	
Vehicles at cost	21,000	
Rent, rates and insurance	5,430	
Lighting and heating	7,980	
Motor expenses	9,260	
Repairs and renewals	1,780	
Wages	14,320	
Trade debtors	1,740	
Trade creditors		1,490
Drawings	2,170	
Capital		70,000
Cash	480	
Bank	1,840	
	174,600	174,600

Stock at 31 December 20*8 £1,010.

Required a) Name the accounts that will be closed down at the end of the financial year by posting the amounts to the trading and profit and loss account.
b) Prepare a trading and profit and loss account for the year ended 31 December 20*8.
c) Prepare a balance sheet at 31 December 20*8.

Answer

a) Purchases sales, rent, rates and insurance, lighting and heating, motor expenses, repairs and renewals and wages.

Patel
Trading and profit and loss account for the year ended 31 December 20*8

	£	£
Sales		103,110
Less cost of sales		
Purchases	41,600	
Less stock	1,010	40,590
Gross profit		62,520

The trading account is 'closed off' by inserting a gross profit of £62,520. The profit and loss account is 'opened' with the gross profit.

	£	£
Gross profit		62,520
Less expenses		
Rent, rates and insurance	5,430	
Lighting and heating	7,980	
Motor expenses	9,260	
Repairs and renewals	1,780	
Wages	14,320	38,770
Net profit		23,750

The profit and loss account is 'closed off' with a net profit of £23,750.

The rules of the double-entry game say that we must have another entry of £23,750 ...

So ...

The net profit is entered in the capital account in the general ledger:

c)

	Patel		
	Balance sheet at 31 December 20*8		
		£	£
Fixed assets			
Land and buildings at cost			60,000
Furniture and fittings at cost			7,000
Vehicles at cost			21,000
			88,000
Current assets			
Stock		1,010	
Trade debtors		1,740	
Bank		1,840	
Cash		480	
		5,070	
Current liabilities			
Trade creditors		1,490	3,580
			91,580
Capital			70,000
Add profit			23,750
			93,750
Less drawings			2,170
			91,580

Draft – an attempt to prepare a statement or document which might need to be amended before it can be said to be a perfect copy.

WORKED EXAMPLE

The following draft trial balance has been extracted from the books of account of McDougal on 30 June 20*8 after her first year of trading.

There are three missing figures. The accounts that will provide the missing figures are shown below the trial balance.

Trial balance at 30 June 20*8		
	£	£
Purchases	128,360	
Sales		317,830
Premises at cost	?	
Fixtures and fittings at cost	17,000	
Vehicles at cost	34,000	
Wages	119,000	
Rent and rates	14,670	
Motor expenses	21,630	
Repairs	?	
Lighting and heating	9,710	
General expenses	?	

Trade debtors	2,460	
Trade creditors		5,400
Drawings	26,300	
Capital		150,000
Bank	3,510	
Cash in hand	640	

Stock 30 June 20*8 was valued at £6,480.

Dr	Repairs account	Cr
3 Apl Bank 348		
19 May Cash 56		
12 June Bank 1,319		
27 June Bank 737		

Dr	General expenses account	Cr
7 Sept Cash 1,467		
24 Nov Bank 1,672		
3 Jan Bank 4,381		
17 Feb Cash 419		
9 May Bank 2,318		
7 June Bank 3,233		

Dr	Premises	Cr
1 July Balance b/d 80,000		

Required a) Complete the trial balance and ensure that it balances.
b) Close the nominal accounts shown.
c) Prepare a trading and profit and loss account for the year ended 30 June 20*8.
d Prepare a balance sheet at 30 June 20*8.

Answer
a) The trial balance totals are £473,230.
b) Repairs closed by credit entry £2,460; general expenses closed by credit entry £13,490.

The premises account should not be closed down – the premises will be used by the business in subsequent years.

c)

McDougall
Trading and profit and loss account for the year ended 30 June 20*8

	£	£
Sales		317,830
Less cost of sales		
Purchases	128,360	
Less stock	6,480	121,880
Gross profit		195,950
Less expenses		
Wages	119,000	
Rent and rates	14,670	
Motor expenses	21,630	
Repairs	2,460	
Lighting and heating	9,710	
General expenses	13,490	180,960
Net profit		14,990

d)

Balance sheet at 30 June 20*8

	£	£
Fixed assets		
Premises at cost		80,000
Fixtures and fittings at cost		17,000
Vehicles at cost		34,000
		131,000
Current assets		
Stock	6,480	
Trade debtors	2,460	
Bank	3,510	
Cash	640	
	13,090	
Current liabilities		
Trade creditors	5,400	7,690
		138,690
Capital		150,000
Add profit		14,990
		164,990
Less drawings		26,300
		138,690

McDougall's capital account in the general ledger would look like this:

Dr			Capital account		Cr
30 June 20*8	Drawings	26,300	1 July 20*7	Bank	150,000
30 June 20*8	Balance b/d	138,690	30 June 20*8	Profit and loss account	14,990*
		164,990			164,990
			1 July 20*8	Balance b/d	138,690

The net profit of £14,990 entered on the profit and loss account needed another entry. The entry is in McDougall's capital account marked *.

It is useful and usual to show all the details contained in the capital account in the balance sheet as we have done above and in previous examples.

● EXAMINATION TIP

If a question asks you to show a capital account it should be in account form, not a list as it would appear in a balance sheet.

QUESTION 1

The following accounts appear in Theresa Gorton's general ledger. (The dates of the transactions have been omitted).

Dr	Advertising account	Cr
Cash	120	
Bank	340	
Bank	720	
Cash	160	

Dr	Rates account	Cr
Bank	1,400	
Bank	1,400	

Dr	Motor expenses account	Cr
Bank	2,160	
Bank	814	
Bank	932	

Dr	Rent receivable account	Cr
	Bank	600
	Bank	600
	Bank	600
	Bank	600

Dr	Purchases account	Cr
Purchases day book	9,000	
Purchases day book	2,000	
Purchases day book	3,000	

Dr	Machinery account	Cr
Bank	14,000	
Bank	12,000	

Dr	Discount received account	Cr
	Cash	121
	Cash	72
	Cash	36

Dr	Sales account	Cr
	Sales day book	4,000
	Sales day book	12,000
	Sales day book	7,000
	Sales day book	4,500

Required
a) Close down the relevant accounts in the general ledger.
b) Show how these entries would appear in the appropriate final accounts and balance sheet

QUESTION 2

The following accounts appear in Ben Halliday's general ledger (the dates of the transactions have been omitted).

Dr	Premises account	Cr
Bank	125,000	

Dr	Purchases account	Cr
Purchases day book	1,320	
Purchases day book	4,581	
Purchases day book	1,007	

Dr	Sales account	Cr
	Sales day book	3,729
	Sales day book	4,516
	Sales day book	7,819

Dr	Rent payable account	Cr
Bank	150	
Bank	150	
Bank	150	

Dr	Discount allowed account	Cr
Cash	124	
Cash	64	

Dr	Purchase returns account	Cr
	Purchases returns day book	43
	Purchases returns day book	51

Dr	Insurance account	Cr
Cash	254	
Bank	2,440	
Cash	120	

Dr	Vehicles account	Cr
Bank	25,690	
Bank	18,450	

Required
a) Close down the relevant accounts in Ben's general ledger.
b) Show how these entries would appear in the appropriate final accounts and balance sheet

STOCK

So far the businesses that we have looked at have, in the main, been in the first year of trading.

As part of our trading account and our closing balance sheet we have had to consider stock.

Stocks are the goods that remain unsold at the end of the financial year.

Stock is valued physically at the end of each financial year. Even if a trader keeps manual or computerised stock records, the figures produced are not used in the end of year accounts. Why not?

Despite what you might think, stock records kept manually or on a computerised system will be inaccurate! Why?

Because stock gets stolen and goods get damaged and deteriorate – these occurrences are not shown in manual or computer records.

The most accurate way to value stock is to count it manually and then value it – but more of that later.

After the trial balance is extracted a value is placed on closing stock. Hence closing stock appears as an afterthought to the trial balance.

The closing stock figure is used to calculate the cost of sales figure for the year. Closing stock is a current asset and must be shown on the balance sheet at the end of the financial year.

Closing stock at the **end** of a financial year is opening stock at the start of the **next** financial year.

Year 1	Year 2	Year 3	Year 4

Closing stock is opening stock
£1,000   £1000

Closing stock is opening stock
£2,000   £2,000

Closing stock is opening stock
£3,000   £3,000

Closing stock is opening stock
£4,000   £4,000

This is fairly straightforward but hardly double-entry bookkeeping!

How is stock recorded in the double-entry system?

We need to open a stock account. Which ledger do we use?

Is stock a customer? No!
Is stock a supplier? No!

So the stock account appears in the **general ledger**.

WORKED EXAMPLE

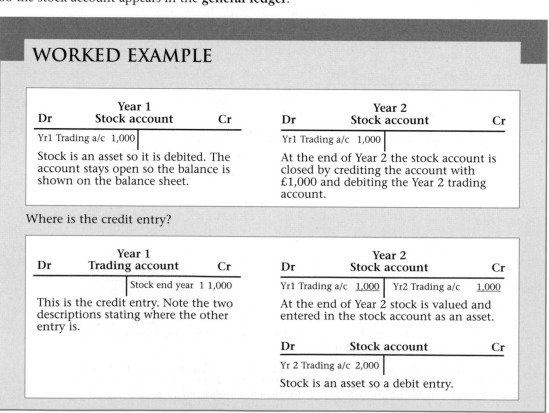

Where is the credit entry?

The account is still open at the end of the year so the balance is shown on the balance sheet as a current asset.

The stock account and the trading account now look like this:

Dr	Stock account		Cr
Yr1 Trading a/c	1,000	Yr 2 Trading a/c	1,000
Yr 2 Trading a/c	2,000		

Dr	Trading account		Cr
Opening stock	1,000	Closing stock	2,000

Year 3

Dr	Stock account		Cr
Yr1 Trading a/c	1,000	Yr2 Trading a/c	1,000
Yr2 Trading a/c	2,000		

At the end of Year 3 the stock account is closed by crediting £2,000 to the account and debiting the Year 3 trading account with £2,000.

Dr	Stock account		Cr
Yr1 Trading a/c	1,000	Yr2 Trading a/c	1,000
Yr2 Trading a/c	2,000	Yr3 Trading a/c	2,000

At the end of Year 3 stock is valued and entered in the stock account as an asset.

Dr	Stock account		Cr
Yr1 Trading a/c	1,000	Yr2 Trading a/c	1,000
Yr2 Trading a/c	2,000	Yr3 Trading a/c	2,000
Yr3 Trading a/c	3,000		

Stock is an asset so a debit entry is needed. The account is still open at the end of the year so the balance is shown on the balance sheet as a current asset.

The stock account and the trading account now look like this:

Dr	Stock account		Cr
Yr1 Trading a/c	1,000	Yr2 Trading a/c	1,000
Yr2 Trading a/c	2,000	Yr3 Trading a/c	2,000
Yr3 Trading a/c	3,000		

Dr	Trading a/c		Cr
Opening stock	2,000		
		Closing stock	3,000

Year 4

Dr	Stock account		Cr
Yr2 Trading a/c	1000	Yr1 Trading a/c	1,000
Yr2 Trading a/c	2,000	Yr3 Trading a/c	2,000
Yr3 Trading a/c	3,000		

At the end of Year 4 the stock account is closed by crediting £3,000 to the account and debiting the Year 4 trading account with £3,000.

Dr	Stock account		Cr
Yr1 Trading a/c	1,000	Yr2 Trading a/c	1,000
Yr2 Trading a/c	2,000	Yr3 Trading a/c	2,000
Yr3 Trading a/c	3,000	Yr4 Trading a/c	3,000

At the end of Year stock is valued and entered in the stock account as an asset.

Dr	Stock account		Cr
Yr1 Trading a/c	1,000	Yr2 Trading a/c	1,000
Yr2 Trading a/c	2,000	Yr 3 Trading a/c	2,000
Yr3 Trading a/c	3,000	Yr4 Trading a/c	3,000
Yr 4 Trading a/c	4,000		

Stock is an asset so a debit entry is needed. The account is still open at the end of the year so the balance is shown on the balance sheet as a current asset.

The stock account and the trading account now look like this:

Dr	Stock account		Cr
Yr1 Trading a/c	1,000	Yr2 Trading a/c	1,000
Yr2 Trading a/c	2,000	Yr3 Trading a/c	2,000
Yr3 Trading a/c	3,000	Yr4 Trading a/c	3,000
Yr4 Trading a/c	4,000		

Dr	Trading account		Cr
Opening stock	3,000		
		Closing stock	4,000

This illustration used a horizontal layout for the trading accounts in order to show the completed double-entry. It may look rather complicated, so try using a couple of sheets of paper and examine each year column one at a time by covering the other columns over with the spare paper. Then talk yourself through it slowly and carefully.

One final point: many years ago it was common practice to present trading accounts as shown in the four examples above. Opening stock was shown as a debit and closing stock was shown as a credit. This practice has now disappeared and the closing stock is deducted from the cost of sales in the trading account – it does give the same result arithmetically.

WORKED EXAMPLE

The following trading account has been prepared for Lhasa Trefta for the year ended 30 September 20*8:

	£		£
Opening stock 1 October 20*7	3,490	Sales	140,720
Purchases	73,400	Closing stock	
		30 September 20*8	3,760
Gross Profit	67,590		
	144,480		144,480

Required Prepare the trading account using a layout that shows cost of goods sold.

Answer

Lhasa Trefta
Trading account for the year ended 30 September 20*8

	£	£
Sales		140,720
Less cost of sales		
Stock 1 October 20*7	3,490	
Purchases	73,400	
	76,890	
Less stock 30 September 20*8	3,760	73,130
Gross profit		67,590

WORKED EXAMPLE

The following information is available at 30 April 20*3 for Tuan:

stock at 1 May 20*7 £1,760; stock at 30 April 20*8 £1,870; purchases for the year ended 30 April 20*8 £24,680; sales for year ended 30 April 20*8 £56,770.

Required a) Prepare a trading account for the year ended 30 April 20*8 showing clearly the cost of goods sold.
b) Prepare the stock account as it would appear in the general ledger at 30 April 20*8.

Answer

a)

Tuan
Trading account for the year ended 30 April 20*8

	£	£
Sales		56,770
Less cost of sales		
Stock 1 May 20*7	1,760	
Purchases	24,680	
	26,440	
Stock 30 April 20*8	1,870	24,570
Gross profit		32,200

b)

Dr			Stock account		Cr
30 April 20*7	Trading account	1,760	30 April 20*8 Trading account		1,760
30 April 20*8	Trading account	1,870			

Note the debit entry in the stock account – it is a current asset (all assets are debit entries) the other entry is deducted from cost of sales.

QUESTION 3

Tom Jackson provides the following information relating to his business for the year ended 29 February 20*8:

stock 1 March 20*7 £2,351; stock 29 February 20*8 £3,722; purchases £52,765; sales £87,503.

Required a) Prepare a trading account for the year ended 29 February 20*8 showing clearly the cost of goods sold.
b) Prepare the stock account as it would appear in the general ledger at 29 February 20*8.

QUESTION 4

Sanaa Malik provides the following information relating to her business for the year ended 31 August 20*8:

stock at 1 September 20*7 £13,579; stock at 31 August 20*8 £14,217; purchases £126,993; sales £203,741.

Required a) Prepare a trading account for the year ended 31 August 20*8 showing clearly the cost of goods sold.
b) Prepare the stock account as it would appear in the general ledger at 31 August 20*8.

QUESTION 5

Cary Thims provides the following information for her business for the year

ended 31 March 20*8:

stock at 1 April 20*7 £1,768; stock at 31 March 20*8 £1,439; purchases £23,771; sales £56,880; returns inward £239.

Required Prepare a trading account for the year ended 31 March 20*8 showing clearly the cost of goods sold.

QUESTION 6

Tom O'Leary provides the following information for his business for the year ended 30 November 20*8:

stock at 1 December 20*7 £8,663; stock at 30 November 20*8 £6,711; purchases £106,734; sales £214,775; returns outward £231.

Required Prepare a trading account for the year ended 30 November 20*8.

STOCK VALUATION

At the end of the financial year a trader will physically count the items that are in stock in his business. He will make a list of all the items. Each category of stock has then to be valued.

The over-riding principle used in the valuation of stock is that it is always valued at the lower of cost price or net realisable value. This is an application of the principle of **prudence** (see Chapter 19).

- If closing stock is overvalued gross profit is overvalued.
- If gross profit is overvalued then net profit is overvalued.
- If closing stock is undervalued then gross profit is undervalued.
- If gross profit is undervalued then net profit is undervalued.

We can check this with a simple example.

EXAMPLE

The following is the trading account of Fergie.

■ Closing stock should be valued at £15.
■ Sales amount to £50.

Stock overvalued		Accurate stock value		Stock undervalued	
	£		£		£
Opening stock	10	Opening stock	10	Opening stock	10
Purchases	25	Purchases	25	Purchases	25
	35		35		35
Less closing stock	20	*Less* closing stock	15	*Less* closing stock	8
Cost of sales	15	Cost of sales	20	Cost of sales	27
Gross profit	35	Gross profit	30	Gross profit	23
Sales	50	Sales	50	Sales	50

Highest closing stock valuation gives highest gross profit. Lowest closing stock valuation gives lowest gross profit.

The use of net realisable value causes problems for many students.

Realisable value is selling price.

Net realisable value is selling price less any expenses incurred by the business to get the stock into a saleable condition.

● EXAMINATION TIP

Make sure you understand net realisable value. In a recent examination it was reported that many candidates were unable to calculate correctly the net realisable value of goods!

WORKED EXAMPLE

The following information is available regarding the stock held by Tina at 29 February 20*8:

Product	Cost price per unit	Selling price per unit
	£	£
Arkers	12	31
Bodins	23	22
Clarts	8	14
Domps	42	40
Eldivs	17	15

Required State the value of each unit of stock held by Tina.

Answer
Arkers	£12
Bodins	£22
Clarts	£8
Domps	£40
Eldivs	£15

WORKED EXAMPLE

The following information is available regarding stock held by John at 31 August 20*8:

Components	Units in stock	Cost price	Selling price
		£	£
PX/117	21	16	20
QR/2138	13	41	50
T/1798C	8	18	15
S/5319	32	10	20

Required Calculate the total value of the stocks of components held at 31 August 20*8.

Answer

Total value of stock of components = £1,309

Workings
PX/117 at cost	*336*
QR/2183 at cost	*533*
T/1798C at realisable value (selling price)	*120*
S/5319 at cost	*320*

Realisable value is selling price – easy!

Net realisable value is realisable value net of (less) any expenses incurred in making the stock ready for sale – easy!

QUESTION 7

Thomas Timms sells furniture. He is uncertain how to value three items of stock.

Article	Cost	Selling price	Notes
Table	145	278	
Chair	54	75	The chair is damaged; before it can be sold it will have to be repaired at a cost of £25.
Bed	170	345	The mattress is dirty and will have to be cleaned at a cost of £2 before it can be sold.

Required Calculate the value to be placed on each of the three items of stock.

QUESTION 8

Kerry Picker sells electrical goods. She is uncertain how to value the following three items of damaged stock.

Article	Cost	Selling price	Notes
Toaster	12	18	The toaster is damaged; before it can be sold it will have to be repaired at a cost of £8.
Fryer	30	50	The fryer needs a new plug and flex costing £4 before it can be sold.
Microwave	140	225	Repairs costing £46 and a government test costing £24 need to be carried out before the appliance can be sold.

Required Calculate the value to be placed on each of the three items of stock.

In Chapter 14, you saw that the payments made to acquire goods and services for a business are not always perfectly matched to the receipt of the actual goods and services. Sometimes goods and services are received during the financial year but are not paid for at the end of the financial period. For example, at the financial year-end, workers may still be owed wages for work that was completed during the financial year; there may be a garage bill still remaining unpaid after the end of the accounting period.

Sometimes cash is paid before a service is provided. Can you think of an example where payment is made before a service is received?

Two examples could be business rates that are paid at the beginning of the local authority financial year and payments made for insurance cover before cover is actually needed.

Accrued expenses and prepaid expenses must be recorded in the books of account.

WORKED EXAMPLE

During the year ended 31 December 20*8 Harold has paid wages of £443,408 to his staff. The summarised entries in the wages account are shown.

Wages account		
Bank	127,938	
Bank	89,267	
Bank	131,442	
Bank	94,761	

At the financial year-end, Harold owes his workers £2,793 for work completed during December 20*8.

Required a) Complete the wages account for the year ended 31 December 20*8.
b) Show appropriate entries in the final accounts.

Workings

At the year-end Harold owed his workers £2,793.

This accrued expense is owed at the year-end – therefore it is a creditor. It has to be shown as a credit balance in the books of account at the start of the next financial year.

Wages account		
	———	
	Balance b/d	2,793
		———

The rules of double-entry mean we cannot make a credit entry without a corresponding debit entry.

Enter a debit entry 'above the line' to complete the double entry.

So . . .

Wages account		
Balance c/d	2,793	
	———	
	Balance b/d	2,793
		———

Total the account and transfer the adjusted amount to the profit and loss account.

The balance left on the account at the end of the year is shown in the balance sheet as a current liability – the amount that still has to be paid to Harold's workers.

Answer

Wages account		
Bank	127,938	
Bank	89,267	
Bank	131,442	
Bank	94,761	P & L a/c	446,201
Balance c/d	2,793	
	446,201	446,201
		Balance b/d	2,793

Extract from the profit and loss account for the year ended 31 December 20*8

£

Expenses
Wages   446,201

Balance sheet extract at 31 December 20*8

Current liabilities
Accrued wages   2,793

WORKED EXAMPLE

Josie has paid £1,798 for insurance at 31 December 20*8. The summarised entries are shown. £340 has been paid in advance for the following year.

Insurance account		
Bank	610	
Bank	720	
Bank	468	

Required a) Prepare the insurance account for the year ended 31 December 20*8.
         b) Show the appropriate entries in the final accounts.

Workings

At the financial year-end the insurance company owes Josie £340 so the insurance company is a debtor to Josie.

Insurance account		
	‾‾‾	‾‾‾
Balance b/d	340	

Remember every debit entry needs a corresponding credit entry.

Insurance account		
		Balance c/d	340
	‾‾‾	‾‾‾
Balance b/d	340	

Now complete the account.

Answer

Insurance account			
Bank	610	P & L a/c	1458
Bank	720		
Bank	468	Balance c/d	340
	1,798		1,798
Balance b/d	340		

QUESTION 9

Alec Rooney made three payments of £900 for rent during the year ended 30 November 20*8. At 30 November he owed his landlord £900.

Required Prepare a rent account for the year ended 30 November 20*8.

QUESTION 10

Thelma Goodyear made three payments to her insurance broker.

13 October 20*7	£458
16 December 20*7	£519
17 May 20*8	£1,314

At 30 September 20*8, her financial year-end, she had paid a £60 insurance premium that related to October and November 20*8.

Required a) Prepare an insurance account for the year ended 30 September 20*8.

b) Show the appropriate entries in the financial statements at 30 September 20*8.

Chapter summary

- At the end of each financial year the nominal accounts in the general ledger are closed by transferring the balances to either the trading account or the profit and loss account.
- Accruals and prepayments are brought down as balances and are shown as liabilities and assets to start the nominal accounts in the next time period.
- Credit balances brought down are shown as current liabilities on the balance sheet; debit balances are shown as credit assets.
- Accounts that are not closed are shown on the balance sheet.
- The trading account is closed by transferring the gross profit to the profit and loss account.
- The profit and loss account is closed by transferring the net profit or loss to the owner's capital account.
- Stock is valued at the lower of cost or net realisable value.
- Net realisable value is the selling price of the items in stock less any costs that might be incurred in making the items ready for sale.

SELF-TEST QUESTIONS

- Name three checks that are used throughout the year to verify the accuracy of parts of the double-entry system.
- A trial balance balances. Is this proof that it is error free?
- Name the type of accounts that are closed down at the end of the financial year.
- In which ledger would you expect to find the trading account of a business?
- In which ledger would you expect to find the profit and loss account of a business?
- Why do some traders keep a private ledger?
- What entries are required to close the following accounts?

Account	Debit	Credit
Rent payable		
Discount received		
Purchases		

- Insurance; returns outward; carriage inward; Orton, a debtor; wages. Identify the account that would not be closed at the end of a financial year.
- Appleby, a creditor; bank; advertising; capital; vehicles. Identify the account that would be closed at the end of a financial year.
- Explain what is meant by the word 'draft' in 'draft profit and loss account'.
- What is the overriding principle used in the valuation of stock?
- The application of this principle is an example of the ....concept. (Fill the space.)
- If closing stock is overvalued gross profit will be .... (Fill the space.)
- Explain how closing stock is dealt with in the 'final accounts'.

TEST QUESTIONS

QUESTION 11

Bob Banger sells second-hand cars. He has yet to value the vehicles listed below.

Make	Cost £	Selling price £	Notes
Ford	1,200	1,500	Needs a new engine costing £320 before it can be sold.
Citröen	450	600	Before it can be sold it needs two new wings costing £100. Spraying both wings will cost £60.
Skoda	560	600	Needs a new tyre costing £24 before it can be sold.

Required Calculate the value placed on each of the three cars in stock.

QUESTION 12

Shirley Burton has a clothes shop. Three items remaining in stock have yet to be valued.

Article	Cost £	Selling price £	Notes
Jeans	24	52	Faulty zip will cost £8 to repair before jeans can be sold.
Gent's suit	64	134	Trousers stolen. Replacement pair will cost £32 before suit can be sold.
Sweater	24	36	Hole in sleeve. Repairs will cost £14 before sweater can be sold.

Required Calculate the value placed on each of the three items of stock.

QUESTION 13

Tammy Mount supplies the following incomplete trial balance and four ledger accounts.

Draft trial balance at 31 March 20*8

	Dr	Cr
	£	£
Capital		17,160
Sales		102,786
Purchases	41,903	
Returns inwards	460	
Returns outwards	?	?
Wages	25,600	
Rates	?	?
Telephone	?	?
Fixtures and fittings at cost	12,500	
Vehicle at cost	17,300	
Trade debtors	3,791	
Trade creditors		4,286
Bank balance	1,248	
Drawings	?	?

Dr	Returns outwards account		Cr
	Purchases returns day book	80	
	Purchases returns day book	25	
	Purchases returns day book	105	

Dr	Rates account		Cr
Bank	625		
Bank	625		

Dr	Telephone account		Cr
Bank	212		
Bank	216		
Bank	248		
Bank	174		

Dr	Drawings account		Cr
Bank	4,075		
Bank	4,075		
Bank	4,075		
Bank	4,075		

Additional information

After completing the trial balance the following account was opened:

Dr	Stock account		Cr
31 March 20*7 Trading a/c	3,240		

At 31 March 20*8 stock was valued at £3,970.

Required a) Complete the trial balance at 31 March 20*8.
b) Close the detailed accounts as necessary.
c) Prepare a trading and profit and loss account for the year ended 31 March 20*8.
d) Prepare a balance sheet at 31 March 20*8.

QUESTION 14

Willie Gill provides the following draft trial balance and four detailed ledger accounts.

Draft trial balance at 30 September 20*8

	Dr	Cr
	£	£
Capital	?	?
Equipment at cost	20,000	
Van at cost	12,000	
Sales		97,612
Trade debtors	4,992	
Purchases	38,614	
Stock	?	?
Trade creditors		3,171
Returns inwards	?	?
Carriage inwards	930	
Drawings	17,500	
Rent and rates	4,612	
Heat and lighting	?	?
Wages	29,360	
Bank	1,280	
Cash in hand	70	

Dr	Capital account		Cr
	Balance b/d	35,957	

Dr	Returns inwards account		Cr
Sales returns day book	136		
Sales returns day book	276		

Dr	Heat and lighting account		Cr
Bank	1,230		
Bank	819		
Bank	716		
Bank	755		

Dr	Stock account		Cr
30 Sep 20*7 Trading a/c	3,450		

Additional information

Stock was valued at £3,760 at 30 September 20*8.

Required a) Complete the trial balance at 30 September 20*8.
b) Complete the stock account showing any transfers to the final accounts.
c) Close the detailed ledger accounts as necessary.
d) Prepare a trading and profit and loss account for the year ended 30 September 20*8.
e) Write up the capital account as it would appear in the general ledger on 30 September 20*8.
f) Prepare a balance sheet at 30 September 20*8.

QUESTION 15

Chetan Nath provides the following draft trial balance as at 31 August 20*8. He also provides four detailed ledger accounts.

Draft trial balance as at 31 August 20*8

	Dr	Cr
	£	£
Sales		172,460
Purchases	81,236	
Stock	?	?
Carriage inwards	1,810	
Carriage outwards	?	?
Drawings	23,100	
Equipment at cost	24,000	
Premises at cost	60,000	
Rent payable	?	?
Rates	1,580	
Wages	32,460	
Advertising	?	?
Trade debtors	8,491	
Trade creditors		3,984
Bank balance	8,701	
Capital	?	?

Dr	Carriage outwards account		Cr
Bank	934		
Cash	127		
Bank	406		
Cash	175		

Dr	Rent payable account		Cr
Bank	1,500		
Bank	1,500		
Bank	1,500		
Bank	1,500		

Dr	Advertising account		Cr
Cash	76		
Bank	211		
Cash	99		
Bank	2,489		

Dr	Stock account		Cr
31 Aug 20*7 Trading a/c	7,621		

Dr	Capital account		Cr
		Balance b/d	83,072

Additional information

Stock was valued at £8,470 at 31 August 20*8.

Required a) Complete the trial balance at 31 August 20*8.
b) Complete the stock account showing any transfers to the final accounts.
c) Close the detailed ledger accounts as necessary.
d) Prepare a trading and profit and loss account for the year ended 31 August 20*8.
e) Write up the capital account as it would appear in the general ledger on 31 August 20*8.
f) Prepare a balance sheet at 31 August 20*8.

QUESTION 16

Dave provides the following draft trial balance. He also provides six ledger accounts.

Draft trial balance at 30 April 20*8

	Dr	Cr
	£	£
Capital	?	?
Vehicles at cost	?	?
Machinery at cost	15,000	
Premises at cost	45,000	
Purchases	?	?
Sales		188,461
Stock	?	?
Returns inwards	499	
Carriage inwards	213	
Returns outwards	?	?
Carriage outwards	?	?
Rent and rates	3,926	
Insurance	4,109	
Trade debtors	12,430	
Trade creditors		7,621
Drawings	29,150	
Heat and light	4,288	
Wages	36,490	
Bank balance	1,284	
Cash in hand	126	

Dr	Purchases account	Cr	Dr	Returns outwards account	Cr
Purchases day book	17,496			Purchases returns day book	84
Purchases day book	23,810			Purchases returns day book	12
Purchases day book	12,567			Purchases returns day book	81
Purchases day book	19,093				

Dr	Carriage outwards	Cr	Dr	Vehicles at cost account	Cr
Bank	432		Balance b/d	2,000	
Bank	618		Bank	6,000	
Cash	75				
Bank	346				

Dr	Capital account	Cr	Dr	Stock account	Cr
	Balance b/d	47,979	30 Apr 20*7 Trading Account 9,286		

Additional information

Stock was valued at £10,140 on 30 April 20*8.

Required a) Complete the trial balance at 30 April 20*8.
b) Complete the stock account showing any transfers to the final accounts.
c) Close the detailed ledger accounts as necessary.
d) Prepare a trading and profit and loss account for the year ended 30 April 20*8.
e) Write up the capital account as it would appear in the general ledger on 30 April 20*8.
f) Prepare a balance sheet at 30 April 20*8.

CHAPTER SIXTEEN

Depreciation of fixed assets

A fixed asset is an item that has been purchased by a business in order to generate profits for the business.

Fixed assets will be used by the business for more than one financial year. They will yield benefits to the business over a prolonged period of time.

A business purchases resources to be used in the generation of profits. Some of the resources are used up in one time period. Other resources will be used over a number of time periods.

- Goods purchased for resale will be used in one time period.
- Petrol purchased for a delivery vehicle will be used in one time period.
- The work provided by staff is used in one time period

Each of the expenses described here can be classified as revenue expenditure. The benefits derived from revenue expenditure will be earned in the year and the expense is entered in the profit and loss account for the year in question.

Depreciation is the apportioning of the cost of an asset over its useful economic life.

- Premises will, generally, be used for more than one time period
- A delivery van will, generally, be used for more than one time period.
- Machinery will, generally, be used for more than one time period.

Expenditure on these items is classified as capital expenditure. Since the benefits derived from capital expenditure will continue to be earned over a number of years, it seems sensible to charge part of the cost of the fixed assets over those years.

Finite life: a limited life span.
Infinite life: an unlimited life span.

All fixed assets (except land) have a finite life.

The Companies Act 1985 says that all assets with a finite life should be depreciated, so the only asset that should not be depreciated is land because land has an infinite life.

- A machine will eventually cease to produce the goods for which it was purchased.
- A delivery vehicle will eventually cease to be useful for the delivery of goods.

The total cost of a fixed asset is never charged to the profit and loss account for the year in which it was purchased. The cost is spread over all the years that it is used in order to reflect in each profit and loss account the cost of using the asset in that particular year.

Fixed assets are recorded in **real accounts** in the general ledger.
Revenues and expenses are recorded in **nominal accounts**.

When a fixed asset is purchased and later sold the amount that is not recovered is called depreciation.

Specification coverage:
AQA Unit 1 and Unit 2
OCR Unit 1

By the end of this chapter you should be able to:
- define 'depreciation'
- calculate depreciation using the straight-line method
- calculate depreciation using the reducing balance method
- Calculate the profit or loss on the disposal of a fixed asset.

WORKED EXAMPLE

Donna purchased a fixed asset for £20,000. She sold it three years later for £2,000.

Calculate the cost of using the asset (the amount of depreciation) for the three years.

Answer

The cost of using the fixed asset (i.e. the depreciation) is £18,000 (£20,000 – £2,000).

This means that the actual depreciation can only be calculated when the fixed asset is no longer being used. The annual depreciation charge is therefore an estimate based on experience.

If we know the cost and can make an estimate of how long the fixed asset will be useful and how much it might be worth at the end of its life, we can calculate the amount of depreciation that will take place over the fixed asset's lifetime. We need to apportion this lifetime cost into each of the years that the fixed asset was used.

There are many methods of dividing the lifetime depreciation charge. We shall only consider the following:

■ straight line method (also known as equal instalment method)
■ reducing balance method.

Residual value is the amount that an asset can be sold for at the end of its useful life.

THE STRAIGHT LINE METHOD OF DEPRECIATING FIXED ASSETS

This requires that the same amount is charged annually to the profit and loss account over the lifetime of the fixed asset.

The formula is $\dfrac{\text{Cost of fixed asset} - \text{any residual value}}{\text{Estimate of number of years' use}}$

To calculate depreciation using the straight line method it is therefore necessary to consider:

■ the cost of the fixed asset
■ the estimated life of the fixed asset
■ the estimated residual value or scrap value.

If we know the life of an asset we can easily calculate the annual rate of depreciation.

If an asset has an expected life of 10 years the annual rate of depreciation would be 10% (100% divided by 10 years).

If an asset has an expected life of 50 years the annual rate of depreciation would be 2% (100% divided by 50 years).

If an asset has an expected life of 2 years the annual rate of depreciation would be 50% (100% divided by 2 years).

WORKED EXAMPLE

A computer is purchased for £2,300. Its useful life is expected to be two years, after which it will be replaced. It is expected that it will have a trade-in value of £100.

Required Calculate the annual depreciation charge using the straight line method.

Answer

Annual depreciation charge = £1,100

Workings

Formula: $\dfrac{\text{Cost of computer £2,300} - \text{residual value £100}}{\text{Estimated years of use 2}}$

WORKED EXAMPLE

A machine is purchased for £17,500. It has an expected life of 10 years, after which it will be scrapped. Its estimated scrap value is thought to be £250.

Required Calculate the annual depreciation charge using the straight line method.

Answer

£1,725

Workings

Formula: $\dfrac{Cost\ of\ machine\ -\ scrap\ value}{Estimated\ years\ of\ use}$ $\quad\dfrac{£17,500\ -\ £250}{10}$

We need to record depreciation in the ledger. In which ledger will we find the account for depreciation?

Is depreciation a credit customer? No.
Is depreciation a credit supplier? No.

The account is found in the general ledger.

A **provision** is an amount set aside out of profits for a known expense, the amount of which cannot be calculated with substantial accuracy.

I know that my car is depreciating (a known expense), but I cannot tell you exactly the amount of annual depreciation. I will only be able to give you an accurate figure in two or three years' time when I change my car.

Net book value is the cost of the asset shown in the general ledger (and therefore the balance sheet), less the total depreciation charged to date.

We have just seen how to calculate depreciation. How is the charge entered in the double-entry system?

Debit: profit and loss account   Credit: provision for depreciation account

---

WORKED EXAMPLE

Tanya purchases a delivery van for £18,000 on 1 January 20*5. She will use the van for four years, after which she estimates she will be able to sell the van for £6,000.

Tanya's financial year-end is 31 December.

Required a) Prepare the delivery van account.
b) Prepare the provision for depreciation account.
c) Prepare the profit and loss account extracts to record the necessary entries.
d) Prepare the balance sheet extracts for the four years.

Answer

Dr	Delivery van account		Cr
1 Jan 20*5 Bank	18,000		

Dr	Provision for depreciation on delivery van account			Cr
31 Dec 20*5 Balance c/d	3,000	31 Dec 20*5 Profit and loss account	3,000	
	3,000		3,000	
		1 Jan 20*6 Balance b/d	3,000	
31 Dec 20*6 Balance c/d	6,000	31 Dec 20*6 Profit and loss account	3,000	
	6,000		6,000	
		1 Jan 20*7 Balance b/d	6,000	
31 Dec 20*7 Balance c/d	9,000	31 Dec 20*7 Profit and loss account	3,000	
	9,000		9,000	
		1 Jan 20*8 Balance b/d	9,000	
31 Dec 20*8 Balance c/d	12,000	31 Dec 20*8 Profit and loss account	3,000	
	12,000		12,000	
		1 Jan 20*9 Balance b/d	12,000	

Profit and loss account extract for the year ended 31 December 20*5

	£	£
Gross profit		....
Less expenses		
Provision for depreciation of delivery van	3,000	

Profit and loss account extract for the year ended 31 December 20*6

	£	£
Gross profit		....
Less expenses		
Provision for depreciation of delivery van	3,000	

Profit and loss account extract for the year ended 31 December 20*7

	£	£
Gross profit		....
Less expenses		
Provision for depreciation of delivery van	3,000	

Profit and loss account extract for the year ended 31 Decmber 20*8

	£	£
Gross profit		....
Less expenses		
Provision for depreciation of delivery van	3,000	

Balance sheet extract at 31 December 20*5

	£
Fixed asset	
Delivery van at cost	18,000
Less depreciation to date	3,000
	15,000

Balance sheet extract at 31 December 20*6

	£
Fixed asset	
Delivery van at cost	18,000
Less depreciation to date	6,000
	12,000

Balance sheet extract at 31 December 20*7
£

Fixed asset
Delivery van at cost 18,000
Less depreciation to date 9,000
9,000

Balance sheet extract at 31 December 20*8
£

Fixed asset
Delivery van at cost 18,000
Less depreciation to date 12,000
6,000

Note

- the double entries – debit profit and loss account; credit provision account
- the equal instalments in each year's profit and loss account
- the delivery van is entered in the balance sheet at cost
- the accumulated (total) depreciation is taken from the fixed asset in the balance sheet
- the total shown at the end of each year in the balance sheet for the delivery van is the net book value (NBV).

THE REDUCING BALANCE METHOD OF DEPRECIATING FIXED ASSETS

A fixed percentage is applied to the cost of the fixed asset in the first year of ownership. The same percentage is applied in subsequent years to the net book value of the asset.

WORKED EXAMPLE

A vehicle was purchased for £18,000 on 1 January 20*6.

Depreciation is to be provided at the rate of 40% per annum, using the reducing balance method.

Required Calculate the annual charge for depreciation in years 20*6, 20*7 and 20*8.

Answer	Workings
Year 20*6 £7,200	£18,000 × 40%
Year 20*7 £4,320	(£18,000 − £7,200) × 40%
Year 20*8 £2,592	(£18,000 − £7,200 − £4,320) × 40%

How is this method entered into the double-entry system? In the same way that we entered the straight line method.

Debit: profit and loss account   Credit: provision for depreciation account

The provision for depreciation account will look very similar no matter which method is used; only the annual charge debited to the profit and loss account will change.

WORKED EXAMPLE

Dev Trater purchased a machine on 1 January 20*6 for £64 000.

Depreciation is to be charged at 20% per annum using the reducing balance method.

Dev's financial year end is 31 December.

Required a) Prepare the machinery account.
b) Prepare the provision for depreciation of machinery account.
c) Prepare the profit and loss account extract to record the necessary entries for three years.
d) Prepare the balance sheet extracts for three years.

Dr		Machinery account			Cr
1 January 20*6	Bank	64,000			

Dr		Provision for depreciation of machinery account			Cr
31 Dec 20*6	Balance c/d	12,800 12,800	31 Dec 20*6 Profit and loss account	12,800 12,800	
			1 Jan 20*7 Balance b/d	12,800	
31 Dec 20*7	Balance c/d	23,040 23,040	31 Dec 20*7 Profit and loss account	10,240 23,040	
			1 Jan 20*8 Balance b/d	23,040	
31 Dec 20*8	Balance c/d	31,232 31,232	31 Dec 20*8 Profit and loss account	8,192 31,232	
			1 Jan 20*9 Balance b/d	31,232	

Profit and loss account extract for the year ended 31 December 20*6

	£	£
Gross profit	....	
Less expenses		
Provision for depreciation of machinery	12,800	

Profit and loss account extract for the year ended 31 December 20*7

	£	£
Gross profit	....	
Provision for depreciation of machinery	10,240	

Profit and loss account extract for the year ended 31 December 20*8

	£	£
Gross profit	....	
Provision for depreciation of machinery	8,192	

Balance sheet extract at 31 December 20*6

	£	£
Fixed asset		
Machinery at cost	64,000	
Less depreciation to date	12,800	
	51,200	

Balance sheet extract at 31 December 20*7

	£
Fixed asset	
Machinery at cost	64,000
Less depreciation to date	23,040
	40,960

Balance sheet extract at 31 December 20*8

	£
Fixed asset	
Machinery at cost	64,000
Less depreciation to date	31,232
	32,768

QUESTION 1

John Frost started in business on 1 January 20*7. He purchased a delivery vehicle costing £28,000 on that day. He expects to keep the vehicle for four years and hopes to sell the vehicle then for £8,000. John will depreciate his vehicle using the straight line method.

Required a) Prepare the delivery vehicles account.
b) Prepare the provision for depreciation of vehicles account for the years ended 31 December 20*7 and 31 December 20*8.

QUESTION 2

Agnes Trotter started in business on 1 March 20*6. She purchased office machinery costing £12,000 on that day. She expects the machinery to last 10 years, by which time she expects it will have a scrap value of £100. Agnes will depreciate her office equipment using the straight line method.

Required a) Prepare the office equipment account.
b) Prepare the provision for depreciation of office equipment account for the years ended 28 February 20*7 and 29 February 20*8.

QUESTION 3

Shajal Patel started in business on 1 April 20*6. Her financial year end is 31 March. She made the following purchases of machinery:

- 1 April 20*6: one machine costing £13,000
- 1 April 20*7: two machines costing £8,000 each
- 1 October 20*7: one machine costing £10,000.

None of the machines is expected to have any value at the end of their useful life.

Shajal charges depreciation at 10% per annum using the straight line method, calculated on a monthly basis.

Required a) Prepare the machinery account.
b) Prepare the provision for depreciation of machinery account.
c) Prepare balance sheet extracts at 31 March 20*7 and 31 March 20*8.

QUESTION 4

Tony Prem started in business on 1 September 20*6. His financial year end is 31 August. He made the following purchases of machinery:

- 1 September 20*6: two machines costing £14,000 each
- 1 March 20*7: one machine costing £12,000
- 1 September 20*7: one machine costing £16,000.

None of the machines is expected to have any value at the end of its useful life.

Tony charges depreciation at 25% per annum using the straight line method, calculated on a monthly basis.

Required a) Prepare the machinery account.
b) Prepare the provision for depreciation of machinery account.
c) Prepare balance sheet extracts at 31 August 20*7 and 31 August 20*8.

THE SALE OR DISPOSAL OF FIXED ASSETS

You will notice that the word 'expected' has been used quite freely in the examples above. The owner of a business tries to guess how many years a fixed asset will be used. The owner will try to guess how much cash will be received when the asset is sold when it is no longer of any use.

When an asset is sold it is highly unlikely that the sum received will be the same as the net book value.

When assets are sold it is likely that a profit or loss based on the net book value will arise.

WORKED EXAMPLE

A machine which cost £32,000 five years ago has been sold for £14,000.

The total depreciation to date was £15,000.

Required Calculate the profit or loss arising from the disposal of the machine.

Answer

	£	
Machine at cost	32,000	The cost of the machine
Depreciation to date	15,000	less depreciation to date
Net book value	17,000	gives the net value recorded in the ledger.
Sale proceeds	14,000	The cash received from the sale
Loss on disposal	3,000	is less than the value shown in the ledger hence the loss on disposal.

WORKED EXAMPLE

A machine cost £18,000 ten years ago. It has now been sold for £1,500. The aggregate (total) depreciation to date was £17,000.

Required Calculate the profit or loss on disposal.

Answer

	£	
Machine at cost	18,000	The cost of the machine
Depreciation to date	17,000	less depreciation to date
Net book value	1,000	gives the net value recorded in the ledger.
Sale proceeds	1,500	The cash received from the sale
Profit on disposal	500	is more than the value shown in the ledger hence the profit on disposal.

● EXAMINATION TIP

If an examination question asks for a calculation you may use this method or you may choose to show a disposal account. However, if a question asks for a disposal account you must show your answer in account format.

If a disposal account is required the following procedure should be followed.

Open a disposal account.
Debit the disposal account with the cost of the asset.   Credit the asset account.
Debit the provision for depreciation account (with   Credit the disposal account
the total depreciation relating to the asset sold).
Debit cash with cash received for sale.   Credit the disposal account.
Debit disposal account with loss on disposal **OR**   Credit the disposal account with the profit.

WORKED EXAMPLE

Marjorie Dawes provides the following information from her general ledger

Dr	Machinery account	Cr		Dr	Provision for depreciation of machinery account	Cr
31 Mar 20*8 Balance b/d 66,000				31 Mar 20*8 Balance b/d 43,000		

Earlier this year Marjorie sold a machine for £3,000 cash. She has entered the cash received in the cash book but has made no other entries in the ledger.

The machine had cost £18,000 some years ago. The aggregate depreciation relating to the machine amounted to £16,500.

Required Prepare the machinery disposal account to record the sale of the machine.

Answer

Dr	Disposal of machinery account			Cr
Machinery	18,000	Provision for depreciation of machinery	16,500
Profit and loss account (profit)	1,500	Cash	3,000
	19,500		19,500

Other entries would be:

- credit machinery account £18,000 Debit provision for depreciation £16,500
- credit Profit and loss account £1,500 Debit Cash book £3,000

QUESTION 5

The following information is available at 30 September 20*7:

- Vehicles account £120,000.
- Provision for depreciation of vehicles account £73,000.
- In July 20*8 a machine that had cost £21,000 was sold for £800.
- The aggregate depreciation relating to the vehicle amounted to £19,000.
- Depreciation is charged at 25% per annum on cost.

Required a) Prepare a disposal of vehicles account to record the sale of the vehicle.
       b) Prepare a balance sheet extract showing the entry for vehicles at 30 September 20*8.

QUESTION 6

The following information is available at 30 June 20*7:

- Premises account £278,000.
- Provision for depreciation of premises account £88,960
- During February 20*8 part of the premises that had cost £56,000 was sold for £68,000. The aggregate depreciation relating to the premises that had been sold amounted to £6,720.
- Depreciation is charged at 1% per annum on cost.

Required a) Prepare a disposal of premises account to record the sale of premises.
       b) Prepare a balance sheet extract showing the entry for premises at 30 June 20*8.

Sometimes when an asset is replaced the 'old' asset is traded in and an allowance is made by the supplier of the 'new' asset.

I recently purchased a new car for £14,000. The garage took my 'old' car in part exchange. They

made an allowance on my 'old' car of £6,500. I paid £7,500 cash for the new car. The garage actually bought my old car from me for £6,500. This, together with my payment of £7,500 made up the total purchase price.

WORKED EXAMPLE

Doris Eden purchased a delivery van DQ57 WDA costing £19,000.

The new van replaced vehicle B19 JJH which cost £11,500. The aggregate depreciation to date amounted to £9,000.

The garage gave an allowance of £2,750 on B19 JJH. The balance due was paid by cheque.

Required Prepare the necessary ledger accounts to record the purchase of the new van.

Answer

	Provision for depreciation on van B19 JJH account					
Dr	Van B19 JJH account		**Cr**	**Dr**		**Cr**
Balance b/d	11,500	Disposal	11,500	Disposal	9,000	Balance b/d 9,000
Dr	Disposal B19 JJH account		**Cr**	**Dr**	Van DQ57WDA account	**Cr**
Van	11,500	Depreciation	9,000	Disposal	2,750	
Profit and loss		Van		Bank	16,250	
Account	250	DQ03 WDA	2,750			
	11,750		11,750			

Note:

The procedure is very similar to that used when a fixed asset is purchased for cash only. The only difference is that the new asset is debited with any allowance being made by the supplier and the disposal account is credited with the allowance.

THE CONNECTION BETWEEN CASH AND DEPRECIATION

There is no direct connection between providing depreciation on fixed assets in the profit and loss account and providing cash to replace the asset when it is no longer of use.

A collector does not visit the business every Friday night asking for cash to pay for the use of each asset being used!

Depreciation is a **non-cash expense**.

Cash flows out of a business when the asset is purchased; the annual depreciation charge is that cost being spread over the life-time of the asset.

A second-hand car was purchased for £2,750 in January 20*5 for cash. It is kept for four years.

- The cash outflow took place in January 20*5.
- No further cash outflows have taken place (apart from the usual running costs) but the car will depreciate each year.
- In the case of a business there is an indirect influence that depreciation has on cash-flows.

Depreciation is debited to the profit and loss account. This non-cash expense reduces profits for each year of ownership. The reduction in profit may cause the owner of the business to withdraw less money from the business for personal use, thus conserving more cash within the business.

EXAMPLE

Tom's business earns around £45,000 profit each year.

His drawings average £25,000 per year.

Tom purchases a new machine for the business costing £80,000. The machine is expected to be used for four years before it needs to be replaced.

When depreciation on the new machine (using the straight line method) is included in the final accounts, annual profits are reduced to £25,000.

Tom may well reduce his cash drawings in recognition of the business's reduced profitability.

Chapter summary

- Depreciation is provided on all fixed assets except land.
- Depreciation represents the use of the fixed asset during each year of ownership.
- The accruals concept is being applied when depreciation is charged to the profit and loss account.
- The two main methods of calculating the annual charge for depreciation are the straight line method and the reducing balance method. Whichever method is used by a business, the provision for depreciation account in the general ledger will look similar; the only difference will be the annual charge.

SELF-TEST QUESTIONS

- Define depreciation.
- What is a provision?
- Fill the following gaps: Fixed assets are shown on the .... side of real accounts in the general ledger. All assets with a .... life should be depreciated. Only the asset of .... has an infinite life.
- Name two methods of calculating annual depreciation.
- Which account is debited and which account is credited with the annual charge for depreciation?
- What is meant by the term 'aggregate depreciation'?
- What is meant by the term 'net book value'?
- What is the abbreviated form of net book value?
- An asset with a net book value of £4,000 is sold for £3,800. Calculate the profit or loss on disposal.

TEST QUESTIONS

QUESTION 7

A machine is purchased for £20,000. It has an expected life of 10 years and an expected scrap value of £1,000.

Required Calculate the annual depreciation charge using the straight line method.

QUESTION 8

A machine is purchased for £40,000. It has an expected life of eight years and an expected trade-in value of £6,000.

Required Calculate the annual depreciation charge using the straight line method.

QUESTION 9

A vehicle is purchased for £30,000. Depreciation is to be provided at 40% per annum using the reducing balance method.

Required Calculate the annual depreciation charge for the first three years of ownership.

QUESTION 10

A vehicle is purchased for £70,000. Depreciation is to be provided at 30% per annum using the reducing balance method.

Required Calculate the annual depreciation charge for the first three years of ownership.

QUESTION 11

Equipment is purchased on 1 January 20*6 at a cost of £60,000. It has an expected life of 10 years, after which it will have no scrap value.

Required Prepare the provision for depreciation of equipment account for the two years ended 31 December 20*6 and 31 December 20*7.

QUESTION 12

Equipment is purchased on 1 August 20*6 at a cost of £50,000. It has an expected life of four years, after which it will have a scrap value of £2,000.

Required Prepare the provision for depreciation of equipment account for the two years ended 31 July 20*7 and 31 July 20*8.

QUESTION 13

A lorry costing £140,000 was purchased on 1 March 20*5. It is depreciated at 60% per annum using the reducing balance method.

Required Prepare the provision for depreciation of lorry account for the three years ended 28 February 20*6, 28 February 20*7 and 29 February 20*8.

QUESTION 14

A lorry costing £112,000 was purchased on 1 April 20*5. It is depreciated at 35% per annum using the reducing balance method.

Required Prepare the provision for depreciation of lorry account for the three years ended 31 March 20*6, 31 March 20*7 and 31 March 20*8

QUESTION 15

A machine which cost £45,000 on 1 January 20*7 had an expected life of 10 years. It has been depreciated using the straight line method. It was sold for £31,000 on 31 December 20*8.

Required Calculate the profit or loss on disposal of the machine.

QUESTION 16

A machine which cost £20,000 on 1 January 20*7 had an expected life of four years. It has been depreciated using the straight line method. It was sold for £5,200 on 31 December 20*8.

Required Calculate the profit or loss on disposal of the machine.

QUESTION 17

When a machine was purchased on 1 October 20*6 for £19,000, it was thought that it would be used for six years and then sold for scrap worth £1,000.

The machine was sold for £13,250 on 30 September 20*8 after only two years' use.

Required Prepare a disposal account for the machine.

QUESTION 18

A vehicle was purchased on 1 June 20*4 for £50,000. It was thought that it would be used for six years and then sold for scrap worth £2,000.

The machine was sold for £16,500 on 31 May 20*8 after only four years' use.

Required Prepare a disposal account for the vehicle.

QUESTION 19

A vehicle was purchased for £26,000. It was depreciated at 40% per annum using the reducing balance method. It was sold after two years of use for £9,500.

Required Prepare a disposal account for the vehicle.

QUESTION 20

Equipment costing £30,000 has been depreciated at 50% per annum using the reducing balance method. It was sold after three years of use for £3,700.

Required Prepare a disposal account for the equipment.

CHAPTER
SEVENTEEN

Bad debts and provision for doubtful debts

In the business world of today a large proportion of all business is conducted on credit. A business that deals with credit customers always runs the risk that some of those customers may not honour their debt.

BAD DEBTS

A bad debt occurs when a debtor cannot pay the amount that is owed. If it is known that a debtor will not or cannot pay his debt we cannot leave the debit balance in his account. If we did:

- the total amount of debtors would be overstated
- the current assets would be overstated
- the total assets would be overstated
- capital would be overstated.

Once we are certain that a debtor is unable to pay, the debt must be written off. This is done by debiting a bad debts account in the general ledger and crediting the debtor in the sales ledger.

Specification coverage:
AQA Unit 2
OCR Unit 1

By the end of this chapter you should be able to:
- account for bad debts
- make provision for doubtful debts.

WORKED EXAMPLE

The following accounts appear in Noel Neil's sales ledger:

Dr	Mike	Cr	Dr	Cindy	Cr
Balance b/d	143		Balance b/d	619	

Dr	Rett	Cr	Dr	Sandy	Cr
Balance b/d	51		Balance b/d	430	

Dr	Deck	Cr	Dr	Tina	Cr
Balance b/d	628		Balance b/d	92	

It has been revealed that Mike and Tina are unable to pay their debts and Noel has decided to write them off at the year ended 31 December 20*8.

Required Show the necessary entries to record the transactions.

Answer

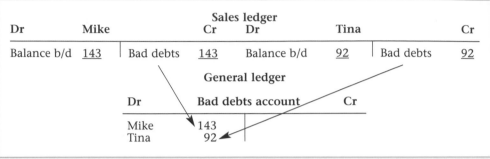

Any entries in the double-entry system must first be entered in a book of prime entry.

We should use the journal to record the transfer of each debtor to the bad debts account before recording the entries in the general ledger.

The journal entries would show:

	Dr	Cr
Bad debts account	143	
Mike		143
Writing off Mike's debt (irrecoverable) to the bad debts account		
Bad debts account	92	
Tina		92
Writing off Tina's debt (irrecoverable) to the bad debts account		

At the end of the financial year the bad debts account is totalled and closed by transferring the amount to the profit and loss account as a revenue expense.

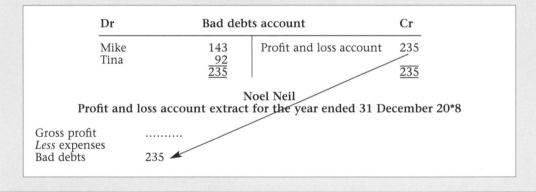

PROVISION FOR DOUBTFUL DEBTS

This is sometimes called a provision for bad debts. Debtors who will definitely not pay their debts are transferred to a bad debts account.

As well as actual bad debts there is always the risk that other debtors *may not* pay.

Those who might not pay are called **doubtful debtors**.

An estimate of amounts owed by those credit customers who might be unable to pay their debt is made.

A prudent business man or woman will not anticipate possible profits but will make provision for likely losses (see Chapter 19).

It therefore seems sensible to make provision for debtors where there is a strong possibility that they will not be able to settle their debt. Remember the definition of a provision: 'an amount set aside out of profits for a known expense, the amount of which is uncertain'.

When we provide for doubtful debts we know that some debtors may not pay but we are not sure who they will be. Therefore we do not know the exact amount of the provision.

How do we calculate the amount to be provided?

We can:

■ examine the sales ledger and try to identify the debtors who are most likely to default on payment
■ take a percentage of total debtors based on experience of bad debts written off in previous years
■ prepare an age profile of debtors and base the provision on the age of each outstanding amount.

WORKED EXAMPLE

Digby has estimated that each year around 2% of his debtors fail to pay. At 31 October 20*8 he has debtors amounting to £31,900. He wishes to make provision for doubtful debts at the rate of 2%.

Required a) Calculate the amount of provision for doubtful debts at 31 October 20*8.
b) Prepare a balance sheet extract at that date showing the details.

Answer

The provision for doubtful debts is £638 *(£31,900 × 2%)*.

Balance sheet extract at 31 October 20*8		
Current assets	£	£
Debtors	31,900	
Less provision for doubtful debts	638	31,262

WORKED EXAMPLE

Deirdre provided the following age profile of her debtors at 31 May 20*8:

The percentage of debtors proving to be bad has been gained from over 20 years' experience in her business.

Time outstanding	0–1 month	1–3 months	3–6 months	6 months- 1 year	over 1 year+
Amount owed	£120,000	£3,000	£400	£300	£1,100
Provision for doubtful debts	1%	3%	5%	20%	50%

Required a) Calculate the amount of provision for doubtful debts at 31 May 20*8.
b) Prepare a balance sheet extract at that date showing the details.

Answer

The provision for doubtful debts is £1,920.

	£
120,000 × 1% =	1,200
3,000 × 3% =	90
400 × 5% =	20
300 × 20% =	60
1,100 × 50% =	550
	1,920

Balance sheet extract at 31 May 20*8		
Current assets	£	£
Debtors	124,800	
Less provision for doubtful debts	1,920	122,880

Note

It is doubtful whether Digby will receive £31,900 from his debtors. From past experience he feels that £31,262 will be a more accurate figure. The creation of the provision allows him to be prudent.

It is also doubtful whether Deirdre will receive £124,800 from her debtors. She feels that £122,880 is a more accurate figure. She is prudent in creating a provision for doubtful debts.

In which ledger would the provision for doubtful debts be found? It is not a person, so the doubtful debts would be found in the general ledger.

Once a provision for doubtful debts account has been opened in the general ledger it stays open from one financial year to the next. Adjustments will be made each year to the balance by either debiting or crediting the profit and loss account with the adjustments.

WORKED EXAMPLE

Lew decides to create a provision for doubtful debts account at 2% of debtors outstanding at the financial year end on 30 June each year. Debtors outstanding at 30 June 20*7: £36,700

Required a) Prepare a provision for doubtful debts account at 30 June 20*7.
  b) Prepare a profit and loss account extract for the year ended 30 June 20*7 showing relevant details.
  c) Prepare a balance sheet extract at 30 June 20*7

Answer

Dr	Provision for doubtful debts account	Cr
	30 June 20*7 Profit and loss account	734

Lew		
Profit and loss account extract for the year ended 30 June 20*7		
	£	£
Gross profit		....
Less expenses		
Provision for doubtful debts	734	

Balance sheet extract at 30 June 20*7

Current assets	£	£
Debtors	36,700	
Less provision for doubtful debts	734	35,966

WORKED EXAMPLE

At the financial year end 30 June 20*8 Lew had outstanding debtors amounting to £41,300. He continues to maintain his provision for doubtful debts account at 2% per annum, based on the debtors outstanding at his year-end.

Required
a) Prepare a provision for doubtful debts account at 30 June 20*8.
b) Prepare a profit and loss extract for the year ended 30 June 20*8 showing relevant details.
c) Prepare a balance sheet extract at 30 June 20*8.

Answer

Dr	Provision for doubtful debts account		Cr
30 June 20*7 Balance c/d	734	30 June 20*7 Profit and loss account	734
		1 July 20*7 Balance b/d	734
30 June 20*8 Balance c/d	826	30 June 20*8 Profit and loss account	92
	826		826
		1 July 20*8 Balance b/d	826

Lew
Profit and loss account extract for the year ended 30 June 20*8

	£	
Gross profit		....
Less expenses		
Provision for doubtful debts	92	

Balance sheet extract at 30 June 20*8

Current assets	£	£
Debtors	41,300	
Less provision for doubtful debts	826	40,474

Note

The amount entered on the profit and loss account is only the increase in the provision account.

It is the amount needed to 'top up' the account to the required level.

QUESTION 1

Darryl has discovered that the three debtors shown below are unable to settle their debts. He has therefore decided to write them off as bad debts in the year ended 31 December 20*8.

Biff	451
Treados Ltd	159
Victor	52

Required Prepare the bad debts account for the year ended 31 December 20*8.

QUESTION 2

Umberto has discovered that the debtors listed below are unable to clear their debts. He has decided to write them off as bad debts in the year ended 30 September 20*8.

Ghuster plc	1,436
Jamie	39
Sally	392

Required Prepare the bad debts account for the year ended 30 September 20*8.

QUESTION 3

Umair wishes to maintain a provision for doubtful debts in his general ledger.

	Year 1	Year 2	Year 3
Provision for doubtful debts	400	420	500

Required Prepare the provision for doubtful debts account for each year.

QUESTION 4

Sheila wishes to maintain a provision for doubtful debts in her ledger at 31 December.

	20*6	20*7	20*8
Provision for doubtful debts	610	660	740

Required Prepare the provision for doubtful debts account for each year.

QUESTION 5

Robin has his financial year-end on 31 January. He provides the following information:

Debtors 31 January 20*6	12,700
Debtors 31 January 20*7	14,500
Debtors 31 January 20*8	16,000

- £700 is to be written off as a bad debt in the year ended 31 January 20*6.
- £200 is to be written off as a bad debt in the year ended 31 January 20*8.
- Robin wishes to make provision for doubtful debts of 2.5% of debtors outstanding at each year-end.

Required Prepare for each year:

a) a bad debts account
b) a provision for doubtful debts account
c) an extract from the profit and loss account
d) an extract from the balance sheet.

QUESTION 6

Mee has her financial year-end on 31 August. She provides the following information:

Debtors 31 August 20*6	42,000
Debtors 31 August 20*7	45,000
Debtors 31 August 20*8	46,000

In each year there have been a number of bad debts which have yet to be written off.

Year ended 31 August	**20*6**	**20*7**	**20*8**
Total bad debts to be written off	437	521	739

Mee wishes to make provision for doubtful debts of 5% of debtors outstanding at each year-end (work to nearest whole number).

Required Prepare for each year:

a) a bad debts account
b) a provision for doubtful debts account
c) an extract from the profit and loss account
d) an extract from the balance sheet.

So far, in each example and question in this chapter there has been an increase in the provision for doubtful debts. A decrease in the provision now needs to be considered.

WORKED EXAMPLE

Bernie maintains a provision for doubtful debts account. His provisions for the last three years are listed below:

Year ended 30 April	20*6	20*7	20*8
Provision for doubtful debts	250	340	270

Required Prepare for each of the three years:

a) a provision for doubtful debts account
b) a profit and loss account extract showing the adjustment to the provision account.

Answer

Dr	Provision for doubtful debts account		Cr
30 April 20*6 Balance c/d	250	30 April 20*6 Profit and loss account	250
		1 May 20*6 Balance b/d	*250
30 April 20*7 Balance c/d	340	30 April 20*7 Profit and loss account	90
	340		340
30 April 20*8 P&L account	70	1 May 20*7 Balance b/d	*340
30 April 20*8 Balance c/d	270		
	340		340
		1 May 20*8 Balance b/d	*270

Note:

* The balance brought down is always equal to the amount of provision needed.

Bernie
Profit and loss account extract for the year ended 30 April 20*6

	£	
Gross profit		....
Less expenses		
Provision for doubtful debts	250	

Bernie
Profit and loss account extract for the year ended 30 April 20*7

	£	
Gross profit		....
Less expenses		
Provision for doubtful debts	90	

Bernie
Profit and loss account extract for the year ended 30 April 20*8

	£	
Gross profit		....
Overprovision for doubtful debts	70 (added to gross profit)	

Mary Green makes a provision for doubtful debts based on 1% of debtors outstanding at her financial year-end.

The table below shows the entries in her final accounts for each of the first five years in business.

End of year	Debtors outstanding £	Provision £	Profit and loss account entry £	Balance sheet detail £	
1	10,000	100	100 expense	10,000 _100	9,900
2	12,000	120	20 expense	12,000 _120	11,880
3	16,000	160	40 expense	16,000 _160	15,840
4	14,000	140	20 'income'	14,000 _140	13,860
5	18,000	180	40 expense	18,000 _180	17,820

QUESTION 7

Try to fill the spaces for the next four years:

End of year	Debtors outstanding £	Provision £	Profit and loss account entry £	Balance sheet detail £
6	23,000			
7	27,000			
8	25,000			
9	26,000			

To summarise:

- The amount needed to increase the provision for doubtful debts is entered as an expense on the profit and loss account.
- The amount needed to decrease the provision for doubtful debts is entered as an 'income' on the profit and loss account.

RECOVERY OF BAD DEBTS

Sometimes a debtor, whose debt has been written off as a bad debt in an earlier year, may subsequently be able to settle his previously outstanding debt.

The simple treatment is as follows:

Debit cash book   Credit bad debt recovery account

Then at the financial year-end:

Debit bad debt recovery account   Show as an income in the profit and loss account.

If an examination question does not require ledger accounts, the result of the transactions above can be recorded in the final accounts as:

- an increase in profit, and
- an increase in cash.

EXAMPLE

Howard owed Bill £237 five years ago. Bill wrote Howard's debt off as bad.

Dr	Howard	Cr	Dr	Bad debts account	Cr
Balance b/d 237	Bad debts 237		Howard 237	Profit and loss account	237

Howard has set up in business again and is now able to pay the £237 that was previously written off.

Howard should be reinstated as a debtor as he is about to pay the debt. This fact should be recorded in Bill's books of account.

This is important to Howard since he may require credit facilities from Bill in the future and the fact that he has repaid his debt may be taken into consideration by Bill.

Dr	Howard	Cr	Dr	Bad debt recovered account	Cr
Bad debt recovered 237				Howard	237

Howard has now been reinstated.

Howard is then credited with the payment made to Bill.

Dr	Howard	Cr	Dr	Cash book	Cr
Bad debt recovered 237	Cash 237			Howard	237

The bad debt recovered account is closed with a debit entry. This amount is added to the gross profit in the profit and loss account, *or* is deducted from any bad debts written off in the current year.

Chapter summary

- Debtors who will definitely not pay their debts are written off to the profit and loss account.
- A provision for doubtful debts is created to take account of credit customers who may not pay their debts. Any increase in the provision is debited to the profit and loss account for the year and any decrease in the provision is credited to the profit and loss account.
- Bad debts recovered are credited to the profit and loss account and debited to the cash book.

SELF-TEST QUESTIONS

- Define debtors.
- Fill the gaps with the words 'debited' or 'credited': When a bad debt is written off, the debtor's account is .... and the bad debts account is ....

- When the provision for doubtful debts is increased, the provision account is .... and the profit and loss account is ....
- When a bad debt is recovered, the debtors account is ....; the bad debts recovered account is ....; when the money is received, the debtor is .... and the cash book is ....
- In which ledger would you find the bad debts account?
- Name the three ways that a trader may use to calculate the amount needed for the provision for doubtful debts.
- The creation of a provision for doubtful debts is a use of which concept?
- In which ledger would you find the provision for doubtful debts account?

TEST QUESTIONS

QUESTION 8

A business has made a gross profit of £126,734 and a net profit of £64,211.

Debtors amount to £32,967 before bad debts of £467 have been written off.

A provision for doubtful debts of 4% is required.

Required Select the correct answer:

The provision for doubtful debts is calculated as 4% of:

A £32,500   B £32,967   C £64,211   D £126,734

QUESTION 9

Pat provides the following information from his sales ledger:

Dr	Defius Ltd	Cr	Dr	Ralph	Cr
Balance b/d	154		Balance b/d	345	

Dr	Gordon	Cr	Dr	Iain	Cr
Balance b/d	87		Balance b/d	620	

All the debtors are bad and need to be written off.

Required Prepare the bad debts account for Pat.

QUESTION 10

Doug informs you that there is no possibility of recovering any cash from the following outstanding debts:

Trish	435
Glaster Ltd	455
Rotrest Ltd	113
Chiter and sons	712

Required Prepare the bad debts account to record writing off the debts.

QUESTION 11

At 31 March 20*8 Morgan has debtors amounting to £40,000. She wishes to make a provision for doubtful debts of 2.5%.

Required a) Calculate the provision for doubtful debts.
b) Prepare a balance sheet extract to show how the provision is treated.

QUESTION 12

At 30 June 20*8 Kingsley has debtors amounting to £68,000. He wishes to make a provision for doubtful debts of 5%.

Required a) Calculate the provision for doubtful debts.
b) Prepare a balance sheet extract to show how the provision is treated.

QUESTION 13

Willie uses an age profile of debtors to calculate his provision for doubtful debts.

He provides the following information for the year ended 31 May 20*8, on which to base the calculation.

Time outstanding	0–1 month	1–3 months	3–6 months	6 months– 1 year	over 1 year
Amount owed	£23,400	£12,900	£1,270	£730	£640
Provision for doubtful debts	1%	2%	3%	5%	20%

Required a) Calculate the provision for doubtful debts.
b) Prepare a balance sheet extract showing how the provision is treated.

QUESTION 14

Hayton uses an age profile of debtors to calculate his provision for doubtful debts.

He provides the following information for the year ended 31 October 20*8, on which to base the calculation.

Time outstanding	0–1 month	1–3 months	3–6 months	6 months– 1 year	over 1 year
Amount owed	£63,400	£32,900	£4,500	£5,700	£450
Provision for doubtful debts	1%	3%	5%	20%	50%

Required a) Calculate the provision for doubtful debts.
b) Prepare a balance sheet extract showing how the provision is treated.

QUESTION 15

Trudy McDuff maintains a provision for doubtful debts equal to 2.5% of outstanding debtors at the end of each financial year. The following information is available:

Total debtors at 1 May 20*7   34,000
Total debtors at 30 April 20*8   44,000

The following bad debts have been written off during the year:

30 June 20*7 P Snow   45
31 October 20*7 J Gatwood   239
31 January 20*8 F Golightly   213
31 March 20*8 D Mark   651

Required Prepare the necessary general ledger accounts to record the entries. Show clearly any amounts to be entered in the profit and loss account for the year ended 30 April 20*8.

Prepare a balance sheet extract at 30 April 20*8 showing debtors and the provision for doubtful debts.

QUESTION 16

Maureen Gill maintains a provision for doubtful debts equal to 5% of outstanding debtors at the end of each financial year. The following information is available:

Total debtors 1 January 20*8   64,000
Total debtors 31 December 20*8   83,500

Bad debts not yet written off at 31 December 20*8

Stephens   1,670
Greatrix   453
Shawcross   2,352
Treew Ltd   25

Required a) Prepare the necessary general ledger accounts to record the entries. Show clearly the amounts to be entered in the profit and loss account

   b) Prepare a balance sheet extract showing debtors and the provision for doubtful debts.

QUESTION 17

During the year a trader receives £288 from Geot Ltd. This amount had been written off as a bad debt some years previously.

Required Prepare the ledger accounts necessary to record the recovery of the bad debt.

QUESTION 18

Jessie receives £761 from Prodo Ltd. Jessie had written the amount off as a bad debt some years ago.

Required Prepare the ledger accounts necessary to record the recovery of the bad debt.

QUESTION 19

Glad Thomson provides the following information for the year ended 31 October 20*8. She maintains a provision for doubtful debts of 5%, based on outstanding debtors at the end of each financial year.

Total debtors 31 October 20*7	35,000
Total debtors 31 October 20*8	41,606

Bad debts not yet written off at 31 October 20*8

Thaker	216
Simms	97
Hurd	184
Fletcher	109

During the year £246 was received from Broadbent. This amount had been written off as a bad debt three years ago.

Required Prepare:

a) a bad debts account
b) provision for doubtful debts account
c) Broadbent's account
d) a bad debt recovered account
e) a profit and loss account extract for the year ended 31 October 20*8.

QUESTION 20

Ryder provides the following information for the year ended 30 April 20*8. He maintains a provision for doubtful debts based on 2.5% of debtors outstanding at his financial year-end.

Total debtors 1 May 20*7	25,200
Total debtors 30 April 20*8	24,952

Bad debts not yet written off at 30 April 20*8

Carson	129
Greer	184
Michael	203
Robinson	36

During the year £197 was received from Tickell. This amount had been written off as a bad debt some four years ago.

Required Prepare:

a) a bad debts account
b) a provision for doubtful debts account
c) Tickell's account;
d) a bad debt recovered account
e) a profit and loss account extract for the year ended 30 April 20*8.

CHAPTER EIGHTEEN

The final accounts revisited

Previous chapters have shown in detail how financial transactions are dealt with through the double-entry bookkeeping system. We have also seen the checks that are undertaken to ensure that errors do not lie undiscovered until the year-end, when they might prove extremely difficult to locate and then correct.

We have also seen how to deal with adjustments to the accounts such as accruals and prepayments and provisions. Until now we have considered and dealt with each type of adjustment in isolation. However, in the real world it is likely that in most businesses many adjustments would be necessary at the end of every financial year. For this reason we need to be able to incorporate these into one set of final accounts.

You have seen and worked through examples for each of the possible adjustments required. Now you will apply your knowledge in more complex situations. Remember, if you get into difficulty with these questions, the answers are detailed in the back of the book, but only look if you really are struggling!

Specification coverage:
AQA Units 1 and Unit 2
OCR Unit 1 and Unit 2

By the end of this chapter you should be able to:
- Prepare a set of final accounts, taking into account:
  - goods for own use
  - accrued expenses and incomes
  - pre-paid expenses and incomes
  - provision for depreciation
  - provision for doubtful debts
  - bad debts recovered.

QUESTION 1

The following trial balance has been extracted from the books of Hanif Mohammed:

Trial balance at 29 February 20*8

	Dr £	Cr £
Stock 1 March 20*7	8,963	
Purchases	56,817	
Sales		123,601
Wages	39,113	
Rent	2,000	
Light and heat expenses	8,617	
General expenses	2,834	
Motor expenses	4,619	
Capital		139,181
Drawings	13,500	
Premises at cost	100,000	
Equipment at cost	16,000	
Delivery van at cost	8,000	
Trade debtors	8,607	
Bank balance	1,281	
Cash in hand	45	
Trade creditors		7,614
	270,396	270,396

Additional information at 29 February 20*8

- Stock was valued at £7,432.
- Rent owing £200.

Required   a) Prepare a trading and profit and loss account for the year ended 29 February 20*8.
      b) Prepare a balance sheet at 29 February 20*8.

QUESTION 2

Siobhan Murgatroyd has extracted the following trial balance from her books of account:

Trial balance at 31 July 20*8

	Dr £	Cr £
Stock 1 August 20*7	840	
Purchases	34,872	
Sales		97,121
Wages	41,483	
Rent and rates	6,490	
Insurances	1,840	
Motor expenses	4,238	
Advertising	2,761	
General expenses	11,218	
Equipment at cost	14,260	
Delivery vehicle at cost	32,700	
Trade debtors	8,641	
Bank balance	2,884	
Cash in hand	236	
Capital		72,718
Drawings	16,340	
Trade creditors		8,964
	178,803	178,803

Additional information at 31 July 20*8

- Stock was valued at £1,166.
- Insurance paid in advance amounted to £315.

Required a) Prepare a trading and profit and loss account for the year ended 31 July 20*8.
b) Prepare a balance sheet at 31 July 20*8.

QUESTION 3

Hibo Ahmed has provided the following trial balance extracted from her books of account:

Trial balance at 31 May 20*8

	Dr £	Cr £
Stock 1 June 20*7	12,461	
Purchases	132,778	
Sales		206,981
Wages	46,337	
Rent payable	6,000	
Insurances	2,387	
Motor expenses	8,123	
Advertising	2,164	
General expenses	8,837	
Office equipment at cost	32,716	
Delivery vehicle at cost	23,500	
Trade debtors	5,871	
Cash in hand	236	
Capital		100,969
Drawings	38,500	
Trade creditors		7,162
Bank overdraft		4,798
	319,910	319,910

Additional information at 31 May 20*8

- Stock was valued at £13,106.
- Wages owing £814.
- Insurance paid in advance £628.

Required a) Prepare a trading and profit and loss account for the year ended 31 May 20*8.
b) Prepare a balance sheet at 31 May 20*8.

QUESTION 4

Helen Duff provides the following information:

Trial balance at 31 December 20*8

	Dr £	Cr £
Stock 1 January 20*7	8,119	
Purchases	98,437	
Sales		196,347
Wages	56,320	
Rent and rates	4,760	
Advertising and insurances	5,982	
Motor expenses	15,135	
Office equipment at cost	27,300	
Delivery vehicle at cost	40,000	
Provision for depreciation		
Office equipment		5,460
Delivery vehicle		10,000
Trade debtors	15,781	
Bank	3,202	
Cash in hand	126	
Capital		68,039
Drawings	19,400	
Trade creditors		14,716
	294,562	294,562

Additional information at 31 December 20*8

- Stock was valued at £9,003.
- Helen provides depreciation on office equipment at 10% per annum using the straight line method; she provides depreciation on her delivery vehicle at 25% per annum using the straight line method.

Required a) Prepare a trading and profit and loss account for the year ended 31 December 20*8.
b) Prepare a balance sheet at 31 December 20*8.

QUESTION 5

Lynn Parker provides the following information:

Trial balance at 31 October 20*8

	Dr £	Cr £
Stock 1 November 20*7	2,468	
Purchases	64,128	
Sales		192,587
Returns inwards	1,111	
Returns outwards		382
Wages	67,491	
Rent and rates	5,400	
Advertising and insurances	3,780	
Light and heat expenses	6,437	
Motor expenses	18,542	
Office equipment at cost	17,400	
Delivery vehicles at cost	46,000	
Provision for depreciation		
Office equipment		8,874
Delivery vehicles		29,440
Trade debtors	14,673	
Bank overdraft		4,372
Cash in hand	430	
Capital		27,706
Drawings	21,300	
Trade creditors		5,799
	269,160	269,160

Additional information at 31 October 20*8

- Stock was valued at £3,199.
- Lynn provides depreciation on all assets using the reducing balance method. The annual charges are: office equipment 20% (round up); delivery vehicles 40%.

Required a) Prepare a trading and profit and loss account for the year ended 31 October 20*8.
b) Prepare a balance sheet at 31 October 20*8.

QUESTION 6

David Lycett provides the following information:

Trial balance at 31 January 20*8

	Dr £	Cr £
Stock 1 February 20*7	4,967	
Purchases	87,328	
Sales		212,439
Returns inwards	726	
Returns outwards		460
Carriage inwards	642	
Carriage outwards	1,723	
Insurance	2,140	
Wages	72,048	
Motor expenses	8,461	
Light and heat expenses	3,487	
Telephone	1,348	
Office equipment at cost	16,500	
Vehicles at cost	30,000	
Provision for depreciation		
Office equipment		9,900
Vehicles		19,710
Trade debtors	18,461	
Bank	8,237	
Cash in hand	252	
Capital		25,992
Drawings	28,500	
Trade creditors		16,319
	284,820	284,820

Additional information at 31 January 20*8

■ Stock was valued at £5,141.
■ Wages owing £312.
■ Light and heat expenses paid in advance £248.
■ Depreciation on office equipment is calculated using the straight line method at 10% per annum.
■ Depreciation on vehicles is calculated using the reducing balance method at 30% per annum.

Required a) Prepare a trading and profit and loss account for the year ended 31 January 20*8.
           b) Prepare a balance sheet at 31 January 20*8.

QUESTION 7

Gladys Jones provides the following information:

Trial balance as at 31 August 20*8

	Dr £	Cr £
Stock 1 September 20*7	18,461	
Purchases	115,268	
Sales		296,431
Returns inwards	816	
Returns outwards		203
Carriage inwards	348	
Insurance	2,400	
Wages	105,892	
Motor expenses	8,420	
Light and heat expenses	2,436	
Telephone	1,348	
General expenses	7,421	
Provision for doubtful debts		280
Discount allowed	436	
Premises at cost	120,000	
Office equipment at cost	15,000	
Vehicles at cost	50,000	
Provision for depreciation		
Premises		52,800
Office equipment		6,000
Vehicles		39,200
Trade debtors	15,200	
Bank	6,132	
Cash	228	
Capital		104,958
Drawings	42,750	
Trade creditors		12,684
	512,556	512,556

Additional information at 31 August 20*8

- Stock was valued at £16,984.
- Insurance paid in advance £180.
- Telephone bill outstanding £351.
- Provision for doubtful debts to be maintained at 2% of debtors outstanding at the year-end.
- Depreciation is to be provided on fixed assets at the following rates:
  - premises 2% per annum straight line
  - office equipment 10% per annum straight line
  - vehicles 40% per annum reducing balance.

Required a) Prepare a trading and profit and loss account for the year ended 31 August 20*8.
b) Prepare a balance sheet at 31 August 20*8.

QUESTION 8

Tom Green provides the following information:

Trial balance at 30 April 20*8

	Dr £	Cr £
Stock 1 May 20*7	819	
Purchases	32,461	
Sales		84,261
Returns inwards	138	
Returns outwards		261
Carriage inwards	412	
Discount received		151
Rent payable	8,300	
Wages	16,272	
Motor expenses	3,420	
Insurance	1,746	
Bad debts	211	
Bad debts recovered		74
General expenses	11,412	
Provision for doubtful debts		361
Office equipment at cost	24,500	
Motor vehicles at cost	20,000	
Provision for depreciation		
Office equipment		14,700
Motor vehicles		6,000
Trade debtors	8,100	
Cash	347	
Capital		33,377
Drawings	17,000	
Trade creditors		3,472
Bank overdraft		2,481
	145,138	145,138

Additional information at 30 April 20*8

- Stock was valued at £612.
- Motor expenses accrued amounted to £182.
- Insurance prepaid £132.
- Provision for doubtful debts is maintained at 5% of year-end debtors.
- Depreciation is provided at 10% on office equipment using the straight line method and at 30% on motor vehicles using the reducing balance method.

Required a) Prepare a trading and profit and loss account for the year ended 30April 20*8.
b) Prepare a balance sheet at 30April 20*8.

QUESTION 9

Isadorah Boom provides the following information:

Trial balance at 31 August 20*8

	Dr £	Cr £
Stock 1 September 20*7	6,483	
Purchases	48,972	
Sales		97,481
Returns inwards	127	
Returns outwards		197
Carriage inwards	348	
Carriage outwards	812	
Bad debts	711	
Bad debts recovered		137
Wages	18,461	
Rent payable	6,500	
Light and heat expenses	3,481	
Telephone	1,856	
General expenses	15,860	
Provision for doubtful debts		276
Discount received		432
Machinery at cost	60,000	
Equipment at cost	36,000	
Trade debtors	6,400	
Trade creditors		2,968
Drawings	13,500	
Bank overdraft		2,487
Cash in hand	136	
Provision for depreciation		
Machinery		36,000
Equipment		31,500
Capital		48,169
	219,647	219,647

Additional information at 31 August 20*8

- Stock was valued at £6,543.
- Wages owing amounted to £380.
- Rent paid in advance £500.
- Provision for doubtful debts is to be maintained at 5% of debtors outstanding at the year-end.
- Depreciation is to be provided on fixed assets at the following rates:
  - machinery at 10% per annum using the straight line method
  - equipment at 50% per annum using the reducing balance method.

Required   a) Prepare a trading and profit and loss account for the year ended 31 August 20*8.
              b) Prepare a balance sheet at 31 August 20*8.

QUESTION 10

The following information is provided for Cindy Ash:

Trial balance as at 30 November 20*8

	Dr £	Cr £
Stock 1 December 20*7	11,461	
Purchases	72,384	
Sales		156,382
Returns inwards	817	
Returns outwards		388
Carriage inwards	278	
Carriage outwards	241	
Discounts allowed	159	
Motor expenses	4,817	
Wages	26,481	
Rent	4,500	
Bad debts	211	
Bad debts recovered		179
Provision for doubtful debts		450
General expenses	7,919	
Telephone	812	
Light and heat expenses	1,487	
Office equipment at cost	48,700	
Motor van at cost	16,000	
Provision for depreciation		
Office equipment		17,045
Motor van		3,200
Trade debtors	6,780	
Bank	4,831	
Cash in hand	199	
Capital		51,053
Drawings	28,100	
Trade creditors		7,480
	236,177	236,177

Additional information at 30 November 20*8

- Stock was valued at £10,177.
- Motor expenses owing amounted to £130.
- Light and heat expenses had been prepaid £102.
- Cindy had withdrawn goods from the business for her private use £1,200.
- Provision for doubtful debts is to be maintained at 10% of debtors outstanding at the year-end.
- Depreciation is to be provided for on fixed assets at the following rates:
  - office equipment at 5% per annum using the straight line method
  - motor van at 20% per annum using the reducing balance method.

Required a) Prepare a trading and profit and loss account for the year ended 30 November 20*8.
b) Prepare a balance sheet at 30 November 20*8.

QUESTION 11

Jack Simms provides the following information:

Trial balance at 30 September 20*8

	Dr £	Cr £
Stock 1 October 20*7	26,381	
Purchases	197,384	
Sales		313,461
Returns inwards	813	
Returns outwards		212
Carriage inwards	277	
Carriage outwards	1,732	
Rates	4,780	
General expenses	8,274	
Wages	59,334	
Motor expenses	13,981	
Bad debts	3,140	
Bad debts recovered		497
Provision for doubtful debts		622
Discounts allowed	814	
Discounts received		1,346
Commission receivable		4,712
Premises at cost	200,000	
Equipment at cost	100,000	
Vehicles at cost	84,000	
Provision for depreciation		
Premises		86,000
Equipment		50,000
Vehicles		53,760
Trade debtors	28,000	
Bank	4,986	
Cash in hand	512	
Capital		91,289
Drawings	32,488	
Trade creditors		16,497
Long term loan		150,000
Loan interest	1,500	
	768,396	768,396

Additional information at 30 September 20*8

- Stock was valued at £27,492.
- Wages owing amounted to £853.
- Rates paid in advance £1,270.
- Jack had withdrawn goods from the business for personal use amounting to £2,500.
- Commission receivable outstanding amounted to £180. This will be paid to Jack in December.
- Provision for doubtful debts is to be maintained at 2.5% of debtors outstanding at the year-end.
- Depreciation is to be provided for on fixed assets at the following rates:
  - premises 1% per annum using the straight line method
  - equipment 10% per annum using the straight line method
  - vehicles 40% using the reducing balance method.

Required   a) Prepare a trading and profit and loss account for the year ended 30 September 20*8.
          b) Prepare a balance sheet at 30 September 20*8.

QUESTION 12

Annie Lim provides the following information:

Trial balance at 30 June 20*8

	Dr £	Cr £
Stock 1 July 20*7	7,481	
Purchases	99,246	
Sales		214,683
Returns inwards	187	
Returns outwards		211
Carriage inwards	1,287	
Carriage outwards	462	
Rates	3,618	
Insurances	2,700	
Wages	81,342	
Discounts allowed	624	
Discounts received		1,438
Commission received		2,500
Rent received		4,250
Motor expenses	8,134	
Bad debts	1,400	
Bad debts recovered		120
Premises at cost	250,000	
Office equipment at cost	68,000	
Vehicles at cost	32,000	
Provision for depreciation		
Premises		150,000
Office equipment		27,200
Vehicles		11,520
Trade debtors	18,300	
Trade creditors		6,422
Bank overdraft		7,968
Cash in hand	714	
Capital		164,857
Drawings	16,500	
Provision for doubtful debts		826
	591,995	591,995

Additional information at 30 June 20*8

- Stock was valued at £9,284.
- Annie has taken goods from the business £1,750 for her personal use.
- Insurance prepaid £350.
- Motor expenses owing £299.
- Commission receivable owing to Annie £500.
- Rent receivable paid in advance £600.
- A provision for doubtful debts is to be maintained at 5% of debtors outstanding at the year-end.
- Depreciation is to be provided for on fixed assets at the following rates:
  - premises 2% per annum using the straight line method
  - office equipment 10% per anum using the straight line method
  - vehicles 20% per annum using the reducing balance method.

Required a) Prepare a trading and profit and loss account for the year ended 30 June 20*8.
          b) Prepare a balance sheet at 30 June 20*8.

NINETEEN

Accounting concepts

Over the years, accounting has evolved rules that all accountants use when preparing the final accounts of a business. These rules are referred to as **accounting concepts** or **accounting principles**. Some of these principles are enshrined in law and in accounting standards laid down by the major accounting bodies. For the moment, we will discuss the broad principles and look at the legal and professional aspects in Book 2.

The application of these rules by all accountants means that the users of the accounts can rely on the information they contain, safe in the knowledge that a set of accounts prepared for a butcher, baker or candlestick maker, or accounts in Penrith, Penzance or Perth, have been prepared using the same ground rules.

The concepts are a popular topic for questions in examinations as they underpin all of the work done by accountants.

GOING CONCERN CONCEPT

This concept means that unless we have knowledge to the contrary, we assume that the business will continue to trade in its present form for the foreseeable future. This means that we value all business assets at cost, not at what they would fetch if sold. If the business is going to continue, the assets will not be sold, so sale value is irrelevant.

> **Specification coverage:**
> AQA Unit 2
> OCR Unit 1
>
> **By the end of this chapter you should be able to:**
> ■ Understand the generally accept accounting concepts of:
> – going concern
> – accruals
> – consistency
> – prudence
> – materiality
> – realisation
> – business entity
> – objectivity.

WORKED EXAMPLE

Land and buildings cost £100,000   They could be sold for £220,000.
Machinery cost £42,000   They have a current scrap value of £3,000.
Vehicles cost £86,000   They could be sold for £55,000.
Warehouse cost £75,000   It has a current market value of £310,000.

Identify the value of each asset to be shown on the balance sheet.

Answer

Required The assets should be shown on the balance sheet as follows:

Land and buildings at cost   £100,000
Machinery at cost   £42,000
Vehicles at cost   £86,000
Warehouse at cost   £75,000

ACCRUALS CONCEPT

As accountants we are concerned with the value of resources used by the business and the benefits derived from the use of those resources by the business in any one financial year. The

value of the resources used in any time period may be different from the price paid to acquire the resources.

WORKED EXAMPLE

Juanita has a financial year-end on 31 December 20*8.

The following amounts have been paid during the year ended 31 December 20*8:

	£
Wages	48,000
Rent	5,500
Rates	1,800
Insurance	2,100
Motor expenses	14,300

Wages due to workers for work completed in the week 24–31 December 20*8 but unpaid amounts to £970.

Rent of £500 for December 20*8 was paid on 19 January 20*9.

Rates have been paid for the period ending 31 March 20*9. £450 relates to 1 January–31 March 20*9.

Insurance includes a premium £300 for the period 1 January – 28 February 20*9

Motor expenses do not include £236 paid on 27 January 20*9 for a vehicle service completed on 15 December 20*8.

Required Calculate the amounts to be included in the profit and loss account for the year ended 31 December 20*8 for Juanita in respect of wages, rent, rates, insurance and motor expenses.

Answer

Wages: £48,970

Juanita has used £48,970 skills and expertise of her workers during the year, even though she has only paid them £48,000.

Rent: £6,000

Juanita has had the use of premises worth £6,000 to her, even though she had only paid £5,500.

Rates: £1,350

Juanita has used local authority facilities valued at £1,350 for the year. She has also paid £450 for the use of facilities in the following year – we are not, at the moment, interested in the figures relating to next year.

Insurance: £1,800

*The payment of £2,100 includes £300 for insurance cover next year. This means that only £1,800 refers to the year ended 31 December 20*8.*

Motor expenses: £14,536

*The service was completed in the year ended 31 December 20*8, even though it was not paid for until the following year.*

Title is the legal term for ownership, e.g. title deeds to premises shows that the holder of the deeds is the owner of the premises.

PRUDENCE

This requires that revenues and profits are only included in the accounts when they are realised or their realisation is reasonably certain. We have already used the concept of prudence when we were valuing stock. If stock is overvalued at the year-end, gross profit will be overstated and net profit will also be overstated. This is why we value stock at the lower of cost or net realisable value.

However, the concept of prudence allows provision to be made for all known expenses or losses when they become known. For example, if damages were awarded against the business in a court case, the business could make a provision on the estimated amount that it might have to pay out in compensation.

REALISATION CONCEPT

This states that profits are normally recognised when the title to the goods passes to the customer, not necessarily when money changes hands. This concept is an extension of the accruals concept.

EXAMPLE

Fiona is an engineer. She is fairly certain that, in July, Jack will sign a contract to purchase lathes valued at £18,000. The £18,000 should not be included in Fiona's accounts until the title to the lathes has passed to Jack.

CONSISTENCY CONCEPT

This concept requires that once a method of treating information has been established, the method should continue to be used in subsequent years' accounts. The application of this concept was seen in Chapter 16, when methods of providing for depreciation of fixed assets were considered.

If information is treated differently each year then inter-year results cannot be compared and trends cannot be determined.

BUSINESS ENTITY CONCEPT

This states that only the expenses and revenues relating to the business are recorded in the business books of account. Transactions involving the private affairs of the owner are not part of the business and should not be included in the business books.

The owner's private electricity bills or private grocery bills should not be included as business expenditure.

If the business cheque book is used to pay the proprietor's private mortgage payments, the amount should be included in the drawings account.

If the proprietor introduces further capital into the business it is included in his capital account.

MATERIALITY CONCEPT

If the inclusion or exclusion of information in a financial statement would mislead the users of that statement, then the information is material.

This concept recognises that some types of expenditure are less important in a business context than others. So, absolute precision in the recording of these transactions is not absolutely essential.

To spend too much time in deciding how to treat a transaction of little consequence in the final accounts is detrimental to the wellbeing of the business – it would be a waste of time and resources.

We have already seen that capital expenditure is spending on fixed assets or their improvement. Revenue expenditure is spending on the normal running costs of a business. Fixed assets are used in a business for more than one time period. If we apply the accruals concept we should spread the cost of a fixed asset over the years it is used to generate the product and hence the profits.

EXAMPLE

A business purchases a ruler. The ruler costs 45p. It is estimated that the ruler should last for three years. Technically, the ruler is a fixed asset and should therefore be classified as capital expenditure, but to do this would be rather silly for such a trivial amount. The 45p would be treated as revenue expenditure and would be debited to either general expenses or office expenses. This treatment is not going to have a significant impact on profits or the valuation of net assets on the balance sheet – the absolute accuracy of its treatment is not material.

DUAL ASPECT

There are two aspects to accounting and they are always equal to each other. The assets of a business are always equal to the liabilities of the business. This means that every financial transaction has a double impact on the financial records of the business. Every debit has a corresponding credit. Every credit has a corresponding debit.

The dual aspect concept has already been encountered earlier in the double-entry system and also as the accounting equation.

OBJECTIVITY

As accountants we should view the business and its transactions in a dispassionate way. The accounts should not be prepared with any personal bias. To avoid this bias, figures should, where possible, be backed by source documents.

EXAMPLE

George owns a 1937 vintage delivery van that cost £8,000 a number of years ago. He could sell it for £23,000 today but he said recently, 'I love that van and I would not sell it if you offered me £100,000'.

The balance sheet value that George should use is £8,000 for two reasons: the £23,000 is based on a non-going concern basis and the £100,000 is a very subjective valuation on his part.

ACCOUNTING BASES

These are methods that have been developed in order to apply accounting concepts and principles to particular accounting transactions. With the publication of accounting standards, the number of alternative bases has been reduced. Examples of accounting bases include the necessity to provide for depreciation over the useful economic life of fixed assets; and the acceptable methods of valuing stocks and work in progress.

ACCOUNTING POLICIES

Accounting policies are the 'most appropriate to its [the business] circumstances for the purpose of giving a true and fair view'.

The policies should be 'consistent with accounting standards but should be appropriate to the particular industry in which the business operates'.

This means that the policies should be:

- relevant
- reliable
- comparable
- understandable.

The policies with regard to depreciation would involve the choice of method that is most appropriate to the particular business and the field that it operates in (i.e. straight line; reducing balance; depletion, etc.).

The choice of which method of stock valuation a business should use is also selection of an accounting policy.

Chapter summary

- Accounting concepts and principles are the basic rules of accounting.
- They should be applied to the recording of all transactions and the preparation of all accounting statements.

TEST QUESTIONS

QUESTION 1

Complete the following statements:

- Although the staff who work in a business are often regarded as one of its most valuable assets, they are not included in the business balance sheet. This is an example of the ……………………….. concept.
- The petrol in the tank of the delivery van, worth £8.50, has not been recorded in the business balance sheet. This is an example of using the concept of ……………… .
- The closing stock has been valued at net realisable value because this is lower than the cost of the stock. This is an example of the ………………concept.
- The owner is using 10% depreciation on all fixed assets in the business because fixed assets have always been depreciated using this percentage. This is an example of the concept of ……………… .

QUESTION 2

Outline one reason why accountants apply accounting concepts when preparing end-of-year financial statements.

QUESTION 3

The owner of a business is planning to include his premises as an asset in the end-of-year balance sheet at cost value of £200,000. However, the finance manager feels that this is too low a value and says that the premises should be included at £250,000, since this is what they could presently be sold for. How should the premises be valued?

QUESTION 4

The business has just purchased a specialised piece of computerised manufacturing machinery for £240,000. It will be used for three years. It would certainly have no resale value because of its specialised nature. How should the machinery be valued? Name the accounting concept that will apply.

- Cost: £240,000
- Resale value: £0
- Average value: £80,000.

QUESTION 5

Rent received for the year is £3,500. The tenant should have paid £4,000.

The amount to be included in the profit and loss account is .... This is an example of using the .... concept.

QUESTION 6

Select the accounting concept to be used in the following circumstances:

(a) Wages outstanding at the end of the financial year: £362.
- accruals
- consistency
- materiality
- going concern

(b) A fixed asset costs £10,000. It is expected to have a life of 10 years with no residual value. Depreciation is to be charged at £1,000 per annum.
- accruals
- business entity
- materiality
- prudence

(c) A customer is expected to place a substantial order worth £8,800 next month.
- realisation
- business entity
- consistency
- realisation

(d) A regular customer who owes £2,720 has just gone into liquidation.
- accruals
- business entity
- materiality
- prudence

(e) Audrey puts some of her home telephone bill on the business profit and loss account, as she regularly uses her home telephone to ring clients.
- accruals
- business entity
- materiality
- prudence

QUESTION 7

Accounting policies should be relevant, ..., comparable and understandable. (Fill the gap.)

QUESTION 8

Select the accounting concept to be used in the following circumstances:

(a) Jim feels that the old 'Olivetti' typewriter valued at cost £47 on the balance sheet could fetch £350 at auction.
- entity
- objectivity
- realisation
- prudence

(b) A new 'Sellotape' dispenser has been purchased. It will be used for at least five years. The purchase price of £8.99 has been included in stationery.
- accruals
- entity
- going concern
- materiality

(c) It has been estimated that the factory cat has saved the business hundreds of pounds by catching mice which previously had caused much damage. The owner of the business wishes to put the cat on the balance sheet at a value of £200, despite the fact that it was purchased for only £3.50.
- accruals
- objectivity
- materiality
- prudence

(d) Tom is to put the family holiday on the profit and loss account because he needs the relaxation to help him cope with the rigours of business.
- accruals
- entity
- going concern
- prudence

(e) Frank believes that about 2% of debts outstanding at the year-end are doubtful. He intends to create a provision for doubtful debts of 2%.
- accruals
- entity
- going concern
- prudence

CHAPTER
TWENTY

The final accounts of limited companies

The main disadvantages of being in business as a sole trader are:

- Liability is not limited to the amount of money invested by the owner. This means that if the business fails and creditors cannot be paid from the proceeds raised from the sale of business assets then the proprietor must provide further finance from his private assets. This could mean that the business failure could result in a sole trader losing both his business assets and some, if not all, of his personal assets.
- Generally, the amount of money that one person can afford to invest in a business is comparatively small.

Limited liability companies came into existence because of the need for businesses to raise capital while at the same time giving investors a degree of security. They appeared when businesses found the need to raise large amounts of capital. A person who invests capital in a limited company is a **shareholder**. Shareholders are the owners of a limited company. They own shares in the company. (Shareholders are sometimes known as members.)

Nominal value is the face value or par value of a share. For example, the nominal value of ordinary shares in Wm Morrison supermarkets plc is 10p, while the nominal value of ordinary shares in Whitbread plc is 50p.

Shares are the equal parts into which a company's capital is divided.

Liquidation is the term used when a limited company is unable to discharge its liabilities.

Limited liability means that the liability of shareholders for the debts of a limited company of which they are members is limited to the amount they have agreed to subscribe.

The capital of a limited company is divided into shares. Shares can have a nominal value of 5p each, 10p each, 50p each, £1 each – in fact any amount!

To become a shareholder a person must buy at least one share.

If a company goes into liquidation each shareholder could lose his or her shares but cannot be asked to contribute further finance to cover the company's debts.

If, however, shareholders have only partially paid for the shares, they can be required to pay the balance outstanding.

Limited companies are treated as separate legal entities. This means that in the eyes of the law, a limited company is a 'person' who can sue others (including its

Specification coverage:
AQA Unit 2

By the end of this chapter you should be able to:
- understand the concept of limited liability
- prepare a profit and loss appropriation account for a limited company
- prepare a balance sheet for a limited company
- distinguish between authorised and issued share capital
- recognise the difference between ordinary and preference shares
- make transfers to reserves
- make the necessary adjustments to record:
  - share premium
  - revaluation of fixed assets
  - the issue of shares
  - dividends.

shareholders), just like you or I can. It also means that we can sue a limited company if we so desire.

There are two kinds of limited company: private and public.

PRIVATE LIMITED COMPANIES

- There are far more private limited companies than public limited companies.
- Private limited companies cannot offer shares to the general public.
- They cannot be listed on the stock market.
- They are often run by a family or a group of friends. The name of a private limited company must end with 'Limited' or 'Ltd'.

PUBLIC LIMITED COMPANIES

- Public limited companies must produce more detailed final accounts than private limited companies.
- They can raise capital from the general public.
- They generally find it easier to raise finance than a private limited company, since members are likely to view them as less risky than private limited companies. This might also result in a lower rate of interest being charged by lenders of finance.
- Companies that issue their shares through the stock market are referred to as quoted or listed companies.
- The name of a public limited company must end in 'plc'.

> **Directors** are the people who are responsible for the day-to-day running of the business. They are appointed by the shareholders at general meetings of the company. They report on their stewardship of the business each year at the company's annual general meeting.

THE ADVANTAGES OF LIMITED LIABILITY STATUS
- Limited liability status for shareholders.
- Larger amounts of capital can be raised by directors for use within the company.

THE DISADVANTAGES OF LIMITED LIABILITY STATUS
- Annual accounts must be audited.
- Directors must complete an annual return and file their accounts with the Registrar of Companies.
- The filed accounts may be inspected by the public.
- Companies are subjected to more 'red tape' than sole traders.
- Copies of the company's annual audited accounts must be sent to each shareholder and debenture holder.

All of these disadvantages involve extra expenditure.

THE INCOME STATEMENT OF A LIMITED COMPANY

> **Dividends** are the rewards paid to shareholders out of the profits of a limited company.

The dividends are paid to individual shareholders in proportion to the size of their holding of shares. Dividends are usually paid annually, but there may be an interim dividend paid based on the half-year profits of the business.

As far as we are concerned, the accounts of both private limited companies and public limited companies are treated in the same manner.

With the introduction of international accounting standards there has been a number of changes to the terminology used in the financial statements (final accounts) prepared by the directors of limited companies. We will use the new terminology in this chapter.

The final accounts of all businesses are similar. In the case of a sole trader, the following final accounts would be prepared:

Profit would then be transferred to the capital section of the balance sheet.

Note:

Since directors are employees of a company overseeing the day-to-day running of the business, payments to them are a profit and loss account expense.

In the case of a limited company, the accounts would show:

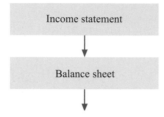

Who is entitled to the profits of a limited company?

Since a company is a legal entity (a 'person' in its own right), it is subject to taxation just like everyone else.

Companies do not pay income tax; they pay corporation tax. The amount of taxation to be levied on a company's profits will be given in an examination question. The tax charged will reduce profits. The adjusted sub-total is shown as profit after tax.

WORKED EXAMPLE

Nota Ltd has made a profit before tax of £287,300 for the year ended 31 March 20*8. Corporation tax due on the profit amounts to £71,400.

Required Calculate the profit after tax for the year ended 31 March 20*8 for Nota Ltd.

Answer

Nota Ltd
Income statement for the year ended 31 March 20*8

	£
Profit for the year before tax	287,300
Corporation tax	71,400
Profit for the year after tax	215,900

Very straightforward – but do identify each figure used.

The corporation tax is due – it will actually be paid to the tax authorities some months later but it needs to be shown as a current liability in the balance sheet.

Who else, apart from HM Revenue and Customs, is entitled to the profit?

When directors have prepared the financial statements (final accounts) of the company they can determine how much of the profits they can afford to pay to the

shareholders. Since the directors work for the shareholders, they can only recommend how much they think should be paid as dividends. This amount has to be agreed by the shareholders at the annual general meeting before it can be paid.

If the shareholders agree the dividend it will be paid by the company some months later. Until it is paid, it is shown on the balance sheet as a creditor.

> **Interim dividends** are dividends that are paid during the financial year. They are based on half-yearly profits.

> **Proposed dividends** – the amount of profit that the directors feel they can pay to their shareholders, based on the end-of-year results.

So, under the heading

Current liabilities

we will find amounts owed to HM Revenue and Customs and amounts owed for final dividends.

The owners are entitled to a share of the profits.

The shareholders are entitled to dividends based on the number of shares they each own. The total amount of dividend is deducted from the profit after tax. Any remaining profit is retained within the company to provide for expansion or the replacement of assets.

WORKED EXAMPLE

Mutar Ltd has made a profit before tax of £482,460 for the year ended 31 August 20*8. Corporation tax due on the profits is £96,000. The directors have paid an interim dividend on ordinary shares of £48,000 and they propose a final dividend on ordinary shares of £120,000.

Required a) Prepare an extract from the income statement for the year ended 31 August 20*8
b) Prepare an extract from the balance sheet at 31 August 20*8 showing any entries under the heading 'Current liabilities'.

Answer

a)

Mutar Ltd
Income statement for the year ended 31 August 20*8

		£
Profit for the year before tax		482,460
Corporation tax due		96,000
Profit for the year after tax		386,460
Interim ordinary dividend paid	48,000	
Ordinary dividend (proposed)	120,000	168,000
Retained profit for the year		218,460

b)

Balance sheet extract at 31 August 20*8

	£
Current liabilities	
Corporation tax due	96,000
Proposed ordinary dividend	120,000

QUESTION 1

The following information relating to GraZeb Ltd for the year ended 31 March 20*8 is given:

	£
Profit for the year before tax	347,320
Corporation tax due	117,450
Directors' fees paid	234,700
Interim ordinary dividend paid	34,500
Final proposed dividend on ordinary shares	112,600

Required Prepare an extract from the income statement for the year ended 31 March 20*8.

QUESTION 2

The information relating to Rutor Ltd for the year ended 31 December 20*8 is given:

	£
Profit for the year before tax	246,821
Interim ordinary dividend paid	42,000
Final proposed dividend on ordinary shares	87,000
Directors' fees paid	126,750
Corporation tax due	74,350

Required Prepare an extract from the income statement for the year ended 31 December 20*8.

THE BALANCE SHEET OF A LIMITED COMPANY

Before proceeding any further we need to consider the construction of the balance sheet of a limited company.

Note

Nowadays when dealing with the balance sheet of a limited company, the word 'inventories' tends to be used rather than 'stocks'.

The balance sheet of Tom Crabb, a sole trader, might look like this:

Tom Crabb
Balance Sheet at 31 December 20*8

	£	£
Fixed assets		
Premises at cost		70,000
Machinery at cost		20,000
Vehicles at cost		15,000
		105,000
Current assets		
Stock	12,000	
Trade debtors	8,000	
Bank	1,000	
	21,000	
Current liabilities		
Trade creditors	6,000	15,000
		120,000
Capital 1 January 20*8		108,000
Add profit		28,000
		136,000
Less drawings		16,000
		120,000

If we draw up the balance sheet of a limited company, Tom Crabb Ltd, it might look like this:

	£	£
Non current assets		
Premises		70,000
Machinery at cost		20,000
Vehicles at cost		15,000
		105,000
Current assets		
Inventories	12,000	
Trade receivables	8,000	
Bank	1,000	
	21,000	
Current liabilities		
Trade payables	6,000	15,000
		120,000
Shareholders' equity		
Ordinary shares of £1 each fully paid		120,000

So you can see that the two are almost identical, except for the difference in the capital section.

> **Incorporation** is the act of forming a registered limited company.

When a limited company is incorporated it raises capital so that it can purchase the fixed assets necessary to enable it to conduct its business. It raises capital through the issue of shares. In the balance sheet this total is called the **share capital**.

There are two main types of shares issued by a limited company: preference shares and ordinary shares.

PREFERENCE SHARES

Preference shareholders receive a fixed dividend which is expressed as a percentage of the nominal value of the share, for example, 7% preference share of £1 each; 8% preference shares of 50p each.

This dividend can only be paid if the company earns sufficient profits, but preference shareholders do receive their dividend before the ordinary shareholders receive theirs.

In the event of a company going into liquidation, the preference shareholders are entitled to receive the nominal value of their shares before the ordinary shareholders are repaid. (Hence their name – they receive preferential treatment in the winding up of a limited company.) Since preference shareholders are entitled to receive the nominal value of their shares before ordinary shareholders in the event of liquidation, preference shares are a less risky form of investment for a shareholder.

Preference shares may be:

- cumulative – if a dividend is not paid in one year, the dividend accumulates until such time as the arrears are able to be paid. These arrears must be paid before ordinary shareholders receive anything (most preference shares are of this type)
- non-cumulative – if a dividend is not paid in any one year, that year's dividend is lost
- redeemable – the company may buy these preference shares back at a stipulated time in the future.

ORDINARY SHARES

These are the most common type of share. The ordinary shareholders are the owners of a company and as such have voting rights. This means that they have control of the company. They appoint and dismiss directors. They also decide whether the dividend proposed by the directors is appropriate (they may reduce the dividend but they cannot increase it). All the profits remaining after preference dividends belong to the ordinary shareholders – although only the part of the profits not retained to expand or replace fixed assets will be paid to them as dividend. Ordinary dividends vary with levels of profits. So you can deduce from this that dividends could be zero with no upper limit.

Note

All dividend payments require:

- sufficient profits being available
- sufficient cash being available to actually pay the dividend.

A **memorandum of association** is a document filed with the Registrar of Companies before a limited company can become incorporated. It defines the external relationship of the company to the outside world.

The details filed include:

- the company's name, address and registered office
- share capital
- the company's objectives.

Articles of association. This document contains the rules that govern the internal organisation of a limited company. It must be filed with the Registrar of Companies together with the Memorandum of Association.

It shows the company's rules with regard to:

- organisation and control
- voting rights
- conduct of directors' meetings
- conduct of shareholders' annual general meeting
- directors' powers
- rights attached to the different classes to shares.

You will encounter a number of headings that relate to a company's share capital.

Authorised share capital (also known as registered share capital or nominal share capital) sets the maximum number of each type of share that a company can issue to its shareholders. It is stated in the company's memorandum and articles of association.

Issued share capital shows the actual number of each type of share that the company has issued to its shareholders. It cannot exceed the authorised share capital.

Paid up capital is the amount of share capital that has been paid by the shareholders.

A balance sheet drawn up immediately after incorporation but prior to any trading activities might look like this:

Reginald Satu Ltd
Balance Sheet at 30 November 20*8

		£
Non current assets:		
Premises at cost		400,000
Machinery at cost		120,000
Vehicles at cost		80,000
		600,000
Current assets:		
Inventories	30,000	
Bank	70,000	100,000
		700,000
Authorised share capital:		
750,000 ordinary shares of £1 each		750,000
1,000,000 6% preference shares of 50p each		500,000
Shareholders' equity:		
500,000 ordinary shares of £1 each		500,000
400,000 6% preference shares of 50p each		200,000
		700,000

QUESTION 3

The following information is given for Arbres Ltd at 30 April 20*8:

authorised share capital 500,000 ordinary shares of 50 pence each; issued share capital 300,000 ordinary shares 50 pence paid; machinery at cost £80,000; vehicle at cost £40,000; inventories £25,000; trade receivables £15,000; bank £1,000; trade payables £11,000.

Required Prepare a balance sheet at 30 April 20*8.

QUESTION 4

The following information is given for Helaminge Ltd at 30 September 20*8:

authorised and issued share capital 800,000 ordinary shares of 25 pence each; premises at cost £80,000; machinery at cost £60,000; vehicle at cost £30,000; inventories £20,000; trade receivables £12,000; bank £6,000; trade payables £8,000.

Required Prepare a balance sheet at 30 September 20*8.

The profit generated by the business of a sole trader belongs to the trader. It is credited to his capital account.

The profits that are removed from the business as drawings are deducted from the capital.

The remainder of the profit is 'ploughed back' and may be used to purchase assets.

The same is true of a limited company. Some profits will leave the business as dividends. The remainder is 'ploughed back' and may be used to purchase assets.

Consider this example:

EXAMPLE

Daphne Baird is a sole trader.	D Baird Ltd is a private limited company.
Her capital account has a balance of £50,000.	The authorised share capital consists of 50,000 £1 ordinary shares.

The business makes a net profit of £35,000.

Her drawings amount to £17,000.

The capital section of her balance sheet would look like this:

The business makes a profit of £35,000.

The directors recommend a dividend of £17,000.

The capital section of the balance sheet would look like this:

Extract from the Balance Sheet of Daphne Baird

	£
Capital	50,000
Add profit	35,000
	85,000
Less drawings	17,000
	68,000

Extract from the Balance Sheet of D Baird Ltd

	£
Shareholders' equity	
50,000 ord. shares of £1 each	50,000
Retained profit	18,000
(£35,000 less £17,000 paid out	
as dividends)	68,000

Not so different!

Retained earnings (profit and loss account) is the name given to a revenue reserve to which the profits of a limited company for each year is credited. It is also known as retained profits.

General reserve is a revenue reserve appropriated from trading profits to strengthen the financial position of a limited company.

Note

The retained profits in the balance sheet of the company cannot be credited to each individual shareholder. In a large public limited company there could be hundreds of thousands of shareholders. The retained profits are shown as one figure – it still belongs to the shareholders and they will receive it if the company is ever wound up.

Retained earnings are a reserve.

WORKED EXAMPLE

The following trial balance has been extracted from the books of Clangitt Co Ltd at 31 July 20*8.

	£	£	
Retained profit for the year		42,000	
Non-current assets at cost	180,000		
Current assets	20,000		
Trade payables		8,000	
Issued share capital			
(50,000 ordinary shares of £1 each)		50,000	
Retained earnings		100,000	profits retained from previous years
	200,000	200,000	

Required Prepare a summarised balance sheet at 31 July 20*8.

Answer

Clangitt Co Ltd
Balance sheet at 31 July 20*8

	£	£
Non-current assets at cost		180,000
Current assets	20,000	
Current liabilities	8,000	12,000
		192,000
Shareholders' equity		
Ordinary shares of £1 each		50,000
Retained earnings		142,000
		192,000

○ EXAMINATION TIP

A common mistake made by examination candidates is to say that reserves are money set aside: **they are not**.
There is one reserve shown in the above balance sheet – the profit and loss account.
Note that it is not a current asset because it is not cash.

Share capital and reserves show how much the company is worth. They show how the assets have been financed – do you remember the accounting equation?

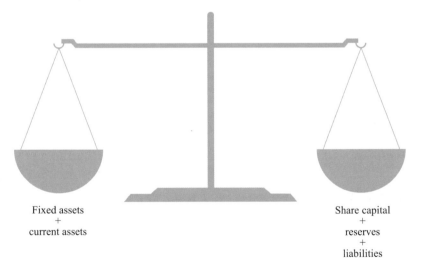

Fixed assets
+
current assets

Share capital
+
reserves
+
liabilities

Reserves are profits. Retained profits are a major source of finance for all successful companies.

WORKED EXAMPLE

The following draft balance sheet at 31 January 20*8 for Vorg Ltd is given.

	£	£
Non-current assets at cost		100,000
Current assets	50,000	
Current liabilities	30,000	20,000
		120,000
Shareholders' equity		
Ordinary shares of £1 each		80,000
Retained earnings		40,000
		120,000

This year's profits have not yet been incorporated into the balance sheet.

The retained profit for the year is £25,000. This has been retained in the business and has been used to purchase additional fixed assets.

£5,000 is to be transferred to a general reserve.

Required Prepare a balance sheet at 31 January 20*8, after making necessary adjustments.

Answer

Vorg Ltd
Balance sheet at 31 January 20*8

	£	£
Non-current assets at cost *(£100,000 + £25,000)*		125,000
Current assets	50,000	
Current liabilities	30,000	20,000
		145,000
Shareholders' equity		
Ordinary shares of £1 each fully paid		80,000
General reserve		5,000
Retained earnings *(£40,000 + £20,000)*		60,000
		145,000

Any transfer to general reserve is an appropriation of profits and is shown as a deduction in the income statement

WORKED EXAMPLE

The following information is given for Bowman Ltd for the year ended 31 October 20*8.

	£
Profit for year before tax	210,000
Corporation tax due	65,000
Interim ordinary dividend paid	36,000
Proposed final ordinary dividend	48,000
Transfer to general reserve	15,000

Required Prepare an extract from the income statement for the year ended 31 October 20*8.

Answer

> **Bowman Ltd**
> **Income statement for the year ended 31 October 20*8**
>
> | | £ | £ |
> |---|---:|---:|
> | Profit for year before tax | | 210,000 |
> | *Less* corporation tax | | 65,000 |
> | Profit for year after taxation | | 145,000 |
> | *Less* transfer to general reserve | 15,000 | |
> | dividends | | |
> | interim ordinary dividend paid | 36,000 | |
> | proposed ordinary dividend | 48,000 | 99,000 |
> | Retained profit for year | | 46,000 |

The balance sheet would show increases in both revenue reserves:

- general reserve would increase by £15,000
- retained earnings would increase by £46,000.

SHAREHOLDERS' EQUITY

This is made up of:

- share capital of the company, and
- all reserves.

All reserves belong to the ordinary shareholders of a company – reserves are part of the shareholder's equity.

Reserves fall into two main categories:

- revenue reserves – these reserves arise from the normal trading activities of the business; they are created at the discretion of the directors of a company. They are profits that have been withheld from dividend distribution in order to strengthen the financial position of the company. If the directors wish to use them they are available for distribution to the shareholders in the form of cash dividends. The two revenue reserves most commonly encountered are:
  - the general reserve
  - retained earnings.
- capital reserves are amounts set aside out of profits but are not provisions. They arise from capital transactions and adjustments to the capital structure of the company. They are not available for transfer to the income statement so they are not available for cash dividend purposes. Capital reserves include:
  - share premium accounts
  - revaluation reserve.

Share premium account is credited when a company issues shares at a price that is greater than the nominal value of the shares.

WORKED EXAMPLE

- 5,000 ordinary shares of £1 each are issued by Boom Ltd at £1.50 each.
- 2 million ordinary shares of 50p each are issued by Gatwood plc at 80p each.
- 90,000 ordinary shares of 10p are issued by Jibe Ltd at 40p each.
- 2,500 ordinary shares of £5 each are issued by Gerrat plc at £8 each.
- 1 million ordinary shares of 5p each are issued by Ken Platt plc at 35p each.

Required Calculate the amounts to be credited to:

a) the ordinary share capital account
b) the share premium account.

Also indicate the total amount of finance raised by the share issue.

Answer

	Ordinary Share Capital Account	Share Premium Account	Finance Raised
	£	£	£
Boom Ltd	5,000	2,500	7,500
Gatwood plc	1,000,000	600,000	1,600,000
Jibe Ltd	9,000	27,000	36,000
Gerrat plc	12,500	7,500	20,000
Ken Platt plc	50,000	300,000	350,000

A share premium account only arises when a company issues shares.

○ EXAMINATION TIP

Always be precise in written questions.
'A share premium account is opened when shares are sold at a price above their par value' is imprecise and would not gain marks.

If you sell some shares through a stock-broker at a higher price than you paid for them this will not give rise to a share premium. This is a private transaction and is not recorded in the company's books of account.

The company will record the change of ownership in its register of shareholdings, otherwise you would continue to receive copies of the annual report and any dividends that the company might pay out in the future.

How does the issue of shares affect the balance sheet of the company?

In some of the examples and questions that follow, the company bank balance is shown separately from other current assets, so that any effect that occurs because of cash transactions can be seen clearly.

WORKED EXAMPLE

The summarised balance sheet at 31 December 20*7 of Swelt plc is as follows:

	£	£
Non-current assets at cost		400,000
Current assets	74,000	
Bank	6,000	
	80,000	
Current liabilities	30,000	50,000
		450,000
Shareholders' equity		
Ordinary shares of £1 each		350,000
Retained earnings		100,000
		450,000

On 1 January 20*8 the company issued a further 200,000 ordinary shares of £1 each at a price of £1.30 each.

Required Prepare a summarised balance sheet at 31 January 20*8 as it would appear immediately after the share issue.

Answer

Swelt plc
Summarised balance sheet at 1 January 20*8

	£	£
Non-current assets at cost		400,000
Current assets	74,000	
Bank *(6,000 + 260,000)*	266,000	
	340,000	
Current liabilities	30,000	310,000
		710,000
Shareholders' equity		
Ordinary shares of £1 each *(350,000 +200,000)*		550,000
Share premium account		60,000
Retained earnings		100,000
		710,000

WORKED EXAMPLE

The summarised balance sheet at 1 October 20*8 for Capdo Ltd is as follows:

	£	£
Non-current assets at cost		17,000
Current assets	10,000	
Bank	2,000	
	12,000	
Current liabilities	10,000	2,000
		19,000
Shareholders' equity		
Ordinary shares of 10p each		10,000
Retained earnings		9,000
		19,000

On l November 20*8 Capdo Ltd issued a further 200,000 ordinary shares of 10p each at a premium of 40p each.

Required Prepare a summarised balance sheet at 1 November 20*8 for Capdo Ltd after the share issue.

Answer

Capdo Ltd
Summarised balance sheet at 1 November 20*8

	£	£
Non-current assets at cost		17,000
Current assets	10,000	
Bank *(£2,000 + £100,000)*	102,000	
	112,000	
Current liabilities	10,000	102,000
		119,000
Shareholders' equity		
Ordinary shares of 10p each *(£10,000 + £20,000)*		30,000
Share premium account *(£200 000 x 40p)*		80,000
Retained earnings		9,000
		119,000

QUESTION 5

The summarised balance sheet of Duvase Ltd at 30 November 20*8 is shown.

	£	£
Non-current assets at cost		120,000
Current assets	22,000	
Bank	15,000	
	37,000	
Current liabilities	8,000	29,000
		149,000
Shareholders' equity		
Ordinary shares of £1 each		100,000
Retained earnings		49,000
		149,000

On 1 December 20*8 Duvase Ltd issued a further 200,000 ordinary shares at £1.60 per share.

Required Prepare a summarised balance sheet at 1 December 20*8 as it would appear after the share issue has been completed.

QUESTION 6

The summarised balance sheet of D Lilly Ltd at 31 March 20*8 is shown.

	£	£
Non-current assets at cost		500,000
Current assets	125,000	
Bank	8,000	
	133,000	
Current liabilities	96,000	37,000
		537,000
Shareholders' equity		
Ordinary shares of 50 pence each		450,000
Retained earnings		87,000
		537,000

On 1 April 20*8 D Lilly Ltd issued a further 400,000 ordinary shares at 80 pence per share. Immediately after the share issue the company purchased additional fixed assets of £300,000, paying by cheque.

Required Prepare the balance sheet at 1 April 20*8 immediately after the share issue and the purchase of the additional fixed assets.

Up to now we have always shown assets at cost on balance sheets.

Which concepts are being applied when assets are being valued at cost? The answer is the going concern concept and objectivity.

REVALUATION RESERVES

Many limited companies revalue some of their fixed assets to reflect an increase in the value of those assets and to ensure that the balance sheet reflects the permanent change in the value of the assets and therefore the capital structure of the business (remember the accounting equation?). Generally, the only asset to be revalued upwards is land and buildings.

Why do companies revalue their assets while sole traders do not?

If the company's assets do not reflect a current market value the company could be subject to a hostile take-over bid by a predatory rival company.

The increase in the value of the non-current assets is matched with an increase in reserves. The revaluation reserve is a capital reserve and is not therefore available for dividend purposes. This reserve is a 'profit' due to inflation that will not be realised as cash until the asset is sold.

The creation of a revaluation reserve clearly illustrates the earlier point about reserves not being cash put aside for use in the future. All that has happened is that the top part of the balance sheet has been increased by the non-current asset being revalued and the bottom part has been increased by the same amount.

EXAMPLE

I purchased my house a number of years ago for £80,000. I am confident that I could now sell it for over £200,000. However, this increase in value cannot be used to buy a new car or to pay for a meal for my family because it is not cash – it is an unrealised profit.

Reserves are not piles of cash waiting to be spent! If only they were!

In the examples that follow, some businesses are private limited companies and others are public limited companies. Treat both types in the same way. Any differences in presentation will be indicated later.

Also notice the par value of the shares. The value ranges from 1 penny to £1. The par value can be any amount; it will not affect your working of a question but it may affect the ability of the company to raise future finance.

WORKED EXAMPLE

The summarised balance sheet of Dox plc at 30 June 20*8 shows:

	£	£
Non-current assets at cost		400,000
Less aggregate depreciation		50,000
		350,000
Current assets	99,000	
Bank	1,000	
	100,000	
Current liabilities	40,000	60,000
		410,000
Shareholders' equity		
Ordinary shares of 25 pence each		400,000
Retained earnings		10,000
		410,000

The non-current assets are revalued at £600,000 on 1 July 20*8.

Prepare the balance sheet of Dox plc at 1 July 20*8 after the assets have been revalued.

Answer

Dox plc
Balance sheet at 1 July 20*8

	£	£
Non-current assets at valuation		600,000
Current assets	99,000	
Bank	1,000	
	100,000	
Current liabilities	40,000	60,000
		660,000
Shareholders' equity		
Ordinary shares of 25 pence each		400,000
Revaluation reserve		250,000
Retained earnings		10,000
		660,000

Workings

Dr	Non current assets account	Cr	Dr	Provision for depreciation of non current assets account	Cr
Bal b/d 400,000					
Revn Res 200,000			Revn Res 50,000	Bal b/d 50,000	

Dr	Revaluation reserve	Cr
	Non-current assets 200,000	
	Depr of non current assets 50,000	

Note:
- The fixed assets are 'at valuation'.
- There has been no change in the bank balance.
- The reserve must be called revaluation reserve.

QUESTION 7

The summarised balance sheet of Ousby Ltd at 31 October 20*8 is given.

	£	£
Non-current assets at cost		250,000
Current assets	40,000	
Bank	8,000	
	48,000	
Current liabilities	36,000	12,000
		262,000
Shareholders' equity		
Ordinary shares of 10 pence each		200,000
Retained earnings		62,000
		262,000

The non-current assets were revalued at £400,000 on 1 November 20*8.

Required Prepare the balance sheet of Ousby Ltd at 1 November 20*8 after the non-current assets were revalued.

QUESTION 8

The summarised balance sheet of Graf Ltd at 29 February 20*8 is given.

	£	£
Non-current assets at cost		75,000
Current assets	12,000	
Bank	2,000	
	14,000	
Current liabilities	9,000	5,000
		80,000
Shareholders' equity		
Ordinary shares of 1 penny each		60,000
Retained earnings		20,000
		80,000

The non-current assets were revalued at £200,000 on 1 March 20*8.

Required Prepare the balance sheet of Graf Ltd at 1 March 20*8 after the non-current assets were revalued.

DEBENTURES

Many limited companies raise additional capital by issuing debentures.

Debentures are long-term loans to the company. A debenture is the legal document issued by the company that is managing the debt. Debentures are generally secured against the company's assets. The security may be fixed, that is it relates to a specific asset or group of assets or it may be a floating charge where no specific assets are identified. If the company was to be wound up the debenture holders are in a safer position than either the preference shareholders or the ordinary shareholders because of this security. Debentures are usually for a fixed time period and are redeemable by the company at the end of that period.

Like all forms of borrowing, the debt has to be serviced and the interest due will normally be paid half-yearly. The interest that the company pays to the holders of the debentures, like all interest payable, is a charge against the profits and appears as an expense on the profit and loss account.

Note:

Debenture interest is not an appropriation of profits. It must be paid whether the company is profitable or not.

An issue of debentures will have the following effect on a balance sheet:

Increase bank balance   Increase non-current liabilities.

OR

Decrease bank overdraft   Increase non-current liabilities.

Debentures are not part of the share capital. Debenture holders are not shareholders.

We show debentures on the balance sheet under the heading 'Non-current liabilities'. The amount is deducted from the total assets less current liabilities.

Here is an example of how debentures should be treated in a balance sheet:

EXAMPLE

Studret plc
Summarised balance sheet at 30 September 20*8

	£	£
Non-current assets at cost		750,000
Current assets	150,000	
Current liabilities	60,000	90,000
Total assets *less* current liabilities		840,000
Non-current liabilities		
7% debentures (2035)		200,000
		640,000
Shareholders' equity		640,000

Debentures should be shown in the balance sheet with all their details, i.e. 7% debentures (2035).

This means that the interest to be paid by the company to the lenders is 7% per annum. The date shown means that the company will redeem the debentures in the year 2035.

Let us put the parts of the final accounts together.

Here are two examples showing the layout.

WORKED EXAMPLE

The following information relates to Becktom plc (all necessary adjustments, transfer and provisions have already been made) for the year ended 31 March 20*8.

	£
Non-current assets at valuation	590,000
Current assets	283,000
Current liabilities	170,000
6% debentures (2022)	90,000
Net profit for the year before tax	207,300
Corporation tax due	73,300
Transfer to general reserve	25,000
Interim dividend paid	
– ordinary shares	8,000
– preference shares	3,000
Proposed dividends	
– ordinary shares	17,000
– preference shares	3,000
Share premium account	20,000
Revaluation reserve	80,000
General reserve at 1 April 20*7	50,000
Retained earnings	138,000
Authorised share capital	
Ordinary shares of £1 each	500,000
6% preference shares of £1 each	250,000
Issued share capital	
Ordinary shares of £1 each fully paid	200,000
6% preference shares of £1 each fully paid	100,000

Required a) Prepare an extract from the income statement for the year ended 31 March 20*8.
b) Prepare the balance sheet at 31 March 20*8.

Answer

a)

Becktom plc
Income statement extract for the year ended 31 March 20*8

	£	£	£
Profit for the year before tax			207,300
Corporation tax			73,300
Profit for the year after tax			134,000
Transfer to general reserve			25,000
			109,000
Dividends: interim paid			
Ordinary shares	8,000		
Preference shares	3,000	11,000	
Dividends: proposed			
Ordinary shares	17,000		
Preference shares	3,000	20,000	31,000
Retained profit for the year			78,000

b)

Balance sheet at 31 March 20*8

	£	£
Non-current assets at valuation		590,000
Current assets	283,000	
Current liabilities	170,000	113,000
		703,000
Non-current liabilities		
6% debentures (2022)		90,000
		613,000
Authorised share capital		
Ordinary shares of £1		500,000
6% preference shares of £1 each		250,000
Shareholders' equity		
Ordinary shares of £1 each fully paid		200,000
6% preference shares of £1 each fully paid		100,000
Share premium account		20,000
Revaluation reserve		80,000
General reserve		75,000
Retained earnings		138,000
		613,000

WORKED EXAMPLE

Kneal plc provides the following trial balance at 31 December 20*8 which has been prepared *after* completion of the income statement for the year ended 31 December 20*8.

	£	£
Profit before tax for the year ended 31 December 20*8		499,000
Retained earnings balance at 1 January 20*8		301,700
General reserve		25,000
Revaluation reserve		85,000
Share premium account		125,000
7% preference shares of £1 each		200,000
Ordinary shares of £1 each		250,000
6% debentures (2020)		110,000
Patents	75,000	
Land & buildings at valuation	1,000,000	
Vehicles	130,000	
Investments 4 1\4% Treasury stock (2032)	150,000	
Inventories	142,000	
Trade receivables	85,000	
Trade payables		18,000
Interim dividends paid 3 August 20*8		
Ordinary shares	28,000	
Preference shares	7,000	
Debenture interest owing		3,300
	1,617,000	1,617,000

Additional information

The directors recommend:

- Transfer to general reserve £50,000.
- A final dividend on ordinary shares of £42,000 be provided.

■ A final dividend on preference shares of £7,000 be provided.
■ A provision for corporation tax of £154,000 be made.

Required a) Prepare an extract from the income statement for the year ended
31 December 20*8.
b) Prepare a balance sheet at 31 December 20*8.

Kneal plc
Income statement extract for the year ended 31 December 20*8

	£	£
Profit for the year before tax		499,000
Corporation tax		154,000
Profit for the year after tax		345,000
Transfer to general reserve		50,000
		295,000
Dividends paid		
Preference shares	7,000	
Ordinary shares	28,000	
Dividend proposed		
Preference shares	7,000	
Ordinary shares	42,000	84,000
Retained profit for the year		211,000

Answer

Balance sheet at 31 December 20*8

	£	£	£
Intangible assets			
Patents			75,000
Non-current assets			
Land & buildings at valuation			1,000,000
Vehicles			130,000
Investments			
4 ¼% Treasury stock (2032)			150,000
			1,355,000
Current assets			
Stock		142,000	
Trade receivables		85,000	
		227,000	
Current liabilities			
Trade payables	18,000		
Corporation tax due	154,000		
Proposed preference dividend	7,000		
Proposed ordinary dividend	42,000		
Debenture interest due	3,300	224,300	2,700
			1,357,700
Non-current liabilities			
6% debenture (2020)			110,000
			1,247,700
Shareholders' equity			
Ordinary shares of £1 each			250,000
7% preference shares of £1 each			200,000
Share premium account			125,000
Revaluation reserve			85,000
General reserve			75,000
Profit and loss account			512,700
			1,247,700

Note

Three types of fixed assets have been identified: intangible, non current and
investments. Capital reserves are shown before revenue reserves.

DIFFERENT TYPES OF FIXED ASSETS

We need to distinguish between the different types of fixed assets in the balance sheet of a limited company.

1 **Intangible assets** – these are non-physical assets, i.e. assets that cannot be seen or touched. Examples include patents and brand names, for example, the brand names Coca Cola, Oxo, etc., would come under this heading.
2 **Non-current assets** – these are physical assets, i.e. those that can be seen and touched, for example, delivery vehicles, premises.
3 **Investments** – if investments are to be kept for a number of years, they are treated as fixed assets. However, if the intention is to sell the investments within the current year, they would be classified as current assets.

The aggregate depreciation on fixed assets should be shown in the balance sheet of a limited company along with any revaluations of fixed assets that have taken place during the year.

The accounts that limited companies produce are used by the managers of that company for decision-making purposes. If the accounts used by the managers were published in this very useful form, rivals might gain access to information that could undermine the company.

Although legally a limited company must send its shareholders and lenders a set of accounts, the law protects the company by allowing it to publish an 'abridged' version.

At this stage of your studies you will not be asked to prepare a set of final accounts for publication. The final accounts of limited companies for publication will be dealt with in Book 2 and may be examined in your A2 examinations.

Some time after the final accounts are prepared and checked for their truthfulness and accuracy, the 'abridged' version is sent to the shareholders and other interested parties.

The published accounts are accompanied by:

■ the directors' report
■ the auditors' report.

DIRECTORS' REPORT

This is rather like a school or college report in that it outlines the progress of the company over the past year and also looks towards performance in the future.

It is a legal requirement that the directors report to the shareholders (Companies Act 1985) and the report must contain the following:

■ a review of performance during the year
■ the position of the company at the end of the year
■ the main activities of the company during the year, plus any major changes in activities that may have taken place during the year
■ important changes to non-current assets that have taken place during the year
■ particulars of important events affecting the company since the financial year-end
■ an indication of any likely future developments in the business of the company
■ an indication of research and development undertaken by the company
■ amounts of recommended dividends and transfers to reserves
■ names of people who were or are directors during the year
■ the number of shares and debentures in the company held by directors
■ any charitable donations or donations to political parties if these donations exceed £200
■ information regarding the health, safety and welfare of employees while at work
■ if the company employs more than 250 people, a statement on its policy regarding the employment of disabled people.

AUDITORS' REPORT

This report is addressed to the shareholders, not to the directors. The auditors must ensure:

■ the company keeps proper books of account
■ proper records are kept
■ the final accounts are in agreement with the records kept.

The Auditors must report on whether, in their opinion:

- the balance sheet and income statement have been prepared in accordance with the requirements of the Companies Act
- the balance sheet gives a 'true and fair view' of the company's affairs at the end of the financial year.
- the income statement gives a 'true and fair view' of the profit or loss for the financial year.

Chapter summary

- A limited company has a legal status separate from that of its shareholders.
- Liability of the members is limited to the amount they have paid or have agreed to pay for their shares.
- Public limited companies may issue shares to the general public but private limited companies cannot.
- Finance is raised by selling shares to preference shareholders and ordinary shareholders; further finance may be raised by issuing debenture stock.
- Reserves are past profits ploughed back into the company.
- Revenue reserves are past profits earned through normal activities of the company.
- Capital reserves are past profits derived through 'non-normal' activities.

SELF-TEST QUESTIONS

- Explain what is meant by limited liability.
- Does a sole trader have limited liability?
- Does a shareholder in a limited company have limited liability?
- Explain what is meant by the 'par value' of a share.
- The owners of a limited company are its directors. True or false?
- The owners of a limited company are its shareholders. True or false?
- ....are the rewards given to shareholders of a limited company. (Fill the gap.)
- Debenture holders earn .... (Fill the gap.)
- How are current liabilities described in the balance sheet of a limited company?
- A limited company must be profitable and also have............in order to pay dividends to shareholders. (Fill the gap.)
- Explain the difference between authorised share capital and issued share capital.
- Reserves are cash put aside for future use. True or false?
- Identify the two components of shareholders funds.
- Identify the two types of reserves.
- Explain what is meant by the term 'share premium account'.
- Identify two reports that must be sent to shareholders along with the final accounts of a limited company.

TEST QUESTIONS

QUESTION 9

Douglas Ltd supplies the following information after the first year of trading:

Trial balance at 29 February 20*8

	Dr £	Cr £
Profit for year before tax		312,000
Non-current assets at cost	300,000	
Current assets	150,000	
Interim dividend paid	40,000	
Ordinary shares of £1 each		178,000
	490,000	490,000

Additional information

The directors wish to transfer £50,000 to general reserve and recommend a final dividend of £60,000. They wish to provide for corporation tax due £82,000.

Required a) Prepare an extract from the income statement for the year ended 29 February 20*8.

b) Prepare a balance sheet at 29 February 20*8.

QUESTION 10

Donald Ltd provides the following information after the first year of trading:

Trial balance at 31 August 20*8

	Dr £	Cr £
Non-current assets at cost	200,000	
Current assets	150,000	
Ordinary shares of 50 pence each		100,000
Net profit for year		276,000
Interim dividend paid	26,000	
	376,000	376,000

Additional information

The directors wish to transfer £40,000 to general reserve and recommend a final dividend of £50,000. They wish to provide for corporation tax due £65,000.

Required a) Prepare an extract from the income statement for the year ended 31 August 20*8
b) Prepare a balance sheet at 31 August 20*8.

QUESTION 11

Hox Ltd provides the following summarised balance sheet at 31 May 20*8:

	£	£
Non-current assets at cost		180,000
Current assets	23,000	
Bank	18,000	
	41,000	
Current liabilities	40,000	1,000
		181,000
Shareholders' equity		
Ordinary shares of 25 pence each		70,000
General reserve		30,000
Retained earnings		81,000
		181,000

The non-current assets were revalued at £300,000 on 1 June 20*8.

Required Prepare a summarised balance sheet at 1 June 20*8 after revaluing the non-current assets.

QUESTION 12

Wong Ltd provides the following summarised balance sheet at 31 December 20*8:

	£	£
Non-current assets at cost		30,000
Current assets	42,000	
Bank	2,000	
	44,000	
Current liabilities	24,000	20,000
		50,000
Shareholders' equity		
Ordinary shares of 10 pence each		40,000
Profit and loss account		10,000
		50,000

The non-current assets were revalued on 1 January 20*9 at £210,000.

Required Prepare a summarised balance sheet at 1 January 20*9 after revaluing the non-current assets.

QUESTION 13

The summarised balance sheet of Norest Ltd at 31 January 20*8 is given.

	£	£
Non-current assets at cost		60,000
Current assets	15,000	
Bank	1,000	
	16,000	
Current liabilities	9,000	7,000
		67,000
Shareholders' equity		
Ordinary shares of 5 pence each		50,000
Retained earnings		17,000
		67,000

On 1 February 20*8 Norest Ltd issued a further 100,000 ordinary shares at a price of 30 pence per share.

Required Prepare a summarised balance sheet at 1 February 20*8 after the new shares were issued.

QUESTION 14

The summarised balance sheet of Trosh Ltd at 31 October 20*8 is given.

	£	£	£
Non-current assets at cost			360,000
Current assets		27,000	
Current liabilities			
Trade payables	12,000		
Bank overdraft	6,000	18,000	9,000
			369,000
Shareholders' equity			
Ordinary shares of £1 each			300,000
General reserve			50,000
Retained earnings			19,000
			369,000

On 1 November 20*8 Trosh Ltd issued a further 200,000 ordinary shares at £1.75 each.

Required Prepare a summarised balance sheet at 1 November 20*8 after the new shares were issued.

QUESTION 15

The summarised balance sheet of Smith-Patel Ltd at 31 March 20*8 is given.

	£	£
Non-current assets at cost		500,000
Current assets	100,000	
Bank	20,000	
	120,000	
Current liabilities	70,000	50,000
		550,000
Shareholders' equity		
Ordinary shares of £1 each		400,000
Retained earnings		150,000
		550,000

On 1 April 20*8 Smith-Patel Ltd issued a further 200,000 £1 ordinary shares at £1.50. On the same date the company revalued the non-current assets at £750,000.

Required Prepare a summarised balance sheet at 1 April 20*8 after the revaluation of non-current assets and the share issue.

QUESTION 16

The summarised balance sheet of Wiley-Fox Ltd at 30 November 20*8 is given.

	£	£	£
Non-current assets at cost			150,000
Less aggregate depreciation			35,000
			115,000
Current assets		16,000	
Current liabilities			
Trade payables	10,000		
Bank overdraft	2,000	12,000	4,000
			119,000
Shareholders' equity			
Ordinary shares of 25 pence			80,000
Retained earnings			39,000
			119,000

On 1 December 20*8 Wiley-Fox Ltd issued a further 100,000 ordinary shares at 40 pence per share. On the same date the company revalued the non-current assets at £200,000.

Required Prepare a summarised balance sheet at 1 December 20*8 after the revaluation of non-current assets and the share issue.

QUESTION 17

The following trial balance has been extracted from the books of Stephanie Hood Ltd on 30 April 20*8.

	Dr £	Cr £
Net profit for the year before tax		267,432
Issued share capital share capital		
Ordinary shares of £1 each fully paid		400,000
6% preference shares of £1 each fully paid		100,000
General reserve		70,000
Retained earnings		80,000
Non-current assets at cost	950,000	
Provision for depreciation of non current assets		230,000
Inventories 30 April 20*8	143,461	
Trade receivables	21,380	
Trade payables		17,211
Bank	34,802	
Interim dividends paid ordinary shares	12,000	
preference shares	3,000	
	1,164,643	1,164,643

Additional information

The directors recommend:

- a transfer to general reserve £50,000
- a final ordinary dividend £26,000 be provided
- a final preference dividend be provided
- provision for corporation tax £58,196 be made.

Required a) Prepare an extract from the income statement for the year ended 30 April 20*8.
         b) Prepare a summarised balance sheet at 30 April 20*8.

QUESTION 18

Pling Ltd has an authorised capital of 500,000 ordinary shares of £1 each and 250,000 10% preference shares of £1 each. The following trial balance has been extracted from the books of account at 30 September 20*8.

	Dr £	Cr £
Issued capital 100,000 ordinary shares of £1 each		100,000
30,000 10% preference shares of £1 each		30,000
Buildings at cost	350,000	
Office equipment at cost	30,000	
Delivery vehicles at cost	60,000	
Provision for depreciation – buildings		180,000
– office equipment		15,000
– delivery vehicles		36,000
Trade receivables	16,840	
Trade payables		6,970
Inventories 1 October 20*7	14,710	
Purchases	183 940	
Sales		412,480
Motor expenses	12,470	
Rent and rates	10,100	
Wages	57,200	
General expenses	18,520	
Retained earnings		27,000
General reserve		10,000
Bank	42,720	
Provision for doubtful debts		550
Interim dividends paid - ordinary shares	20,000	
- preference shares	1,500	
	818,000	818,000

Additional information at 30 September 20*8

- Inventories were valued at £16,320.
- Wages accrued and unpaid amounted to £1,550.
- Rates paid in advance amounted to £600.
- Provision for doubtful debts is to be maintained at 5% of trade receivables outstanding at the year-end.
- Depreciation is to be provided on non-current assets at the following rates:
  - buildings 2% on cost
  - office equipment 10% on cost
  - delivery vehicles 20% on cost.
- The directors recommend
  - a transfer to general reserve £10,000
  - a final dividend on ordinary shares of £25,000 be provided
  - a final preference dividend be provided
  - provision for corporation tax £28,420 be made.

Required a) Prepare an income statement for the year ended 30 September 20*8.
b) Prepare a balance sheet at 30 September 20*8.

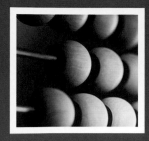

CHAPTER
TWENTY ONE

Accounting ratios

Accounting is a medium of communication. Financial statements are prepared to convey information. The statements that we have prepared up to now have contained much information, but, as yet, we have been unable to make judgements as to whether business performance has been good, bad or indifferent. In order to make judgements we need to make comparisons.

A business has made £230,000 profit for the year ended 31 December 20*8. is this a good profit?

You would need to have more information before you could give an intelligent answer to this question.

If the profit for the year was generated by BP plc, what is your verdict?

If the profit for the year has been generated by Sandra, my wife, selling cosmetics to her friends, what would your reaction be?

Even if we can make comparisons we still may not be able to make a judgement on whether or not the business is performing well or badly.

Specification coverage:
AQA Unit 2
OCR Unit 2

By the end of this chapter you should be able to:
- define and calculate basic profitability and liquidity ratios
- explain the significance of the ratios
- comment on the performance of businesses
- make year-on-year comparisons
- make comparisons with other businesses
- explain the limitations of using ratio analysis.

EXAMPLE

Mark Allen owns and runs a general store in Ousby, a small village in the north of England. His profits for the year ended 31 March 20*8 are £17,500.

Marllen plc is a large supermarket chain that has 72 stores throughout the country. Its profits for the same financial year were £132,000,000. Which business has been run most efficiently during the year?

On the basis of the information given, it is very difficult to say. The only thing we can say with any certainty is that the overall business profits were greater in the case of Marllen plc. But you would, generally, expect a business with 72 outlets to have a larger profit than a small village store.

How can we overcome the problems of comparing businesses of differing sizes, operating in different locations, etc.?

We do not compare raw data, that is the actual results as they appear in the final accounts. Instead we convert the data to a common base.

Consider Pat in class 4B. She scores 12 out of 20 in this week's history test. Danny, her friend, is in class 4D and scores 23 out of 50 in a similar history test. Clearly Danny has scored a higher mark in the weekly test, but who has done better?

By converting both results to the same base, out of 100 (i.e. converting them both into a percentage) we can make a very easy comparison.

Pat scores 60 % and Danny scores 46%.

The use of percentages is one of the approaches we use when comparing the results of one business with another, or if we are comparing the results of one business in two different time periods.

Who would be interested in the results of a business? Many groups of people, including:

- bank managers
- creditors
- HM Revenue & Customs
- debtors
- employees
- press
- students.

What are these people and any other users of accounting information interested in?

They are interested, in the main, with the survival of the business. Survival depends on the ability of the businesses to:

- generate profits – its profitability
- generate positive cash flows – its liquidity.

Why is it necessary for a business to be profitable?

A business needs to be profitable to ensure its long-term survival. In the short term a business can make a loss but losses cannot be sustained over long periods of time.

Why is it necessary for a business to have a positive cash flow?

A business needs a positive cash flow in order to meet its everyday commitments, i.e. in order to pay wages and creditors.

> **Ratio** is the term applied to a variety of calculations used to compare the results of a business over time or to compare the results of two or more businesses in the same business sector.

How do the users of accounting information assess whether or not the profitability and/or liquidity of a business are acceptable? They use precisely the same techniques that you would use in deciding whether the rate of pay in your part-time job was acceptable:

- you *compare* your earnings with what you earned last year
- you *compare* your earnings with those earned by your friends and relatives
- you *compare* your earnings with the average earnings in the sector in which you work
- you may even *compare* your earnings with what you thought you might earn and what you think you might spend your earnings on.

Performance evaluation is about **making comparisons**.

Ratio analysis and interpretation of ratios is about **making comparisons**.

When trying to evaluate the performance of a business, the users of accounting information go through the same processes that you would go through when considering your weekly wages slip.

The users will compare the performance of the business with:

- its performance in earlier years
- that of similar businesses
- the sector as a whole.

Some users such as managers of the business and bank managers, for example, may also compare *actual* performance with the performance that has been predicted in any budgets drawn up for the business.

Comparing the results of a business with its previous results is fairly straightforward.

Comparing the results of a business with the results achieved in the whole sector in which the business operates also is reasonably straightforward. However, inter-firm comparisons are difficult in that a true 'like with like' comparison is impossible.

Why?

Because all businesses have a different:

- level of turnover
- sales mix
- location
- set of employees
- set of managers.

The list of differences can go on and on.

Some text books sub-divide ratios into:

- profitability ratios
- financial ratios
- utilisation of resources ratios
- investment ratios.

In some cases they may also sub-divide into:

- primary
- secondary
- tertiary.

Although these are important categories, examination questions will not generally ask you for such a classification.

● EXAMINATION TIP

It is essential you learn the formula used for each calculation. You *must* learn the basic ratios if you are to gain a good result in your examination.

The following set of final accounts for Fradtly plc will be used to calculate and explain each ratio.

Fradtly plc
Income statement for the year ended 31 October 20*8

	£000	£000
Sales		25,200
Less cost of sales		
Inventories at 1 November 20*7	1,730	
Purchases	8,900	
	10,630	
Less inventories at 31 October 20*8	1,600	9,030
Gross profit		16,170
Less Expenses		
Distribution expenses	7,752	
Administration costs	4,316	12,068
Operating profit on ordinary activities		4,102
Finance costs		210
Profit for year before taxation		3,892
Taxation		960
Profit for year after taxation		2,932
Interim preference dividend paid	35	
Interim ordinary dividend paid	360	
Proposed final preference dividend	35	
Proposed final ordinary dividend	520	950
Retained profit for the year		1,982

Balance sheet at 31 October 20*8

	£000	£000	£000
Non-current assets			
Freehold land and buildings			5,400
Plant and machinery			4,500
Vehicles			1,800
Office equipment			200
			11,900
Current assets			
Inventories		1,600	
Trade receivables		2,320	
Bank		40	
		3,960	
Current liabilities			
Trade payables	965		
Taxation	960		
Proposed dividends	555	2,480	
			1,480
			11,380
Non-current liabilities			1,400
			9,980
Shareholders' equity			
Ordinary shares of 50 pence each			2,500
7% preference shares of £1 each			1,000
Share premium account			900
Profit and loss account			5,580
			9,980

All sale and purchases are on credit.

THE RATIOS

RETURN ON CAPITAL EMPLOYED (ROCE)

(Profitability in relation to capital employed.)

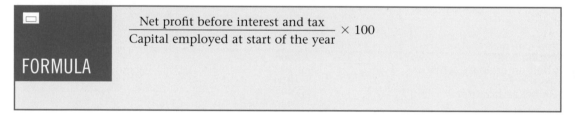

FORMULA

$$\frac{\text{Net profit before interest and tax}}{\text{Capital employed at start of the year}} \times 100$$

Return on capital employed $= \dfrac{4,102}{9,398} \times 100 = 43.65\%$

This ratio measures the return (profit earned) in relation to the total amount of money invested in the business by all the providers of long-term finance.

Net profit is taken before interest and tax, since neither interest nor tax are common elements in the final accounts of some businesses with whom we may wish to compare our ratios.

Long-term finance is provided by lenders and all shareholders. In the case of

Fradtly plc, long-term finance amounts to £11,380,000 (£9,980,000 plus £1,400,000), but we need to deduct this year's retained profit of £1,982,000.

The return on capital employed should be compared to the return from similar businesses and may also be compared to the return that could be obtained from risk-free investments.

The ratio tells us that for every £1 invested in the business the company earns a return of over 43 pence.

This ratio is sometimes calculated for different parts of a business. If a department or a branch has a return that is below the average for the business as a whole, or is deemed by managers to be unacceptable, then remedial measures should be taken.

In some examination questions it may not be possible to arrive at the capital employed at the start of the year. In these questions use the closing capital as shown in the balance sheet. But do remember to show the formula that you have used.

GROSS PROFIT MARGIN

FORMULA

$$\frac{\text{Gross profit}}{\text{Sales}} \times 100$$

Gross profit margin $= \dfrac{16,170}{25,200} \times 100 = 64.17\%$

This shows that for every £1 of sales Fradtly plc earns just over 64 pence. Each £1 of sales earns 64.17 pence towards covering company overheads.

The gross profit margin will be affected by both the cost price of purchases and the selling price charged by the business.

To improve the gross profit margin a business could buy goods for resale more cheaply while maintaining its selling price. Alternatively, the business could buy at the price presently being charged and put up the selling price, if their customers will accept the increase without reducing quantity demanded.

GROSS PROFIT MARK-UP

FORMULA

$$\frac{\text{Gross profit}}{\text{Cost of sales}} \times 100$$

Mark-up $= \dfrac{16,170}{9,030} \times 100 - 179.07\%$

This tells us that every £1 of purchases made by Fradtly plc is sold for just over £2.79. Every £1 of purchases earns £1.79 towards covering the company overheads.

Mark-up and margin are different perspectives on the same data. So, improvements to mark-up would be achieved by using the same policies with regard to purchase and selling price strategies as those outlined in improving margin.

NET PROFIT MARGIN

(Net profit in relation to turnover.)

FORMULA

$$\frac{\text{Net profit before interest and taxation}}{\text{Sales}} \times 100$$

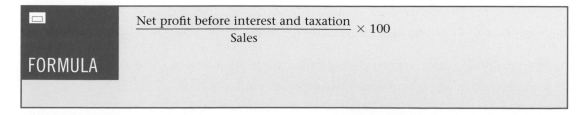

Net profit margin $= \dfrac{4{,}102}{25{,}200} = 16.28\%$

Each £1 sales that Fradtly plc makes earns just over 16 pence. This will pay corporation tax and provide dividends and any profits to be ploughed back for expansion or purchase of further assets.

Probably the greatest impact on this ratio is the level of gross profit earned. If gross profit margins improve, one would expect the net profit margin to also improve. However, this will depend on the behaviour patterns of the overhead costs.

OVERHEADS IN RELATION TO TURNOVER

Overheads are another way of describing expenses incurred by a business.

FORMULA

$$\dfrac{\text{Overheads}}{\text{Sales}} \times 100$$

Overheads in relation to turnover $= \dfrac{12{,}068}{25{,}200} = 47.89\%$

This ratio tells us that out of every £1 of sales, almost 48 pence goes to paying Fradtly's expenses (wages, rent, rates, etc.).

This ratio will be adversely affected by changes in the expenses incurred by the business, for example, a wage rise, an increase in rent paid or an increase in business rates.

The ratio would improve should any of the expenses incurred fall or if any resources were used more efficiently.

Note

Remember that:

$$\text{gross profit} - \text{expenses} = \text{net profit} \, .$$

So,

$$\text{gross profit margin} - \text{overheads in relation to turnover} = \text{net profit margin}$$

Let us check the calculation that we have done:

$$64.17\% - 47.89\% = 16.28\%$$

RATE OF STOCK TURNOVER

(Stock turn or stock turnover or inventory turnover.)

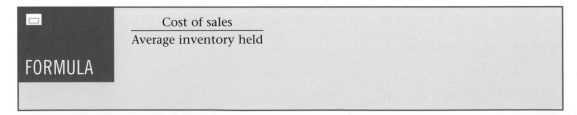

FORMULA

$$\dfrac{\text{Cost of sales}}{\text{Average inventory held}}$$

Rate of stock turnover $= \dfrac{9{,}030}{1{,}665^{*}} = 5.42$ *times* (*Note*: this is not a %)

*(1,730 opening stock + 1,600 closing stock = 3,330 divided by 2)

This shows that on average, Fradtly sells its stocks 5.42 times per year.

If we divide a year by 5.42 it will tell us how long, on average, Fradtly plc keeps stock. So,

Fradtly keeps stocks on average for about 67 days $\dfrac{365 \text{ days}}{5.42} = 67.34$

or for about nine and a half weeks $\dfrac{52 \text{ weeks}}{5.42} = 9.59$

or for about two and a quarter months $\dfrac{12 \text{ months}}{5.42} = 2.21$

We cannot really say whether these figures are good or bad. We can only comment if we know the type of business that the figures relate to. If Fradtly plc deals with perishable goods (fruit, flowers, etc.) it would seem that to hold stocks for over two months is a little excessive!

This calculation gives the average time taken for stock to be sold. The result may conceal very slow-moving stocks.

If the business is selling a variety of different products it may be beneficial to calculate the rate of stock turnover for each different category of stock. It can then be seen which type of stock is selling slowly and which products are being sold more quickly.

There is an element of profit wrapped up in each 'bundle' of stock; there is also cash tied up in it. The quicker stock is being turned round the quicker the profits are earned and the more often cash is released for use within the business.

QUESTION 1

The information given relates to the business of Sean Brady.

Summarised trading and profit and loss account for the year ended 30 November 20*8

	£	£
Sales		213,000
Less cost of sales		
Stock 1 December 20*7	22,000	
Purchases	142,000	
	164,000	
Stock 30 November 20*8	18,000	146,000
Gross profit		67,000
Expenses		39,000
Net profit		28,000

Required Calculate:

a) gross profit margin
b) net profit margin
c) overheads in relation to turnover
d) rate of stock turnover.

QUESTION 2

The information given relates to the business of May Styles.

Summarised trading and profit and loss account for the year ended 28 February 20*8

	£	£
Sales		313,500
Less cost of sales		
Stock 1 March 20*7	39,000	
Purchases	167,000	
	206,000	
Stock 28 February 20*8	41,000	165,000
Gross profit		148,500
Expenses		88,500
Net profit		60,000

Required Calculate:

a) mark-up
b) net profit margin
c) overheads in relation to turnover
d) rate of stock turnover.

NET CURRENT ASSET RATIO

(Current ratio or working capital ratio.)

FORMULA

$$\frac{\text{Current assets}}{\text{Current liabilities}}$$

This ratio is a 'true' ratio in that it is always expressed as 'something' to one. For example, 2.4:1, 1.65:1.

$$\text{Current ratio} = \frac{3,960}{2,480} = 1.597 \text{ expressed as } 1.6:1$$

This means that for each £1 owed the company can cover this with current assets 1.6 times.

There is no ideal current ratio. Some businesses work very effectively with very low ratios; others have what could be considered very high ratios, so do avoid stating categorically that this ratio should be 2:1. Many examination candidates quote this – it will not gain a mark for you.

It can be said that a high current ratio is wasteful of resources. Current assets do not generally yield a return, unlike fixed assets, so the reduction of a high current ratio could release resources that might be more efficiently converted into fixed assets that can be used to earn greater profits.

LIQUID CAPITAL RATIO

(Acid test ratio or quick asset ratio.)

FORMULA

$$\frac{\text{Current assets } less \text{ inventories}}{\text{Current liabilities}} \quad \text{or} \quad \frac{\text{Current assets } less \text{ stock}}{\text{Current liabilities}}$$

$$\text{Liquid ratio} = \frac{2,360}{2,480} = 0.95 \text{ expressed as } 0.95:1$$

This means that for every £1 owed Fradtly plc can only raise 95 pence by way of liquid assets. Stocks are ignored because they are the least liquid form of current asset; that is, they are the least easily converted into cash resources.

DEBTORS' COLLECTION PERIOD

(Average collection period.)

FORMULA

$$\frac{\text{Trade receivables} \times 365}{\text{Credit sales}} \quad \text{or} \quad \frac{\text{Trade debtors} \times 365}{\text{Credit sales}}$$

$$\text{Debtors' collection period} = \frac{2,320 \times 365}{25,200} = 34 \text{ days (33.60 but always round up)}$$

This means that on average debtors are taking 34 days before settling their debts.

Because the result of this calculation is an average figure, it could conceal a number of debts that have been outstanding for some time.

The compilation of an age profile of debtors on a regular basis would reveal debtors whose debts were outstanding for an unacceptable length of time.

A high average debtor collection period could indicate a number of 'older' debts. Old debts are more likely to become bad debts. This means that in reality the current asset figure shown in the balance sheet might be lower than the figure indicated.

CREDITORS' PAYMENT PERIOD

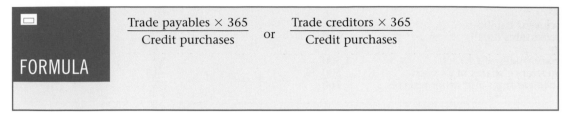

FORMULA

$$\frac{\text{Trade payables} \times 365}{\text{Credit purchases}} \quad \text{or} \quad \frac{\text{Trade creditors} \times 365}{\text{Credit purchases}}$$

$$\text{Creditors' payment period} = \frac{965 \times 365}{8,900} = 40 \text{ days (39.58 but rounded up)}$$

This tells us how much time Fradtly is taking to pay its creditors.

This is a valuable source of finance for any business, so the longer that can be taken before making a payment the better. However, care must be taken not to upset suppliers in this respect.

It is worth noting that Fradtly plc are, on average, settling their debts in 40 days, while their debtors are taking, on average, 34 days to pay. This is a good situation for any business to be in as it aids liquidity.

GEARING RATIO

The owner's stake in a business may be at risk if the business's capital is provided mainly by outsiders in the form of loans. The gearing ratio calculates the proportion of the total finance available to the business that is provided by outside sources.

High borrowing might be risky because all types of borrowing must be serviced, i.e. interest has to be paid on a regular basis to the provider of the finance. This is fine if the business is highly profitable. In fact, it makes sound business sense to borrow funds if the interest to be paid is less than the return that the borrowed capital can earn when used in the business. For example, I would be prepared to borrow £1,000,000 at 15% interest per annum, if I could put the £1,000,000 to use to earn me a return of 25%. I would make a profit of £100,000!

However, in times of poor profits or even losses, the interest on long-term finance still has to be paid in full. If the interest cannot be paid then the consequences could be very serious. The business may be forced into liquidation by its creditors

FORMULA

$$\frac{\text{Fixed cost capital}}{\text{Total capital}} \times 100$$

WORKED EXAMPLE

Anthea is a sole trader and she has a capital account balance of £42,000. She has a long-term bank loan of £50,000.

Required Calculate the gearing ratio for the business.

Answer

$$\text{Gearing ratio} = \frac{\text{Fixed cost capital}}{\text{Total capital}} = \frac{50,000}{92,000} \times 100 = 54.35\%$$

WORKED EXAMPLE

The directors of Wharma plc provide the following information:

	£
Non-current liabilities	
8% debentures (2049)	300
Equity	
Ordinary shares of £1 each	1,500
7% preference shares of £1 each	500
Retained earnings and other reserves	760

Required Calculate the gearing ratio for Wharma plc.

Answer

$$\text{Formula} = \frac{\text{Fixed cost capital}}{\text{Total capital}} =$$

$$\frac{\text{Long-term loans} + \text{preference shares}}{\text{Long-term loans} + \text{preference share capital} + \text{ordinary share capital} + \text{all reserves}} \times 100$$

$$= \frac{300 + 500}{300 + 500 + 1500 + 760} \times 100 = 26.14\%$$

The gearing of a business is:

- high when the ratio is more than 50%
- neutral when the ratio is 50%
- low when the ratio is less than 50%.

So high geared =

- high borrowing
- high debt
- high risk.

Low geared =

- low borrowing
- low debt
- low risk.

QUESTION 3

Look back at the worked examples above.

Is Fradtly plc high geared or low geared?
Is Anthea's business high geared or low geared?
Is Wharma plc a high geared company or is it low geared?

QUESTION 4

Milly has provided £130,000 capital for her business. She has borrowed £30,000 for business use, from BHSC Bank plc.

Required Calculate the gearing ratio for Milly's business.

QUESTION 5

The directors of Shuttlemann plc provide the following information:

	£
Non-current liabilities	
5% debentures (2031)	800
Shareholders' equity	
Ordinary shares of £1 each	700
6% preference shares of £1 each	200
Retained earnings and other reserves	115

Required Calculate the company's gearing ratio.

When dealing with sole traders' accounts, remember that the descriptions that you learned earlier will still hold good. You will still use profit and loss account as a heading and encounter the terms fixed assets, debtors and creditors.

QUESTION 6

The information given is for the business of Agnes Tutin.

Summarised balance sheet at 30 September 20*8

	£	£
Fixed assets		170,000
Current assets		
Stock	23,500	
Trade debtors	13,500	
Bank balance	13,000	
	50,000	
Current liabilities		
Trade creditors	10,000	40,000
		210,000
Capital		210,000

Additional information

Purchases all on credit £160,000; sales all on credit £350,000.

Required Calculate:

a) net current asset ratio
b) liquid capital ratio
c) debtors' collection period
d) creditors' payment period.

QUESTION 7

The information given is for the business of Trefor Johns.

Summarised balance sheet at 31 January 20*8

	£	£	£
Fixed assets			450,000
Current assets			
Stock		34,000	
Trade debtors		26,500	
		60,500	
Current liabilities			
Trade creditors	19,460		
Bank overdraft	11,540	31,000	29,500
			479,500
Capital			479,500

Additional information

Purchases all on credit £291,900; sales all on credit £450,500.

Required Calculate:

a) net current asset ratio
b) liquid capital ratio

c) debtors' collection period

d) creditors' payment period.

Many students are good at calculating the ratios and so score good marks. However, they are less confident in analysing the results of their calculations.

Examiners and teachers alike expect students to reach earth-trembling conclusions from their calculations and analysis. Try not to be daunted by this prospect. We can only analyse at a very basic level. Even city fund managers are not very good at analysing the results of major businesses; otherwise the scores of pension funds and other investment portfolios would not be in such a mess at the moment!

Let us consider how to tackle the written sections of a question. The presenter of a popular quiz programme on television coined the saying 'Say what you see'. Remember the saying when you are making observations and comments.

The pattern to follow is:

- state the formula
- do the calculation
- state whether the ratio shows an improvement or a worsening of performance
- quantify the change identified
- suggest reasons for any changes.

These five headings should be considered when comparing different businesses and when trying to identify the trends that have occurred within a single business.

WORKED EXAMPLE

The following information is given for Breen Ltd.

Income statement for the year ended 31 December 20*8

	£	£
Sales (all on credit)		500,000
Less cost of sales		
Inventories at 1 January 20*8	18,000	
Purchases (all on credit)	184,000	
	202,000	
Inventories at 31 December 20*8	22,000	180,000
Gross profit		320,000
Expenses		156,000
Net profit for year		164,000

Balance sheet at 31 December 20*8

Non-current assets		400,000
Current assets		
Inventories	22,000	
Trade receivables	23,000	
Bank balance	11,000	
	56,000	
Current liabilities		
Trade payables	20,000	36,000
		436,000
Non-current liabilities		
6% debentures (2018)		100,000
		336,000
Equity		
Ordinary shares of £1 each		100,000
Retained earnings		236,000
		336,000

Additional information

The following ratios were calculated for the year ended 31 December 20*7:

Gross profit margin	60%
Mark-up	150%
Net profit margin	29.23%
Return on capital employed	37.61%
Overheads in relation to turnover	30.77%
Rate of stock turnover	8 times
Net current assets ratio	2.6:1
Liquid capital ratio	1.47:1
Debtors' collection period	22 days
Creditors' payment period	35 days
Gearing ratio	32.81%

Required Calculate the ratios shown above for the year ended 31 December 20*8.

Comment on the ratios for the two years.

Note:

In each case the formula should be stated.

Ratios should be calculated to two decimal places since two decimal places have been used for the previous year's results.

Answer

	31 December 20*7	31 December 20*8
Gross profit margin	60%	64%
Mark-up	150%	177.78%
Net profit margin	29.23%	32.8%
Return on capital employed	32.68%	37.61%
Overheads in relation to turnover	30.77%	31.2%
Rate of stock turnover	8 times	9 times
Net current assets ratio	2.6:1	2.8:1
Liquid capital ratio	1.47:1	1.7:1
Debtors' collection period	22 days	17 days
Creditors' payment period	35 days	40 days
Gearing ratio	32.81%	22.95%

Let us follow the pattern. Have the ratios improved or worsened? How much of an improvement or deterioration?

There has been an improvement in the **gross margin**; it has gone up from 60% to 64%. This means that in 20*7 every £1 sales yielded 60p gross profit; in 20*8 every £1 sales yielded 64p gross profit.

What are the possible reasons for the improvement?

The improvement could be due to Breen Ltd increasing the selling price of their products with cost of sales remaining the same (or even going down); or selling price remaining the same as in the previous year but Breen Ltd's buyers purchasing the goods to be sold at a lower price.

Since the **mark-up** and **margin** are very closely related the comments are identical.

Net profit margin has also improved. It has increased from 29.23% to 32.8%. After expenses, every £1 sales now gives the business 32.8p net profit; in the previous year each £1 sales gave 29.23p net profit. This is due to the increase in the gross profit.

The proportion of **expenses** taken from each £1 of sales has increased from 30.77p to 31.2p, so the position has worsened. Although this is a very small amount, the ratio should be monitored to ensure that the position does not deteriorate further. The reason for the increase could be due to certain overheads increasing without a corresponding increase in productivity.

The **return on capital employed** has improved from 32.68% to 37.61%. This means that every £1 invested in the business in 20*8 gave a return of 37.61p. This is due to the improved profits. (In certain circumstances the increase could be due to a decrease in capital employed. We have no indication that this is the case and we can only 'say what we see'!)

The **rate of stock turnover** has improved. It has risen from 8 times per year to 9 times per year. Breen is selling 'bundles' of stock in 41 days (365 ÷ 9) this year. Stock was sold on average every 46 days (365 ÷ 8) last year. This will have improved cash flows and the magnitude of the profits (though it will not change either of the margins).

Notice that we are still following the pattern:

- Has the ratio improved or worsened?
- Quantify the change.
- Give reasons for any change.

Net current asset ratio has improved. It has increased from 2.6:1 to 2.8:1. This could be due to increases in any of the current assets or a reduction in short-term creditors. We have not been given the details for 20*7 so we can't say what we see! We could perhaps comment on the fact that for every £1 owed Breen now has £2.80 covering liabilities. Is this excessive? Could some current assets be converted into fixed assets in order to increase earning power?

Liquid capital ratio has improved. It has risen from 1.5:1 to 1.7:1. For every £1 owed Breen has current assets (not including stock) of £1.70. In the previous year, for every £1 owed Breen had £1.50. Is the proportion of resources held as liquid assets too high? Could some of those liquid assets be converted into fixed assets and improve earning power? The proportion of stock held as current assets remains static at £1.10 for every £1 owed.

The **debtors' collection period** has improved. It has fallen from an average of 22 days to an average of 17 days. Is this average masking some debts that are outstanding for much longer? Is this too short a time? Has too much pressure been put on debtors to pay up quickly? If too much pressure is put on credit customers they may desert Breen and use a supplier with a much more relaxed credit management policy.

Creditors' payment period has improved. Breen Ltd is now settling its debts on average in 40 days; in the previous year it settled in 35 days. Care must be taken to ensure that suppliers are not alienated by not paying them within the agreed terms.

It is generally worth comparing the debtors' collection period with the creditors' payment period.

Consider this situation: you owe your brother £10 and your sister owes you £12.

Which situation would you prefer?

You pay your brother on Monday and your sister pays you on Friday?

Or

Your sister pays you on Monday and you pay your brother on Friday?

The same principle applies in business. The debtors' collection period should be shorter than the creditors' payment period.

Gearing ratio has decreased indicating that there is slightly less reliance on borrowed capital than in the previous year. The business would not be classified as a high-risk business in either of the years shown. The ratio has fallen and this could be due to an increase in the retained earnings.

LIMITATIONS OF USING RATIO ANALYSIS FOR ASSESSING BUSINESS PERFORMANCE

- Ratio analysis uses historic information; that is, the results are based on events that have already taken place.
- The merit of using historic cost is that it is objective. However, its use does throw doubt on results compared over a long time period. In Dickens' time an annual average salary was £20, so presumably one could buy a house for less than £100. Salaries and house prices have risen substantially since those days. In the case of sole traders and partnerships, assets are valued at cost. Will the use of historic cost invalidate some ratios if the assets are valued at 1970s prices?
- The emphasis on past results provides indications for future results but nothing is guaranteed. A football team may win the premiership. This does not mean that it will necessarily win it for the next five or ten years.
- The bases of the ratios, that is the published accounts, only give an overview of the whole business. One department or product may yield a return on capital employed of 45%, while another yields 2%, yet overall the business may be earning an acceptable 20%.
- The ratios only consider the monetary aspects of the business. They do not record management and/or staff strengths and weaknesses.
- The final accounts are prepared on a particular day. This could mean that a balance sheet may well be unrepresentative of the normal position of the business.
- The external environment facing the business is constantly changing. Some changes may take a considerable time to impact on the business. An increase in the price of raw materials may only be incorporated into costing calculations in a few months' time.
- Organisations vary in their structure, method of financing their operations, expense and revenue patterns and they may use different accounting bases. No matter how similar businesses may appear to outsiders, they are all different and so inter-firm comparison can prove to be misleading.

However, despite all the limitations of using ratios it is the most widely recognised tool for comparing, analysing and evaluating results.

Chapter summary

- Ratio analysis is a valuable way of analysing the performance of a business.
- To be of any value, ratios must be compared to previous years' performance to determine trends.
- Ratios are used to compare the performance of businesses in the same industry.
- Ratios are used to make judgements about the likely future performance of a business.
- Although it is very difficult to compare 'like with like', it is the best measure that is available.
- Remember:
  - show the formula
  - do the calculation
  - state whether better or worse
  - quantify
  - give likely reasons for change.

SELF-TEST QUESTIONS

- Why do we use ratios rather than actual results to evaluate business performance?
- 'A profit of £87,000 is very good.' Comment on this statement.
- Identify three groups of people who might use ratios.
- Gross profit ÷ sales is a ....ratio. (Fill the gap.)
- Current assets: current liabilities is a ....ratio. (Fill the gap.)
- What does ROCE stand for?
- Give alternative names for the following ratios:
  - net profit in relation to turnover
  - overheads in relation to turnover
  - profitability in relation to capital employed

- net current asset ratio
- liquid capital ratio
- working capital ratio
- acid test ratio.
- Identify two weaknesses in using ratios to evaluate the performance of a business.

TEST QUESTIONS

QUESTION 8

The following information is given for Sadie Lolly for the year ended 31 August 20*8:

	£
Sales all on credit	145,000
Stock 1 September 20*7	23,000
Stock 31 August 20*8	27,000
Purchases all on credit	110,000
Gross profit	39,000
Expenses	25,000
Net profit	14,000
Fixed assets	92,000
Trade debtors	18,000
Bank balance	5,000
Trade creditors	12,500
Drawings	23,000
Capital 1 September 20*7	138,500

Required Calculate the following ratios:

a) gross profit margin
b) net profit margin
c) overheads in relation to turnover ratio
d) return on capital employed
e) rate of stock turnover
f) net current asset ratio
g) liquid capital ratio
h) debtors' collection period
i) creditors' payment period.

QUESTION 9

The following information is given for Hemal Limbachia for the year ended 31 December 20*8:

	£
Sales (80% credit sales)	250,000
Stock 1 January 20*8	11,000
Purchases (all on credit)	141,000
Gross profit	139,000
Expenses	78,000
Fixed assets	120,000
Trade debtors	15,000
Bank balance	8,000
Trade creditors	20,000
Drawings	30,000
Capital 1 January 20*8	127,000

Required Calculate the following ratios:

a) mark-up
b) net profit margin
c) overheads in relation to turnover ratio
d) rate of stock turnover
e) net current asset ratio
f) liquid capital ratio
g) debtors' collection period
h) creditors' payment period.

QUESTION 10

The following information is given for Zena Paul:

Trading account for the year ended 30 November 20*8

	£	£
Sales		234,000
Less cost of sales		
Stock 1 December 20*7	14,000	
Purchases	98,000	
	112,000	
Stock 30 November 20*8	16,000	96,000
Gross profit		138,000
Balance sheet at 30 November 20*8		
Fixed assets		300,000
Current assets		
Stock	16,000	
Trade debtors	19,000	
Bank balance	3,000	
	38,000	
Current liabilities		
Trade creditors	15,000	23,000
		323,000
Capital		264,000
Add profit		86,000
		350,000
Less drawings		27,000
		323,000

Additional information

All purchases and sales are on credit.

The net profit margin for the year ended 30 November 20*7 was 29.48%.

The net current asset ratio at 30 November 20*7 was 2.78:1.

Required Calculate the following ratios:

a) gross profit margin
b) net profit margin
c) overheads in relation to turnover ratio
d) return on capital employed
e) rate of stock turnover
f) net current asset ratio
g) liquid capital ratio
h) debtors' collection period
i) creditors' payment period.

Comment on the results revealed by the net profit margin and net current asset ratio.

QUESTION 11

The following information is given for Chris Tynan:

Trading account for the year ended 31 March 20*8

	£	£	£
Sales			560,000
Less cost of sales			
Stock 1 April 20*7		45,000	
Purchases		368,000	
		413,000	
Stock 31 March 20*8		43,000	370,000
Gross profit			190,000
Balance sheet at 31 March 20*8			
Fixed assets			312,000
Current assets			
Stock		43,000	
Trade debtors		36,000	
		79,000	
Current liabilities			
Trade creditors	42,000		
Bank overdraft	21,000	63,000	16,000
			328,000
Capital			309,000
Add profit			61,000
			370,000
Less drawings			42,000
			328,000

Additional information

All purchases and sales were on credit.

The gross margin for the year ended 31 March 20*7 was 35.62%.

The liquid asset ratio at 31 March 20*7 was 0.63:1.

The debtors' collection period at 31 March 20*7 was 21 days.

Required Calculate the following ratios:

a) gross margin
b) net profit margin
c) overheads in relation to turnover ratio
d) return on capital employed
e) net current asset ratio
f) liquid capital ratio
g) debtors' collection period
h) creditors' payment period.

Comment on the results revealed by the gross margin; the liquid capital ratio; and the debtors' collection period.

QUESTION 12

The following information is given for the business of Selena Chulk:

Trading account for the year ended 31 July 20*8

	£	£
Sales		758,000
Less cost of sales		
Stock 1 August 20*7	65,400	
Purchases	452,000	
	517,400	
Stock 31 July 20*8	64,600	452,800
Gross profit		305,200

Balance sheet at 31 August 20*8

	£	£
Fixed assets		450,000
Current assets		
Stock	64,600	
Trade debtors	37,000	
Bank	4,400	
	106,000	
Trade creditors	56,000	50,000
		500,000
Capital		451,000
Profit		103,000
		554,000
Less drawings		54,000
		500,000

Additional information

80% of total sales were on credit.

75% of total purchases were on credit.

The gross margin for the year ended 31 August 20*7 was 48.63%.

The net margin for the year ended 31 August 20*7 was 14.77%.

The rate of stock turnover for the year ended 31 August 20*7 was 10.4 times.

The debtors' collection period at 31 August 20*7 was 22 days.

The creditors' payment period at 31 August 20*7 was 45 days.

Required Calculate the following ratios:

a) gross margin
b) net profit margin
c) overheads in relation to turnover ratio
d) return on capital employed
e) rate of stock turnover
f) net current assets ratio
g) liquid capital ratio
h) debtors' collection period
i) creditors' payment period.

Comment on the results revealed by the gross margin; the net margin; the rate of stock turnover; the debtors' collection period; and the creditors' payment period.

QUESTION 13

The following information is given for two businesses in the same industry for the year ended 30 June 20*8:

	Jim Flack	Josie Chan
	£	£
Sales (all credit)	230,000	896,000
Stock 1 July 20*7	12,400	32,000
Stock 30 June 20*8	11,600	30,000
Purchases (all credit)	58,600	515,000
Overhead expenses	84,600	126,000
Fixed assets	200,000	450,000
Trade debtors	14,000	80,000
Trade creditors	16,000	47,000
Bank balance	2,400	4,000
Capital 1 July 20*7	142,000	332,000
Drawings	16,000	68,000

All purchases and sales were on credit.

Required Prepare a summarised trading and profit and loss account for the year ended 30 June 20*8 for each business.

Prepare a summarised balance sheet at 30 June 20*8 for each business.

Required Calculate the following ratios for each business:

a) gross profit margin
b) net profit margin
c) return on capital employed
d) overheads in relation to turnover ratio
e) rate of stock turnover
f) net current asset ratio
g) liquid capital ratio
h) debtors' collection period
i) creditors' payment period.

Compare the performance of each business.

QUESTION 14

The following financial statements have been produced for Lisus Ltd at 31 March 20*8:

Income statement for the year ended 31 March 20*8

	£000	£000	£000
Revenue			16,620
Less cost of sales			12,630
Gross profit			3,990
Less expenses			2,254
Operating profit			1,736
Finance costs			266
Profit for the year before tax			1,470
Taxation		800	
Dividends		640	1,440
Retained profit for the year			30
Balance sheet at 31 March 20*8			
Assets			
Non-current assets at NBV			14,200
Current assets			
Inventories		4,120	
Trade receivables		4,070	
		8,190	
Current liabilities			
Trade payables	3,850		
Tax and dividends	1,440		
Loans repayable within 12 months	2,480	7,770	420
			14,620
Non-current liabilities			
7% debentures (2013)			3,800
			10,820
Shareholders' equity			
Ordinary shares of £1 each			8,300
Retained earnings and other reserves			2,520
			10,820

All sales are credit sales.

Required Calculate:

a) gross margin
b) net profit margin
c) return on capital employed
d) net current asset ratio
e) liquid (acid test) ratio
f) rate of stock turnover (use closing inventory)
g) debtors' collection period
h) gearing ratio.

QUESTION 15

The following financial statements are provided for Bredgol plc at 31 January 20*9:

	£000	£000	£000
Revenue			16,550
Less cost of sales			8,380
Gross profit			8,170
Less expenses			5,325
Operating profit			2,845
Finance costs			88
Profit for the year before tax			2,757
Taxation			850
Profit for the year after tax			1,907
Dividends			650
Retained profit for the year			1,257
Balance sheet at 31 January 20*9			
Non-current assets			18,000
Current assets			
Inventory		706	
Trade receivables		4,800	
Cash and cash equivalents		81	
		5,587	
Current liabilities			
Trade payables	5,100		
Taxation and dividends	1,500	6,600	(1,013)
			16,987
Non-current liabilities			
8% debentures (2017)			1,100
			15,887
Shareholders' equity			
Ordinary shares of £1 each			8,000
Retained earnings and other reserves			7,887
			15,887

All sales are credit sales

Required Calculate:

a) gross margin
b) net profit margin
c) return on capital employed
d) net current asset ratio
e) liquid (acid test) ratio
f) rate of stock turnover (use closing inventory)
g) debtors' collection period
h) gearing ratio.

QUESTION 16

Compare the results of Lisus Ltd (Question 14) and Bredgol plc (Question 15).

CHAPTER
TWENTY TWO

Budgeting and budgetary control

A **budget** is a short-term financial plan. It is defined by CIMA as 'a plan expressed in money'.

Specification coverage:
AQA Unit 2

By the end of this chapter you should be able to:
- understand the need for budgeting
- explain the benefits of budgetary control
- explain the limitations of budgetary control
- prepare cash budgets.

We have already said that accounting fulfils two purposes:

- the stewardship function
- the management function.

The management function can be broken down into:

- planning
- coordinating
- communicating
- decision-making
- controlling.

Budgets help to achieve all five of these functions.

- The budgets produced by a business are 'plans expressed in money'. The budgets show what management hope to achieve in a future time period, both in terms of overall plans as well as departmental plans.
- The individual budgets are intertwined with each other – they depend on each other and influence each other. There is a need to ensure that the individual budgets are not contradictory or in conflict.
- Because of the inter-dependency and the coordination of the budgets, managers must communicate with each other when preparing budgets. They must also communicate the plans to staff below and management above.
- The nature of forecasting means that decisions have to be made. If profits are to increase then decisions must be made regarding sales, production levels, etc.
- Budgets will be compared with actual results. Remedial action can then be taken when actual results are worse than budgeted results. In cases where actual results are better than those budgeted, examples of good practice may be identified and copied elsewhere in the organisation.

BENEFITS OF BUDGETING

- The preparation of individual budgets means that planning must take place.
- These plans need to be prepared in a coordinated way and this requires communication throughout all levels of the business.
- The budgeting process defines areas of responsibility and targets to be achieved by different personnel.
- Budgets can act as a motivating influence at all levels – this is generally only true when all staff are involved in the preparation of budgets. If budgets are imposed on staff they might have a demotivating effect on morale.
- Budgets are a major part of the overall strategic plan of the business and as such individual departmental and personal goals are more likely to be an integral part of the 'bigger picture'.
- Budgets generally lead to a more efficient use of resources at the disposal of the business – leading to better control of costs.

LIMITATIONS OF BUDGETING

- Budgets are only as good as the data being used – if data is inaccurate the budget will be of little use. Should one departmental budget be overoptimistic or pessimistic, this will have a 'knock-on effect' to other associated budgets.
- Budgets might become an overriding goal – this could lead to a misuse of resources or incorrect decisions being made.
- Budgets might act as a demotivator if they are imposed rather than negotiated.
- Budgets might be based on plans that can be easily achieved – so making departments/managers appear to be more efficient than they really are. There is also a possibility that this could lead to complacency and/or underperformance.
- Budgets might lead to departmental rivalry.

CASH BUDGETS

A cash budget shows estimates of future cash incomes and cash expenditures. It is usually prepared monthly and includes both capital and revenue transactions. It is drawn up to help management be aware of any potential shortages or surpluses of cash resources that could occur, thus allowing management to make any necessary financial arrangements.

The preparation of a cash budget:

- helps to ensure that there is always sufficient cash available to allow the normal activities of the business to take place
- will highlight times when the business will have cash surpluses, thus allowing management time to arrange short-term investment of those surpluses in order to gain maximum return
- will highlight times when the business might have cash deficits, thus allowing management to arrange short-term alternative sources of finance through the arrangement of overdraft facilities, the arrangement of extended periods of credit or the restructuring of existing longer-term debts.

WORKED EXAMPLE

The following budgeted figures relate to Cropp Ltd for the three months ending 30 September.

	July	August	September
	£	£	£
Cash sales	10,000	10,000	12,000
Cash received from debtors	26,000	28,000	27,000
Payments made to creditors	9,000	11,000	12,000
Cash purchases	6,000	6,000	7,000
Payment for rent		21,000	
Payment for rates			1,200
Payment of wages	8,000	8,000	8,000
Payments for other expenses	2,750	3,750	2,800

It is expected that cash in hand at 30 June will be £820.

Required Prepare a cash budget for each of the three months ending 30 September.

WORKED EXAMPLE *continued*

Answer

	July	August	September
	£	£	£
Receipts:			
Cash sales	10,000	10,000	12,000
Cash received from debtors	26,000	28,000	27,000
	36,000	38,000	39,000
Payments:			
To creditors	9,000	11,000	12,000
Cash purchase	6,000	6,000	7,000
Rent		21,000	
Rates			1,200
Wages	8,000	8,000	8,000
Other expenses	2,750	3,750	2,800
	25,750	49,750	31,000
Balance brought forward	820	11,070	(680)
Receipts	36,000	38,000	39,000
	36,820	49,070	38,320
Payments	25,750	49,750	31,000
Balance carried forward	11,070	(680)	7,320

The cash budget shows that overdraft facilities must be arranged during August.

Note

There are alternative layouts. The one shown above is the version most frequently used.

● EXAMINATION TIP

Cash budgets are the most popular type of budget examined. It is well worth practising the layout shown.

Note

- Cash budgets include bank transactions. It is therefore possible to have negative balances in a cash budget.
- Only cash and bank items are included.
- The cash budget deals only with transactions involving the movement of cash. It therefore will not include any non-cash expenses such as a provision for depreciation or provision for doubtful debts.
- Some business studies textbooks refer to cash budgets as cash flow forecasts – these are the same.

WORKED EXAMPLE

Bradley Ltd sells one type of lathe at a selling price of £6,600 each. Fifty per cent is payable in the month of sale and 50% the following month. The lathes are purchased from a supplier at a cost of £1,500, paid in the month following purchase.

WORKED EXAMPLE *continued*

	Dec 20*8	Jan 20*9	Feb 20*9	March 20*9	April 20*9
Budgeted sales (in units)	4	6	3	5	7
Budgeted purchases	6	3	5	7	8
Budgeted operating costs are	£	£	£	£	£
Rent	1,500	1,500	1,500	1,500	1,650
Wages	16,000	19,000	19,000	19,000	19,000
Other expenses	4,700	5,200	5,100	4,800	5,000
Depreciation	2,500	2,500	2,500	2,500	2,500

All operating costs are paid in the month in which they occur.

The balance of cash in hand at 1 January 20*9 is expected to be £1,800.

Required Prepare a cash budget for each of the three months ending 31 March 20*9.

Answer

	January	February	March
	£	£	£
Receipts:			
Cash received from debtors	13,200 (Dec)	19,800 (Jan)	9,900 (Feb)
Cash received from debtors	19,800 (Jan)	9,900 (Feb)	16,500 (Mar)
	33,000	29,700	26,400
Payments:			
Payments to creditors	9,000 (Dec)	4,500 (Jan)	7,500 (Feb)
Rent	1,500	1,500	1,500
Wages	19,000	19,000	19,000
Other expenses	5,200	5,100	4,800
	34,700	30,100	32,800
Balance brought forward	1,800	100	(300)
Receipts	33,000	29,700	26,400
	34,800	29,800	26,100
Payments	34,700	30,100	32,800
Balance carried forward	100	(300)	(6,700)

Note

Depreciation has not been included – it is a NON-cash expense.

QUESTION 1

The following budgeted information relates to Rajpoot Ltd for the three months ending 30 October 20*9.

The cash balance at 1 August 20*9 is expected to be £2,100.

	August	September	October
	£	£	£
Cash sales	90,963	106,125	116,230
Payments to creditors	29,650	35,050	38,400
Payments for wages	19,100	28,000	21,500
Rent and rates	2,800	2,800	2,800
Other expenses	5,700	5,500	5,300
Payment for purchase of machine		84,000	
Depreciation on machine		700	700

Required Prepare a cash budget for each of the three months ending 30 October 20*9.

QUESTION 2

The following budgeted information relates to Chin Ltd for the three months ending 31 July 20*9.

The cash balance at 1 May 20*9 is expected to be £120.

	May	June	July
Cash sales	6,400	8,000	8,000
Receipts from debtors	36,800	59,200	56,000
Payments to creditors	25,600	28,800	27,200
Cash purchases	3,680	4,320	3,840
Rent	3,200	3,200	3,200
Wages	12,800	12,800	12,800
Other expenses	2,800	5,696	4,960
Purchase of shop fittings	3,000		
Depreciation of shop fittings	250	250	250

Required Prepare a cash budget for each of the three months ending 31 July 20*9.

MASTER BUDGET

Just like all the individual ingredients that are put together to make a successful meal, after all the separate budgets are prepared they are drawn together to prepare the master budget.

The master budget provides a summary of all the planned operations of the business for the period covered by the budgets. It is a sum of all the individual budgets prepared by the different parts of the business.

The master budget is made up of:

■ a budgeted manufacturing account (where appropriate)
■ a budgeted trading account
■ a budgeted profit and loss account
■ a budgeted balance sheet.

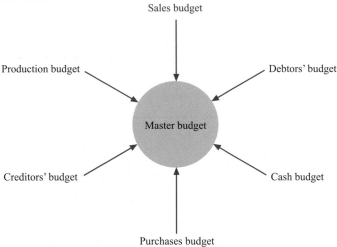

EXAMINATION TIP

Always show the months separately when preparing a cash budget.
The heading should be precise and must include the word 'budgeted' as well as the time period covered.

BUDGETARY CONTROL

Budgetary control delegates financial planning to managers. It evaluates their performance by continuously comparing actual results achieved by their departments against those set in the budget.

Variances arise when there is a difference between actual and budgeted figures.
Favourable variances increase profits.
Adverse variances reduce profits.

Responsibility for variances rests with departmental heads. The process requires that variances are analysed and in the case of adverse variances any necessary remedial action is taken.

The benefits and limitations of budgeting outlined at the start of the chapter also apply to budgetary control.

Chapter summary

- Budgets are an important part of the management function.
- They are plans expressed in money.
- Budgets help with planning and control of a business.
- Individual departmental budgets are summarised in the master budget.
- Cash budgets are the most frequently examined budget.

SELF-TEST QUESTIONS

- Define a budget.
- Identify two functions of budgeting.
- Identify two benefits of budgeting.
- Identify two limitations of budgeting.
- Identify one reason why a cash budget might be prepared.
- Explain why depreciation is not included in a cash budget.
- What is meant by the term 'master budget'.
- Name one component of a master budget.
- Explain the term 'variance'.

TEST QUESTIONS

QUESTION 3

The following budgeted information is available for Hunter Ltd:

	January	February	March	April
	£	£	£	£
Credit sales	21,000	28,000	30,000	31,000
Cash purchases	8,000	12,000	9,000	10,000
Cash expenses	21,000	20,000	22,000	18,000
Cash purchase of office machinery		24,000		
Depreciation of office machinery		200	200	200

It is expected that the cash balance at 1 February will be £3,200.

Debtors are expected to settle their debts one month after sales have taken place.

Required Prepare a cash budget for each of the three months ending 30 April.

QUESTION 4

The following budgeted information is available for Slipper Ltd:

	February	March	April	May
	£	£	£	£
Sales	40,000	38,000	39,000	41,000
Cash purchases	14,000	12,000	13,000	15,000
Cash expenses	16,000	18,000	17,000	19,000
Cash purchase of machinery		60,000		
Depreciation of machinery		500	500	500

It is expected that the cash balance at 1 March will be £2,900.

Cash sales are expected to be 10% of total sales.

Debtors are expected to settle their debts one month after the sales have taken place.

Required Prepare a cash budget for each of the three months ending 31 May.

QUESTION 5

The following budgeted information is given for Singh Ltd:

	March	April	May	June
	£	£	£	£
Cash sales	50,000	40,000	50,000	56,000
Purchases	20,000	30,000	25,000	35,000
Cash expenses	21,000	16,000	24,000	20,000
Depreciation of fixed assets	1,000	1,000	1,000	1,000

It is expected that the cash balance at 1 April will be £1,500 overdrawn.

Five per cent of purchases are expected to be for cash.

Creditors will be paid in the month following purchase.

Required Prepare a cash budget for each of the three months ending 30 June.

QUESTION 6

The following budgeted information is given for O'Casey Ltd:

	April	May	June	July
	£	£	£	£
Cash sales	40,000	60,000	80,000	30,000
Purchases	20,000	20,000	30,000	30,000
Cash expenses	15,000	10,000	14,000	13,000
Depreciation of fixed assets	1,500	1,500	1,500	1,500

It is expected that the cash balance at 1 May will be £800 overdrawn.

Ten per cent of purchases are expected to be for cash.

Creditors will be paid in the month following purchase.

Required Prepare a cash budget for each of the three months ending 31 July.

QUESTION 7

The following budgeted information relates to the business of Pierre:

	May	June	July	August	September
	£	£	£	£	£
Sales	64,000	62,000	60,000	65,000	64,000
Purchases	30,000	32,000	38,000	42,000	39,000
Wages	12,500	12,500	13,000	12,500	12,500
Other expenses	8,500	8,700	8,300	8,500	8,500
Cash purchase of shop fittings			14,000		
Depreciation of shop fittings	150	150	150	150	150

It is expected that:

- the cash balance at 1 June will be £350 overdrawn
- 5% of sales will be for cash
- 10% of purchases will be cash purchases
- debtors will pay one month after sale
- creditors will be paid two months after purchase
- wages and other expenses are paid as incurred.

Required Prepare a cash budget for each of the three months ending 30 September.

QUESTION 8

The following information relates to the business of Marcel:

	June	July	August	September	October
	£	£	£	£	£
Sales	34,000	36,000	35,000	34,000	37,000
Purchases	15,000	16,000	15,000	15,000	16,000
Wages	5,600	5,700	5,600	5,800	5,600
Rent	2,000	2,000	2,000	2,000	2,000
Other expenses	4,800	4,900	4,300	4,000	5,000
Cash purchase of delivery van			17,000		
Depreciation of vehicles	300	300	600	600	600

It is expected that:

- the cash balance at 1 August will be £2,570
- 10% of sales will be cash sales
- 10% of purchases will be for cash
- debtors will pay two months after sale
- creditors will be paid one month after purchase
- wages, rent and other expenses will be paid as incurred.

Required Prepare a cash budget for each of the three months ending 31 October.

QUESTION 9

Tommy Chan supplies the following budgeted information relating to his business:

	August	September	October	November	December
	£	£	£	£	£
Sales	23,000	24,000	29,000	34,000	43,000
Purchases	12,000	13,000	15,000	24,000	35,000
Wages	4,500	4,500	4,500	6,000	6,500
Rent	200	200	200	225	225
Other expenses	1,750	1,850	3,400	1,600	980
Depreciation of office equipment	450	450	450	450	450

It is expected that:

- the cash balance at 1 October will be £670
- 10% of all sales will be on credit
- 10% of purchases will be for cash
- debtors will settle their debts in the month following sale
- creditors will be paid two months after purchase
- rent is payable monthly in advance
- wages and other expenses will be paid as incurred.

Required Prepare a cash budget for each of the three months ending 31 December.

QUESTION 10

Andy Gillespie supplies the following budgeted information relating to his business:

	May	June	July	August	September
	£	£	£	£	£
Sales	34,000	35,000	37,000	40,000	35,000
Cash sale of old office machine			150		
Profit on sale of machine			50		
Purchases	16,000	16,500	17,000	19,000	15,000
Cash purchase of new office machine			1,800		
Wages	5,600	5,500	5,600	5,500	5,600
Other expenses	4,570	4,700	3,950	4,780	5,400
Depreciation of office equipment	250	250	265	265	265

It is expected that:

- the cash balance at 1 July will be £580 overdrawn
- 30% of sales will be cash sales
- 20% of purchases will be for cash

- 50% of credit sale customers will pay in the month following sale and the remainder will pay the following month
- creditors will be paid two months after purchase
- wages will be paid in the month after they are incurred
- other expenses will be paid for as incurred.

Required Prepare a cash budget for each of the three months ending 30 September.

INTRODUCING ACCOUNTING FOR AS

CHAPTER ONE

1 Money owed to Kellogs. HP debt.

3 Capital £58,000; fixed assets £60,000; capital £15,000; current liabilities, £4,000; current assets £15,000.

5 CA; FA; CA; CA; FA; FA.

7 Carole's capital: £214,000.

9 **Sandeep**

Balance Sheet at 31 January 20*8

	£
Fixed assets	
Tools at cost	250
Vehicle at cost	8,000
	8,250
Current assets	
Stock of paint	110
	8,360
Capital	4,300
Long term liability	
Bank loan	4,000
Current liability:	
Creditor	60
	8,360

11 **Sandra**

Balance sheet at 31 March 20*8

	£
Fixed assets	
Premises at cost	40,000
Machinery at cost	10,000
Office equipment at cost	4,000
Vehicle at cost	9,000
	63,000
Stock	4,000
Debtors	1,200
Bank	800
	6,000
Current liabilities	
Creditors	500
	5,500
	68,500
Capital	50,500
Long term liability	
Bank loan	18,000
	68,500

13 Capital shows the amount that the business 'owes' the proprietor, so the accountant is correct.

CHAPTER TWO

1 A balance sheet can be drawn up at any time.

3 Flowers, crisps and vegetables are all drawings.

5 Profit £5,400

7 Loss £37,300

9 Loss £18,250

11 Profit £8,000

CHAPTER THREE

1 Capital; worth.

3 Jeans; sweatshirts, trainers and leather jackets are all purchases.

---

5 **Biddulph**

Trading Account for the year ended 31 March 20*8

	£	£
Sales		84,350
Less cost of sales		
Stock	4,560	
Purchases	47,800	
	52,360	
Stock	5,050	
		47,310
Gross profit		37,040

7 **Clary**

Trading account for the year ended 30 April 20*8

	£	£
Sales		52,900
Less cost of sales		
Stock	340	
Purchases	23,560	
	23,900	
Stock	530	
		23,370
Gross profit		29,530

9 **Joe**

Trading account for the year ended 31 December 20*8

	£	£
Sales		54,760
Less cost of sales		
Stock	238	
Purchases	34,930	
	35,168	
Stock	432	
		34,736
Gross profit		20,024

11 **Rob Berry**

Trading account for the year ended 30 November 20*8

	£	£	£
Sales			98,651
Returns inwards			421
			98,230
Less cost of sales			
Stock		1,657	
Purchases	54,672		
Returns outward	803		
		53,869	
		55,526	
Stock		2,004	
			53,522
Gross profit			44,708

13 Trading account for the year ended 30 April 20*8
Balance sheet at 31 December 20*8

15 Gross profit; £110,000.

17 Returns inwards; carriage inwards; opening stock.

19 Opening stock plus purchases minus returns outwards plus carriage inwards.

21

	£
Stock 1 July 20*8	256
Purchases	71,006
Goods available for sale	71,262

23 Del
Trading account for the year ended 31 January 20*3

	£	£
Sales		56,710
Stock	970	
Purchases	35,780	
	36,750	
Stock	1,050	
		35,700
Gross profit		21,010

25 Natalie
Trading Account for the year ended 31 January 20*8

	£	£	£
Sales			176,040
Returns inward			360
			175,680
Less cost of sales			
Stock		1,560	
Purchases	65,090		
Carriage inwards	960		
	66,050		
Returns outward	770		
	65,280		
		66,840	
Stock		1,640	
		65,200	
Gross profit			110,480

27 Mao
Trading account for the year ended 31 December 20*8

	£	£	£
Sales			342,960
Returns inward			4,532
			338,428
Less cost of sales			
Stock		12,651	
Purchases	175,873		
Carriage inwards	733		
	176,606		
Returns outward	1,364		
	175,242		
		187,893	
Stock		11,537	
		176,356	
Gross profit			162,072

CHAPTER FOUR

1 Your answer could include payments for rent, business rates, insurance, wages, electricity, gas, advertising, motor expenses, etc. Your answer should not have included capital expenditure, i.e. spending on the purchase of delivery vehicles; money spent on extending the store, etc.

3 Pierre Roi
Trading account for the year ended 31 December 20*8

	£	£
Sales		25,047
Less cost of sales		
Stock	613	
Purchases	14,661	
	15,274	
Stock	770	
		14,504
Gross profit		10,543

5 Jack
Profit and loss account for the year ended 31 January 20*8

	£	£
Gross profit		43,719
Less expenses		
Wages	15,437	
Motor expenses	2,864	
Rent and rates	1,442	
Insurances	3,669	
General expenses	8,742	
		32,154
Net profit		11,565

7 Terry
Trading and profit and loss account for the year ended 31 May 20*8

	£	£
Sales		65,782
Less cost of sales		
Stock	1,329	
Purchases	23,664	
	24,993	
Stock	1,275	
		23,718
Gross profit		42,064
Less expenses		
Wages	12,674	
Motor expenses	6,710	
General expenses	441	
Heat and light	1,375	
Advertising	2,674	
		23,874
Net profit		18,190

ANSWERS

9 Gwenelle
Trading and profit and loss account for the year ended 30 November 20*8

	£	£
Sales		325,007
Less cost of sales		
Stock	12,453	
Purchases	157,994	
	170,447	
Stock	10,661	
	159,786	
Gross profit		165,221
Less expenses		
Wages	56,743	
Rates	6,740	
Heat and light	5,441	
Advertising	1,250	
Insurance	6,750	
General expenses	7,531	
	84,455	
Net profit		80,766

11 Helen
Trading and profit and loss account for the year ended 31 March 20*8

	£	£
Sales		51,311
Returns inwards		367
		50,944
Less cost of sales		
Stock		1,554
Purchases	23,887	
Returns outwards	541	
	23,346	
		24,900
Stock		977
		23,923
Gross profit		27,021
Less expenses		
Wages	8,712	
Rates	2,350	
Heat and light	1,458	
Advertising	2,350	
Insurance	2,005	
General expenses	4,637	
		21,512
Net profit		5,509

13 Janice
Trading and Profit and Loss Account for the year ended 31 August 20*8

	£	£	£
Sales			93,673
Returns inwards			276
			93,397
Less cost of sales			
Stock		673	
Purchases	29,041		
Carriage inwards	452		
	29,493		
Returns outwards	450		
		29,043	
		29,716	
Stock		891	
			28,825
Gross profit			64,572
Less expenses			
Carriage outwards		5,675	
Wages		23,774	
General expenses		2,563	
Motor expenses		3,600	
Rent		895	
Rates		779	
Telephone		1,250	
Advertising		2,588	
Heat and light		772	
			41,896
Net profit			22,676

15 Catherine
Trading and profit and loss account for the year ended 31 March 20*8

	£	£
Sales		127,773
Returns inwards		321
		127,452
Less cost of sales		
Stock		1,549
Purchases	54,772	
Carriage inwards	270	
	55,042	
Return outwards	84	
	54,958	
		56,507
Stock		1,471
		55,036
Gross profit		72,416
Less expenses		
Carriage outwards	129	
Wages	41,005	
Motor expenses	2,756	
Rent	4,750	
Rates	1,254	
Insurance	2,674	
Advertising	1,547	
Heat and light	2,541	
Telephone	3,428	
General expenses	6,539	
		66,623
Net Profit		5,793

CHAPTER FIVE

1 Ashley Peacock
Trading and profit and loss account for the year ended 30 June 20*8

	£	£
Sales		175,672
Less cost of sales		
Stock	7,854	
Purchases	70,031	
	77,885	
Stock	9,004	
		68,881
Gross profit		106,791
Less expenses		
Wages and general expenses	38,962	
Repairs and renewals	7,459	
Rent and rates	5,350	
Insurance and advertising	5,312	
Motor expenses	13,674	
		70,757
Net profit		36,034

Balance sheet at 30 June 20*8

	£	£
Fixed assets		
Premises at cost		150,000
Machinery at cost		45,000
Van at cost		17,500
		212,500
Current assets		
Stock	9,004	
Debtors	13,563	
Bank	1,245	
	23,812	
Current liabilities		
Creditors	8,734	
		15,078
		227,578
Long term liability		
Loan		100,000
		127,578
Capital		108,044
Add profit		36,034
		144,078
Less drawings		16,500
		127,578

3 Leslie Harris
Trading and profit and loss account for the year ended 31 December 20*8

	£	£	£
Sales			102,367
Less cost of sales			
Stock		3,691	
Purchases	48 775		
Carriage inwards	693		
		49,468	
		53,159	
Stock		4,187	
			48,972
Gross profit			53,395
Less expenses			
Carriage outwards		528	
Wages and salaries		28,570	
Motor expenses		6,371	
Heat and light		2,448	
Advertising and insurance		3,691	
General expenses		7,999	
			49,607
Net profit			3,788

Balance sheet at 31 December 20*8

	£	£	£
Fixed assets			
Machinery at cost			85,750
Vehicles at cost			50,000
			135,750
Current assets			
Stock		4,187	
Debtors		5,367	
		9,554	
Current liabilities Creditors	3,753		
Bank o/draft	872		
		4,625	
			4,929
			140,679
Long-term liabilities			
Loan			100,000
			40,679
Capital			58,591
Add profit			3,788
			62,379
Less drawings			21,700
			40,679

CHAPTER SIX

1

Cash	
1634	899
	180
	328

Wages	
899	

Sales	
	1634
	65

Drawings	
180	

Motor expenses	
328	

Squash club	
65	

Bank	
671	350
	478
	345

Sales	
	671

3

Purchase	
350	

Insurance	
478	

Cash	
15	

Display unit	
	15

DVD player	
345	

5

Debit	Credit
Rent	Cash
Purchases	Knight
Cash	Sales
Wages	Bank
Fixed assets	Bank
Carriage inwards	Cash
Purchases	Cash
Motor expenses	Bank
Drawings	Cash
Fixed assets	Lock
Carriage outwards	Bank

7

Cash	
211	349
	62
	109
	210

Wages	
349	

Sales	
	211

Telephone	
62	

Purchase	
109	

Drawings	
210	

9

Sales GL	
1,287	
1,473	

Cash GL	
	1,287

Vehicle GL	
42 500	

Rekers PL	
	42,500

Purchase GL	
3,538	

Esso PL	
	3,538

I. Hurry SL	
1,473	

Cash register GL	
	2,650

Bank GL	
	2,650

---

5 Dratesh Narewal

Trading and profit and loss account for the year ended 31 March 20*8

	£	£
Sales		102,453
Returns inwards		743
		101,710
Less cost of sales		
Stock		995
Purchases	48,661	
Carriage inwards	1,539	
	50,200	
Returns outwards	911	49,289
		50,284
Stock		1,007
		49,277
Gross profit		52,433
Less expenses		
Carriage outwards	332	
Salaries	28,749	
Motor expenses	5,673	
Advertising	1,350	
Insurances	3,764	
Heat and light	2,479	
Rates	1,245	
General expenses	941	44,533
Net profit		7,900

Balance sheet at 31 March 20*8

	£	£	£
Fixed assets			
Premises at cost			65,000
Office equipment at cost			18,750
Motor vehicles at cost			35,000
			118,750
Current assets			
Stock		1,007	
Debtors		4,601	
		5,608	
Current liabilities			
Creditors	1,955		
Bank overdraft	351	2,306	
			3,302
			122,052
Long-term liability			
Loan			40,000
			82,052
Capital			98,827
Add profit			7,900
			106,727
Less drawings			24,675
			82,052

CHAPTER SEVEN

1

Andrew PL | 460
Peter PL | 742
Kijah PL | 593
Zara PL | 34
Purchase GL | 1829

3

PDB
Froot	213
Acme	54
Dixon	730
Gold	107
	1,104

Froot PL | 213
Acme PL | 54
Dixon PL | 730
Gold PL | 107
Purchase GL | 1,104

5

Parker SL | 439
Fitton SL | 29
Clive SL | 51
Gray SL | 882
Sales GL | 1,401

7

SDB
Rowan	91
Ash	631
Holly	76
Berry	522
	1,320

Rowan SL | 91
Ash SL | 631
Holly SL | 76
Berry SL | 522
Sales GL | 1320

9

Samson PL | 23
Suchard PL | 14
Tardy PL | 54
Returns outwards GL | 91

11

Sales GL | 3,642 | 188
Cash GL | 784
Dorak Ltd PL | 24 | 340
Purchase returns GL | 24

Bank GL | 3,642 | 166 | 320
Hitters Squash Club SL | 188
Telephone GL | 166

Wages GL | 784
Purchase GL | 340
Drawings GL | 320

13

Purchase GL | 457, 265
Bank GL | 395 | 421
Returns outward | 43

Cash GL | 759 | 457
Noel PL | 43 | 265
GL Wages GL | 421

Sales GL | 759, 395, 511
Daser Ltd SL | 511 | 165
Returns inwards GL | 165

11

Randall SL | 38
Returns inwards GL | 156

Frame SL | 103

13

Hamilton SL | 15

		Dr £	Cr £
15 June	Delivery van account	£35,000	
	Fogg's garage		£35,000

Delivery van purchased on credit from Fogg's garage

15

		Dr £	Cr £
6 January	Tippers Ltd	£200	
	Machinery account		£200

Sale of machine on credit to Tippers Ltd.

17

Cash book	Cash	Fixed asset
PDB	Purchases	Supplier's accounts
Cash book	Cash	Sales
Cash book	Purchases	Cash
Cash book	Bank	Customers' accounts
Cash book	Drawings	Cash
Cash book	Insurance	Cash
Journal	Buyer's account	Fixed asset
Cash book	Wages	Cash

19 PDB   CB   SRDB   J

CHAPTER EIGHT

1 £14 Cr; £14 Dr; £80 Dr; as brought down.

3

Sales
Bal c/d 798	750		
	48		
798	798		
	Bal b/d 798		

Chas | 48

Cash
750	100		
	78		
	69		
	Bal c/d 503		
750	750		
Bal b/d 503			

Purchases
330			
69	Bal c/d 399		
399	399		
Bal b/d 399			

Wages | 78

Rent | 100

Duncan | 330

Trial balance

	Dr £	Cr £
Sales		798
Cash	503	
Rent	100	
Chas (Debtor)	48	
Wages	78	
Duncan (Creditor)		330
Purchases	399	
	1,128	1,128

5

Motor Vehicle	GL	Asset	Debit
Rates	GL	Expense	Debit
Mortgage	GL	Liability	Credit
Carriage inwards	GL	Expense	Debit
Premises	GL	Asset	Debit
Quentin	SL	Asset	Debit
Capital	GL	Liability	Credit
Tara	PL	Liability	Credit
Purchases	GL	Expense	Debit
Insurance	GL	Expense	Debit
Sales	GL	Income/benefit	Credit
Carriage outwards	GL	Expense	Debit

7

	Gross profit	Net profit
Rent	No	Yes
Mortgage	No	No
Insurance	No	Yes
Drawings	No	No
Advertising	No	Yes
Returns outwards	Yes	Yes
Carriage outwards	No	Yes
Purchases	Yes	Yes

9 **Trial balance at 31 August 20*8**

	Dr £	Cr £
Capital		45,578
Vehicles at cost	43,500	
Office equipment at cost	17,600	
Debtors	4,656	
Creditors		2,873
Stock 1 September 20*7	4,502	
Purchases	56,221	
Sales		132,448
Wages	34,662	
Motor expenses	3,189	
Rent and rates	4,692	
Insurances	1,634	
Advertising	2,654	
General expenses	4,654	
Carriage inwards	543	
Carriage outwards	511	
Returns inwards	1,985	
Returns outwards		588
Bank balance	346	
Cash in hand	138	
	181,487	181,487

11 Compensating Commission Principle Omission.

13 **Journal**

	Dr £	Cr £
Rent	200	
Rates		200
Wages	400	
Suspense		400
Tom	146	
Suspense		146
Insurance	546	
Cash		546

Suspense account

	Dr £		Cr £
Trial balance difference	546	Wages	400
		Tom	146
	546		546

The credit side was the larger side.

15 **Journal**

	Dr £	Cr £
Suspense	642	
Beatrice		642
Returns inwards	100	
Suspense		100
Purchase	1,461	
Suspense		1,461
Sales	1,010	
Suspense		1,010

b)

Suspense account			
Beatrice	642	Returns inwards	100
Trial balance difference	1,929	Purchases	1,461
	2,571	Sales	1,010
			2,571

c) The credit side was the larger side.

d)

	£
Gross profit	48,712
Returns inwards	(100)
Purchases	(1,461)
Sales	(1,010)
Corrected gross profit	46,141

e)

	£
Net profit	13,467
Returns inwards	(100)
Purchases	(1,461)
Sales	(1,010)
Corrected net profit	10,896

CHAPTER NINE

1 PDB PRDB CB SDB CB.

3

SDB

Fallon	217
Slee	52
Earley	770
	1,039

PDB

Westby	179
Rawstron	731
Coulson	229
	1,139

Earley	
	770

Slee	
	52

Coulson	
	229

Rawstron	
	731

Sales ledger

Fallon	
217	

Purchase ledger

Westby	
	179

Purchase	
1,139	

General ledger

Sales	
	1,039

5

SDB

Davidson	59
Nixon	563
Nismo	518
	1,140

PDB

Sellars	911
Garewal	187
Chan	67
	1,165

SRDB

| Davidson | 19 |

PRDB

Sellars	45
Garewal	12
	57

Sales ledger

Davidson	
59	19

Nixon	
563	

Nismo	
518	

Purchase ledger

Sellars	
45	911

Garewal	
12	187

Chan	
	67

General ledger

Sales	
	1140

Purchase	
1165	

Returns inwards	
19	

Returns outwards	
	57

7

Purchase day book

Crosby	598
Cox	674
Patel	771
Freer	50
	2,093

Purchase returns day book

| Crosby | 140 |

Sales day book

Clements	456
Lycett	53
Clements	437
	946

Sales returns day book

| Clements | 34 |

Journal

	Dr		Cr
Delivery Van	23,580		
Austen			23,580

Sales Ledger

Clements	
456	34
437	

Lycett	
53	

Purchase ledger

Crosby	
140	598

Cox	
	674

Freer	
	50

Patel	
	771

Austen	
	23,580

General ledger

Sales	
	946

Returns inwards	
34	

Returns outwards	
	140

Van	
23,580	

Purchase	
2,093	

9

Purchase day book

Tunk	573
Tupp	880
Rult	349
	1,802

Sales day book

Thomas	97
Shah	254
	351

Sales returns day book

Thomas	97

Purchase returns day book

Tupp	108

Journal

	Dr	Cr
Display units	3,750	
Sheep Ltd		3,750

Cash book

752	
893	
439	
1,065	

Note: Debit entries in cash book. Cash book is a book of prime entry as well as being part of the double-entry system.

Sales ledger

Thomas	
97	97

Shah	
254	

Purchase ledger

Tunk	
	573

Tupp	
108	880

Rult	
	349

Sheep	
	3,750

General ledger

Sales	
	351
	752
	893
	439
	1,065

Purchases	
1,802	

Returns inwards	
97	

Returns outwards	
	108

Display units	
	3,750

CHAPTER TEN

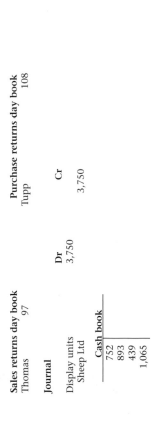

1

Cash book

Cling	176		Cleaning	94	
Sales	522		Motor expenses	51	
Laker	83		Wages	317	

3

Cash book

Hanks		138	Insurance		548
Sales		2,693	Wages		752
Kann		198	Drawings		150

5 Cash balance £746 debit.
Bank balance £2,066 debit.

7

Cash book

Sales		349		Electricity		163	
Ed			561	Bank	C	500	
Sales		670		Wages			471
Cash	C		500	Stationery		112	
				Balances c/d		244	590
		1,019	1,061			1,019	1,061
Balances b/d		244	590				

9

Cash book

Sales		1,792		Bank	C	1,500	
Cash	C		1,500	Rent			240
Burgess			286	Insurance		110	
Sales		135		Repairs			892
				Balances c/d		317	654
		1,927	1,786			1,927	1,786
Balances b/d		317	654				

11

Cash book

Sales			3,487	Motor expenses			345
Thompson		172		Rates			210
Sales		1,372		Bank	C	1,000	
Cash	C		1,000	Motor expenses		48	
				Balance c/d		496	3,932
		1,544	4,487			1,544	4,487
Balance b/d		496	3,932				

13

Cash book

Sales		2,380		Stationery		120	
Cash	C		1,950	Motor expenses		38	
Sales			2,785	Bank	C	1,950	
Bank	C	2,500		Todd			490
				Cash	C		2,500
				Wages		1,988	
				Balances c/d		784	1,745
		4,880	4,735			4,880	4,735
Balances b/d		784	1,745				

CHAPTER ELEVEN

1

Cash book

Balances b/d		217	1,132	Mowlem			834
Sales		912		Laker			137
McAllister			138	Purchases		126	
Sales		468		Purchases		488	
Tyson			1,172	Bank	C	750	
Cash	C		750	Balance c/d		233	221
		1,597	3,192			1,597	3,192
Balance b/d		233	2,221				

Sales ledger

McAllister	
	138

Tyson	
	1172

General ledger

Purchases	
126	
488	

Sales	
	912
	468

Purchase ledger

Mowlem	
834	

Laker	
137	

CHAPTER TWELVE

1 Credit bank £200; Debit cash £1730; Credit bank £190; Credit discount received £10; Debit bank £3430; Credit cash £435; Debit cash £2000 and Credit bank £2000 contra.

3 Bank reconciliation statement at 31 July

Balance at bank as per cash book	189
Add un-presented cheque	312
Balance at bank as per bank statement	501

5 Bank reconciliation statement at 30 November

Balance at bank as per cash book	85
Less lodgements not yet credited	29
Balance at bank as per bank statement	56

7 Bank reconciliation statement at 31 January

Balance at bank as per cash book	452
Add unpresented cheques	456
	908
Less lodgements not yet credited	412
Balance at bank as per bank statement	496

9 Cash book

	£		£
Bal b/d	146.44	Bank chgs	12.52
		Overdraft	26.78
		Interest	246.38
		Electricity	432.12
Bal c/d	432.12		432.12
	432.12	Bal b/d	432.12

Bank reconciliation statement at 31 January

	£	£
Balance at bank as per cash book		(432.12)
Add unpresented cheques	129.81	
	17.26	147.07
		(285.05)
Less lodgement not yet credited		530.22
Balance at bank as per bank statement		(815.27)

11 Cash book

	£		£
Balance b/d	180	Lodgements	180
Lodgement	200		
Cr. Trans	165	Balance c/d	365
	545		545
Balance b/d	365		

Bank reconciliation statement at 30 April

Balance at bank as per cash book	365
Add un-presented cheques	493
Balance at bank as per bank statement	858

3

Cash book

Dr			Cr		
Balance b/d	30	376	Purchases	88	308
Gholar		600	Purchases	845	613
Sales		210	Breem		250
Tempest	12	120	Bank	466	
Trevor	8		Balance c/d	250	1,516
Sales C	50	1,556		1,399	1,556
	1,399				
Balance b/d	228			228	

Purchase ledger

Breem

	40		40

Gholar

Bank	600		
Dis Al	30		

Sales ledger

Tempest

Bank	210		
Dis Al	12		

Trevor

Bank	120		
Dis Al	8		

General ledger

Sales

			845
			466

Purchases

	308		
	613		

Discount allowed

	50		

5

Cash book

Dr			Cr		
Balance b/d	237	2,875	Balance b/d C	1,500	
Sales	1,658		Bank C	3,500	3,500
Cash C	3,500		Cash	657	345
Bank C			Wages	812	563
Biggs	3		Foggerty	65	
Nelson	13		Electricity		
Mandosa	3		Bank C	2,500	
Sales C	2,319		Balance c/d	1,749	
Cash					
Balance c/d	29	7,283		5	7,714
	7,714				7,283
Balance b/d	152			152	1,749

Purchase ledger

Foggerty

CB	345		
DR	5		

Biggs

CB	657		
DA	13		

Sales ledger

Nelson

		CB	812
		DA	13

Mandosa

		CB	65
		DA	3

General ledger

Sales

			1,658
			2,319

Discount received

			5

Discount allowed

	29		

Wages

	3,562		

Electricity

	563		

13 Cash book

	£		£
Rodders	66	Balance b/d	590
		Interest	83
		Water	31
Balance c/d	638		704
	704		
		Balance b/d	638

Bank reconciliation statement at 31 March

	£
Balance at bank as per cash balance	(638)
Add un-presented cheques	938
	300
Less lodgements not yet credited	206
Balance at bank as per bank statement	94

CHAPTER THIRTEEN

1 Purchases ledger; Sales ledger; General ledger.

3 Sales ledger control account for July 20*8

	£		£
Balance b/d	3,830	Cash	7,200
Sales	9,600	Discount allowed	910
		Returns inwards	340
		Balance c/d	4,980
	13,430		13,430
Balances b/d	4,980		

5 Purchase ledger control account for April 20*8

	£		£
Cash	9,300	Balance b/d	2,445
Discount received	700	Purchases	9,200
Returns outwards	150		
Balance c/d	1,495		
	11,645		11,645
		Balance b/d	1,495

7 Purchase ledger control account for October 20*8

	£		£
Cash	9,779	Balance b/d	3,741
Discount received	1,230	Purchases	10,452
Balance c/d	3,184		
	14,193		14,193
		Balances b/d	3,184

9 Sales ledger control account for December 20*8

	£		£
Balance b/d	1,006	Cash	4,921
Sales	5,408	Discount allowed	561
		Balance c/d	932
	6,414		6,414
Balance b/d	932		

11 Purchase ledger control account for May 20*8

	£		£
Cash	109,621	Balance b/d	22,556
Discount received	3,551	Purchases	117,004
Returns outwards	1,572		
Balance c/d	24,816		
	139,560		139,560
		Balance b/d	24,816

13 Sales ledger control account for August 20*8

	£		£
Balance b/d	456	Cash	8,634
Sales	10,674	Discount allowed	1,329
		Returns inwards	566
		Balance c/d	601
	11,130		11,130
Balance b/d	601		

15 Purchase ledger control account for October 20*3

	£		£
Balance b/d	37	Balance b/d	3,551
Cash	12,440	Purchases	15,338
Discount received	1,084		
Returns outwards	32		
Balance c/d	5,450	Balance c/d	154
	19,043		19,043
Balance b/d	154	Balance b/d	5,450

17 Sales ledger control account for December 20*8

	£		£
Balance b/d	7,449	Balance b/d	247
Sales	43,650	Cash	39,754
		Discount allowed	166
		Returns inwards	510
		Transfers to purchase ledger	300
Balance c/d	188	Balance c/d	10,310
	51,287		51,287
Balance b/d	10,310	Balance b/d	188

Purchase ledger control account for December 20*8

	£		£
Cash	19,003	Balance b/d	342
Discount received	251	Purchases	20,005
Returns outwards	543		
Transfers to sales ledger	300		
Balance c/d	4,163	Balance c/d	45
	24,602		24,602
Balance b/d	45	Balance b/d	4,163

CHAPTER FOURTEEN

1

	Profit and loss entry	Current liability
	£	£
Wages	43,872	872
Motor expenses	9,350	750
Telephone	2,680	280
Advertising	2,360	560
Heating and lighting	2,391	391

3 Profit and loss account extract for the year ended 30 November 20*8

	£	
Gross profit		72,385
Commission receivable		8,775
		81,160

Balance sheet extract at 30 November 20*8

	£
Current asset	
Commission receivable owing	1,775

5 Ben Trent

Trading and profit and loss account for the year ended 31 March 20*8

	£	£
Sales		123,563
Less cost of sales		
Purchases	44,832	
Stock	8,459	
		36,373
Gross Profit		87,190
Less expenses		
Rent	5,600	
Rates	2,340	
Wages	48,766	
Motor expenses	2,357	
General expenses	7,459	
		66,522
Net profit		20,668

Balance sheet as at 31 March 20*8

	£	£
Fixed assets		
Equipment at cost		8,000
Van at cost		12,000
		20,000
Current assets		
Stock	8,459	
Trade debtors	8,564	
Bank	1,340	
	18,363	
Current liabilities		
Trade creditors	5,430	
Accruals	874	
	6,304	
		12,059
		32,059
Capital		26,061
Add profit		20,668
		46,729
Less drawings		14,670
		32,059

7 Toby Moore

Trading and profit and loss account for the year ended 31 July 20*8

	£	£	£
Sales			134,908
Returns inwards			453
			134,455
Less cost of sales			
Stock		8,756	
Purchases	54,731		
Returns outwards	612		
		54,119	
		62,875	
Stock		9,315	
		53,560	
Gross profit			80,895
Less expenses			
Wages		34,770	
Motor expenses		1,443	
Insurance		822	
General expenses		4,119	
		41,154	
Net profit		39,741	

Balance sheet at 31 July 20*8

	£	£	£
Fixed assets			
Premises at cost			65,000
Machinery at cost			16,000
Vehicles at cost			7,400
			88,400
Current assets			
Stock		9,315	
Trade debtors		811	
Prepayment		58	
Cash in hand		282	
		10,466	
Current liabilities			
Trade creditors		2,678	
Bank overdraft		4,637	
		7,315	
			3,151
			91,551
Capital			76,810
Add profit			39,741
			116,551
Less drawings			25,000
			91,551

9 Seok Chin
Trading and profit and loss account for the year ended 30 April 20*8

	£	£	£
Sales			407,843
Returns inwards			1,453
			406,390
Less cost of sales			
Stock		23,510	
Purchases	238,056		
Returns outwards	573		
		237,483	
		260,993	
Stock		26,449	
			234,544
Gross profit			171,846
Less expenses			
Carriage outwards		1,323	
Rates		1,318	
Wages		75,016	
Motor expenses		32,540	
Telephone		3,760	
General expenses		8,116	
			122,073
Net Profit			49,773

Balance sheet as at 30 April 20*8

	£	£	£
Fixed assets			
Premises at cost			80,000
Equipment at cost			23,000
Vehicles at cost			84,000
			187,000
Current assets			
Stock		26,449	
Trade debtors		34,534	
Prepayments		342	
Cash		377	
		61,702	
Current liabilities			
Creditors	23,665		
Bank overdraft	7,439		
Accruals	2,007		
		33,111	
			28,591
			215,591
Long-term liability			
Bank loan			120,000
			95,591
Capital			72,318
Add profit			49,773
			122,091
Less drawings			26,500
			95,591

11 Julie Wreak
Trading and profit and loss account for the year ended 31 May 20*8

	£	£	£
Sales			407,563
Returns inwards			1,554
			406,009
Less cost of sales			
Stock		36,734	
Purchases	239,075		
Carriage inwards	347		
		239,422	
Returns outwards		658	
		238,764	
		275,498	
Stock		34,897	
			240,601
Gross profit			165,408
Rent receivable			3,000
			168,408
Less expenses			
Carriage outwards		1,453	
Wages		90,580	
Motor expenses		34,527	
Stationery		3,642	
Rates		2,345	
Insurances		4,111	
Loan interest		3,000	
			139,658
Net profit			28,750

Balance sheet at 31 May 20*8

	£	£	£
Fixed assets			
Premises at cost			240,000
Office equipment at cost			17,000
Lorry at cost			45,000
			302,000
Current assets			
Stock		34,897	
Trade debtors		28,976	
Prepayments		1,397	
Cash		754	
		66,024	
Current liabilities			
Trade creditors	18,785		
Bank overdraft	2,457		
Accruals	6,838		
		28,080	
			37,944
			339,944
Long-term Liability			
Bank loan			250,000
			89,944
Capital			95,894
Add net profit			28,750
			124,644
Less drawings			34,700
			89,944

CHAPTER FIFTEEN

1

Advertising

	120	P & L a/c	1,340
	340		
	720		
	160		
	1,340		1,340

Rates

	1,400	P & L a/c	2,800
	1,400		
	2,800		2,800

Motor expenses

	2,160	P & L a/c	3,906
	814		
	932		
	3,906		3,906

Rent received

P & L a/c	2,400		600
			600
			600
			600
	2,400		2,400

Purchases

	9,000	Trading a/c	14,000
	2,000		
	3,000		
	14,000		14,000

Machinery

	14,000	Bal c/d	26,000
	12,000		
	26,000		26,000
Bal b/d	26,000		

Sales

Trading a/c	27,500		4,000
			12,000
			7,000
			4,500
	27,500		27,500

Discount received

P & L a/c	229		121
			72
			36
	229		229

Trading account

Purchases	14,000	Sales	27,500

Profit and loss account

Advertising	1,340	Rent received	2,400
Rates	2,800	Discount rec'd	229
Motor expenses	3,906		

Balance sheet

Fixed assets
Machinery 26,000

3 Tom Jackson

Trading account for the year ended 29 February 20*8

	£	£
Sales		87,503
Less cost of sales		
Stock	2,351	
Purchases	52,765	
	55,116	
Stock	3,722	51,394
Gross profit		36,109

Stock account

28 Feb 20*7 Trading a/c	2,351	29 Feb 20*8 Trading a/c	2,351
29 Feb 20*8 Trading a/c	3,722		

5 Cary Thims

Trading account for the year ended 31 March 20*8

	£	£
Sales		56,880
Returns inwards		239
		56,641
Less cost of sales		
Stock	1,768	
Purchases	23,771	
	25,539	
Stock	1,439	24,100
Gross Profit		32,541

7

Table	£145
Chair	£50
Bed	£170

9

Rent account

Bank	900	P & L a/c	3,600
Bank	900		
Bank	900		
Balance c/d	900		
	3,600		3,600
		Balance b/d	900

11

Ford	£1180
Citröen	£440
Skoda	£560

13

Trial balance totals £124,442 after including returns outwards £210 credit; rates £1,250 debit; telephone £850 debit; drawings £16,300 debit; stock £3,240 debit. Accounts are closed with a debit entry £210 in returns outwards account; credit entry rates account £1,250; credit entry telephone account £850; credit entry drawings account £16,300 (debited in capital account); credit entry £3,240.

Stock

Dr			Cr
31 Mar 20*7 Trading a/c	3,240	31 Mar 20*8 Trading a/c	3,240
21 Mar 20*8 Trading a/c	3,970		

Tammy Mount
Trading and profit and loss account for the year ended 31 March 20*8

	£	£
Sales		102,786
Returns inwards		460
		102,326
Less cost of sales		
Stock	3,240	
Purchases	41,903	
Returns outwards	210	41,693
		44,933
Stock		3,970
		40,963
Gross profit		61,363
Less expenses		
Wages	25,600	
Rates	1,250	
Telephone	850	27,700
Net profit		33,663

Balance sheet at 31 March 20*8

	£	£
Fixed assets		
Fixtures and fittings at cost		12,500
Vehicles at cost		17,300
		29,800
Current assets		
Stock	3,970	
Trade debtors	3,791	
Bank balance	1,248	
	9,009	
Current liabilities		
Trade creditors	4,286	
		4,723
		34,523
Capital		17,160
Add profit		33,663
		50,823
Less drawings		16,300
		34,523

15 Trial balance totals £259,516 after including:
Debits – Carriage outwards £1,642; Rent £6,000; Advertising £2,875; Stock £7,621.
Credit – Capital £83,072.

Stock account

31 Aug 20*7 Trading a/c	7,621	31 Aug 20*8 Trading a/c	7,621
31 Aug 20*8 Trading a/c	8,470		8,470

Carriage outwards

	934	P & L a/c	1,642
	127		
	406		
	175		
	1,642		1,642

Rent payable

	1,500	P & L a/c	6,000
	1,500		
	1,500		
	1,500		
	6,000		6,000

Advertising

	76	P & L a/c	2,875
	211		
	99		
	2,489		
	2,875		2,875

Capital account

	83,072

Chetan Nath
Trading and profit and loss account for the year ended 31 August 20*8

	£	£
Sales		172,460
Less cost of sales		
Stock	7,621	
Purchases	81,236	
Carriage inwards	1,810	
	83,046	
	90,667	
Stock	8,470	
		82,197
Gross profit		90,263
Less expenses		
Carriage outwards	1,642	
Rent	6,000	
Rates	1,580	
Wages	32,460	
Advertising	2,875	44,557
Net profit		45,706

Balance sheet at 31 August 20*8

	£	£
Fixed assets		
Premises at cost		60,000
Equipment at cost		24,000
		84,000
Current assets		
Stock	8,470	
Debtors	8,491	
Bank	8,701	
	25,662	
Current liabilities		
Creditors	3,984	
		21,678
		105,678
Capital		83,072
Add Profit		45,706
		128,778
Less drawings		23,100
		105,678

CHAPTER SIXTEEN
1

Delivery vehicles account

1 January 20*7 Bank	28,000

Provision for depreciation of delivery van

31 December 20*8 Balance c/d	10,000	31 December 20*7 Profit and loss a/c	5,000
		31 December 20*8 Profit and loss a/c	5,000
	10,000		10,000
		1 January 20*9 Balance b/d	10,000

CHAPTER SEVENTEEN

1

Bad debts account

Biff	451	31 December 20*8 Profit and loss a/c	662
Treadus	159		
Victor	52		
	662		662

3

Provision for doubtful debts account

		Year 1 Profit and loss a/c	400
		Year 2 Profit and loss a/c	20
Year 2 Balance c/d	420		420
	420		420
		Year 3 Balance b/d	420
Year 3 Balance c/d	500	Year 3 Profit and loss a/c	80
	500		500
		Year 4 Balance b/d	500

5

Bad debts account

31 January 20*6 Debtor	700	31 January 20*6 P & L a/c	700
31 January 20*8 Debtor	200	31 January 20*8 P & L a/c	200

Provision for doubtful debts account

31 January 20*7 Balance c/d	362.50	31 January 20 *6 P & L a/c	300.00
		31 January 20*7 P & L a/c	62.50
	362.50		362.50
31 January 20*8 Balance c/d	395.00	1 February 20*7 Bal b/d	362.50
		31 January 20 *8 P & L a/c	32.50
	395.00		395.00
		1 February 20 *8 Bal b/d	395.00

7

Profit and loss account extracts for year ended

31 January 20*6	£	31 January 20*7	£	31 January 20*8	£
Bad debts	700	Provision for doubtful debts	62.50	Bad debts	200.00
Provision for doubtful debts	300			Provision for doubtful debts	32.50

Balance sheet extracts at

31 January 20*6	£	£	31 January 20*7	£	£
Debtors	12,000		Debtors	14,500.00	
Less provision	300	11,700	less provision	362.50	14,137.50

31 January 20*8	£	£
Debtors	15,800	
Less provision	395	15,405

Provision	Profit and loss a/c entry	Balance sheet detail		
230	50 expense	Drs	23,000	
		less prov	230	22,770
270	40 expense	Drs	27,000	
		less prov	270	26,730
250	20 income	Drs	25,000	
		less prov	250	24,750
260	10 expense	Drs	26,000	
		less prov	260	25,740

3

Machinery account

1 April 20*6 Bank	13,000	
1 April 20*7 Bank	16,000	
1 Oct 20*7 Bank	10,000	

Provision for depreciation of machinery

31 March 20 *7 Profit and loss a/c	1,300
31 March 20 *8 Profit and loss a/c	3,400

Balance Sheet extracts

at 31 March 20*7			at 31 March 20*8		
Machinery at cost	13,000		Machinery at cost	39,000	
Less depreciation	1,300	11,700	Less depreciation	4,700	34,300

5

Disposal of vehicles account

Vehicle	21,000	Depreciation	19,000
		Cash	800
		P & L a/c	
		Loss on disposal	1,200
	21,000		21,000

Balance sheet extract at 30 September 20*8

Vehicles at cost	99,000	
Depreciation	78,750	20,250

7 £1,900

9 £12,000; £7,200; £4,320.

11

Provision for depreciation of equipment

31 December 20*6 Profit and loss a/c	6,000
31 December 20*7 Profit and loss a/c	6,000

13

Provision for depreciation of lorry account

28 February 20*7 Balance c/d	117,600	28 February 20*6 Profit and loss a/c	84,000
		28 February 20*7 Profit and loss a/c	33,600
	117,600		117,600
		1 March 20*7 Balance b/d	117,600
		29 February 20* Profit and loss a/c	13,440

15

Disposal of machinery account

Machinery	45,000	Depreciation	9,000
		Cash	31,000
		Profit and loss a/c loss on disposal	5,000
	45,000		45,000

17

Disposal of machinery account

Machinery	19,000	Depreciation	6,000
Profit and loss a/c profit on disposal	250	Cash	13,250
	19,250		19,250

19

Disposal of vehicle account

Vehicle	26,000	Depreciation	16,640
Profit and loss account profit on disposal	140	Cash	9,500
	26,140		26,140

9

Bad debts account

Defius	154	Profit and loss a/c	1,206
Ralph	345		
Iain	620		
Gordon	87		
	1,206		1,206

11 Provision for doubtful debts £1,000.

Balance sheet extract at 31 March 20*8

	£	£
Debtors	40,000	
Provision for doubtful debts	1,000	39,000

13 £234 + £258 + £38.10 + £36.50 + £128 = £694.60

Balance sheet extract at 31 May 20*8

	£	£
Trade debtors	38,940.00	
Provision for doubtful debts	694.60	38,245.40

15

Provision for doubtful debts

30 April 20*8 Balance c/d	1,100	1 May 20*7 Balance b/d	850
		30 April 20*8 Profit and loss a/c	250
	1,100		1,100
		1 May 20*8 Balance b/d	1,100

Bad debts account

P Snow	45		
J Gatwood	239		
F Golightly	213		
D Mark	651	30 April 20*8 Profit and loss a/c	1,148
	1,148		1,148

Profit and loss account extract for the year ended 30 April 20*8

	£
Bad debts	1,148
Provision for doubtful debts	250

Balance sheet extract at 30 April 20*8

	£	£
Debtors	44,000	
Provision for doubtful debts	1,100	42,900

17

Geot Ltd

Bad debt recovered	288	Cash	288

Cash

Geot	288		288

Bad debt recovered account

P & L a/c	288	Geot	288

19

Provision for doubtful debts account

31 October 20*8 Balance c/d	2,050	1 November 20*7 Balance b/d	1,750
		31 October 20*8 Profit and loss a/c	300
	2,050		2,050
		1 November 20*8 Balance b/d	2,050

Bad debts account

Thaker	216	P & L a/c	606
Simms	97		
Hurd	184		
Fletcher	109		
	606		606

Broadbent

Bad debt recovered a/c	246	Cash	246

Bad debt recovered account

Profit and loss a/c	246	Broadbent	246

Profit and loss account extract for the year ended 31 October 20*8

	£
Bad debts (606 – 246)	360
Provision for doubtful debts	300

CHAPTER EIGHTEEN

1 Hanif Mohammed

Trading and profit and loss account for the year ended 29 February 20*8

	£	£
Sales		123,601
Less cost of sales		
Stock	8,963	
Purchases	56,817	
	65,780	
Stock	7,432	58,348
Gross profit		65,253
Less expenses		
Wages	39,113	
Rent	2,200	
Light and heat	8,617	
General expenses	2,834	
Motor expenses	4,619	57,383
Net profit		7,870

Balance sheet at 29 February 20*8

	£	£
Fixed assets		
Premises at cost	100,000	
Equipment at cost	16,000	
Delivery van at cost	8,000	124,000
Current assets		
Stock	7,432	
Debtors	8,607	
Bank	1,281	
Cash	45	
	17,365	
Less current liabilities		
Creditors	7,614	
Accrued expenses	200	
	7,814	9,551
		133,551
Capital		139,181
Add profit		7,870
		147,051
Less drawings		13,500
		133,551

3 Hibo Ahmed

Trading and profit and loss account for the year ended 31 May 20*8

	£	£
Sales		206,981
Less cost of sales		
Stock	12,461	
Purchases	132,778	
	145,239	
Stock	13,106	
		132,133
Gross profit		74,848
Less expenses		
Wages	47,151	
Rent	6,000	
Insurance	1,759	
Motor expenses	8,123	
Advertising	2,164	
General expenses	8,837	
		74,034
Net profit		814

Balance Sheet at 31 May 20*8

		£	£
Fixed assets			
Office equipment at cost			32,716
Delivery vehicle at cost			23,500
			56,216
Current assets			
Stock		13,106	
Debtors		5,871	
Prepayment		628	
Cash		236	
		19,841	
Less current liabilities			
Bank overdraft	4,798		
Creditors	7,162		
Accrued expenses	814		
		12,774	
			7,067
			63,283
Capital			100,969
Add profit			814
			101,783
Less drawings			38,500
			63,283

5 Lynn Parker

Trading and profit and loss account for the year ended 31 October 20*8

	£	£	£
Sales		192,587	
Less returns inwards		1,111	
			191,476
Less cost of sales			
Stock		2,468	
Purchases	64,128		
Less returns outwards	382		
		63,746	
		66,214	
Stock		3,199	
			63,015
Gross profit			128,461
Less expenses			
Wages		67,491	
Rent and rates		5,400	
Advertising and insurances		3,780	
Light and heat		6,437	
Motor expenses		18,542	
Depreciation: office equipment		1,706	
vehicles		6,624	
			109,980
Net profit			18,481

Balance sheet at 31 October 20*8

	£	£	£
Fixed assets			
Office equipment		17,400	
Less depreciation		10,580	
			6,820
Delivery vehicles		46,000	
Less depreciation		36,064	
			9,936
			16,756
Current assets			
Stock		3,199	
Trade debtors		14,673	
Cash		430	
		18,302	
Less current liabilities			
Trade creditors	5,799		
Bank overdraft	4,372		
		10,171	
			8,131
			24,887
Capital			27,706
Add profit			18,481
			46,187
Less drawings			21,300
			24,887

7 Gladys Jones

Trading and profit and loss account for the year ended 31 August 20*8

	£	£	£
Sales			296,431
Less returns inwards			816
			295,615
Less cost of sales			
Stock		18,461	
Purchases	115,268		
Carriage inwards	348		
	115,616		
Less returns outwards	203	115,413	
		133,874	
		16,984	116,890
Gross profit			178,725
Less expenses			
Insurance		2,220	
Wages		105,892	
Motor expenses		8,420	
Light and heat		2,436	
Telephone		1,699	
General expenses		7,421	
Provision for doubtful debts		24	
Discount allowed		436	
Depreciation: premises		2,400	
office equipment		1,500	
vehicles		4,320	136,768
Net profit			41,957

Balance sheet at 31 August 20*8

	£	£	£
Fixed assets			
Premises	120,000		
Depreciation	55,200		64,800
Office equipment	15,000		
Depreciation	7,500		7,500
Vehicles	50,000		
Depreciation	43,520		6,480
			78,780
Current assets			
Stock		16,984	
Trade debtors	15,200		
Less provision	304	14,896	
Prepayment		180	
Bank		6,132	
Cash		228	
		38,420	
Less current liabilities			
Trade creditors	12,684		
Accrued expenses	351	13,035	25,385
			104,165
Capital			104,958
Add profit			41,957
			146,915
Less drawings			42,750
			104,165

9 Isadorah Boom

Trading and profit and loss account for the year ended 30 April 20*8

	£	£	£
Sales			97,481
Less returns inwards			127
			97,354
Less cost of sales			
Stock		6,483	
Purchases	48,972		
Carriage inwards	348		
	49,320		
Less returns outwards	197	49,123	
		55,606	
Stock		6,543	49,063
Gross profit			48,291
Discount received			432
			48,723
Less expenses			
Carriage outwards		812	
Bad debts		574	
Wages		18,841	
Rent		6,000	
Light and heat		3,481	
Telephone		1,856	
General expenses		15,860	
Provision for doubtful debts		44	
Provision for depreciation:			
machinery	6,000		
equipment	2,250	8,250	55,718
Net loss			6,995

Balance sheet at 30 April 20*8

	£	£	£
Fixed assets			
Machinery	60,000		
Depreciation	42,000		18,000
Equipment	36,000		
Depreciation	33,750		2,250
			20,250
Current assets			
Stock		6,543	
Debtors	6,400		
Less provision	320	6,080	
Prepayment		500	
Cash		136	
		13,259	
Less current liabilities			
Creditors	2,968		
Bank overdraft	2,487		
Accrued expenses	380	5,835	7,424
			27,674
Capital			48,169
Less loss			6,995
			41,174
Less drawings			13,500
			27,674

11 Jack Simms
Trading and profit and loss account for the year ended 30 September 20*8

	£	£
Sales		313,461
Less returns inwards		813
		312,648
Less cost of sales		
Stock		26,381
Purchases	197,384	
Less goods for own use	2,500	
	194,884	
Carriage inwards	277	
	195,161	
Less returns outwards	212	
	194,949	
	221,330	
Stock	27,492	193,838
Gross profit		118,810
Discount received		1,346
Commission received		4,892
		125,048
Less expenses		
Rates	3,510	
General expenses	8,274	
Wages	60,187	
Motor expenses	13,981	
Bad debts	2,643	
Provision for doubtful debts	78	
Loan interest	1,500	
Discount allowed	814	
Carriage outwards	1,732	
Depreciation: premises	2,000	
equipment	10,000	
vehicles	12,096	116,815
Net profit		8,233

Balance sheet at 30 September 20*8

	£	£	£
Fixed assets			
Premises	200,000		
Less depreciation	88,000	112,000	
Equipment	100,000		
Less depreciation	60,000	40,000	
Vehicles	84,000		
Less depreciation	65,856	18,144	170,144
Current assets			
Stock		27,492	
Debtors	28,000		
Less provision	700	27,300	
Prepayments		1,270	
Commission owed		180	
Bank		4,986	
Cash		512	
		61,740	
Less current liabilities			
Creditors	16,497		
Accrued expenses	853	17,350	44,390
			214,534
Capital			91,289
Add profit			8,233
			99,522
Less drawings			34,988
			64,534
Long term liability			
Loan			150,000
			214,534

CHAPTER NINETEEN

1 Objectivity; materiality; prudence; consistency.
3 £200,000; prudence/objectivity concept.
5 £4,000; accruals concept.
7 Reliable.

CHAPTER TWENTY

1 Grazeb Ltd
Income statement extract for the year ended 31 March 20*8

	£	£
Profit for the year before tax		347,230
Corporation tax		117,450
Profit for the year after tax		229,780
Ordinary dividends:		
Paid	34,500	
Proposed	112,600	147,100
Retained profit for year		82,680

3 Arbres Ltd
Balance sheet at 30 April 20*8

	£	£
Non-current assets:		
Machinery at cost		80,000
Vehicle at cost		40,000
		120,000
Current assets:		
Stock	25,000	
Trade receivables	15,000	
Bank	1,000	
	41,000	
Current liabilities		
Trade creditors	11,000	30,000
		150,000
Authorised share capital:		
500 000 Ordinary Shares of 50p each		250,000
Shareholders' equity:		
300 000 Ordinary shares of 50p each fully paid		150,000

5 Duvase Ltd
Balance sheet at 1 December 20*8

	£	£
Non current assets at cost		120,000
Current assets	22,000	
Bank	335,000	
	357,000	
Current liabilities		
Trade payables	8,000	349,000
		469,000
Shareholders' equity		
Ordinary shares of £1 each		300,000
Share premium account		120,000
Retained earnings		49,000
		469,000

7 Ousby Ltd
Balance sheet at 1 November 20*8

	£	£
Non-current assets at valuation		400,000
Current assets	40,000	
Bank	8,000	
	48,000	
Current liabilities	36,000	12,000
		412,000
Shareholders' equity		
Ordinary shares of 10p each fully paid		200,000
Revaluation reserve		150,000
Retained earnings		62,000
		412,000

9 Douglas Ltd
Income statement for the year ended 29 February 20*9

	£	£
Profit for the year before tax		312,000
Corporation tax		82,000
Profit for the year after tax		230,000
Transfer to general reserve		50,000
		180,000
Ordinary dividends: paid	40,000	
Proposed	60,000	100,000
Retained profit for year		80,000

Balance sheet at 29 February 20*9

	£	£
Non-current assets at cost		300,000
Current assets	150,000	
Current liabilities		
Corporation tax	82,000	
Proposed dividend	60,000	
	142,000	8,000
		308,000
Shareholders' equity		
Ordinary shares of £1 each fully paid		178,000
General reserve		50,000
Retained earnings		80,000
		308,000

11 Hox Ltd
Balance sheet at 1 June 20*8

	£	£
Non-current assets at valuation		300,000
Current assets	23,000	
Bank	18,000	
	41,000	
Current liabilities	40,000	1,000
		301,000
Shareholders' equity		
Ordinary shares of 25 pence each fully paid		70,000
Revaluation reserve		120,000
General reserve		30,000
Profit and loss account		81,000
		301,000

13 Norest Ltd
Balance sheet at 1 February 20*8

	£	£
Non-current assets at cost		60,000
Current assets	15,000	
Bank	31,000	
	46,000	
Current liabilities	9,000	37,000
		97,000
Shareholders' equity		
Ordinary shares of 25p each		55,000
Share premium account		25,000
Retained earnings		17,000
		97,000

15 Smith-Patel Ltd
Balance sheet at 1 April 20*8

	£	£
Non-current assets at valuation		750,000
Current assets	100,000	
Bank	320,000	
	420,000	
Current liabilities	70,000	350,000
		1,100,000
Shareholders' equity		
Ordinary shares of £1 each		600,000
Share premium account		100,000
Revaluation reserve		250,000
Retained earnings		150,000
		1,100,000

17 Stephanie Hood Ltd
Income statement for the year ended 30 April 20*8

	£	£
Net profit for the year before tax		267,432
Corporation tax		58,196
Profit for the year after tax		209,236
Less transfer to general reserve		50,000
		159,236
Preference dividends		
paid	3,000	
proposed	3,000	
Ordinary dividends		
paid	12,000	
proposed	26,000	44,000
Retained profit for year		115,236

Balance sheet at 30 April 20*8

	£	£
Fixed assets at cost		950,000
Less depreciation		230,000
		720,000
Current assets:		
Inventories	143,461	
Trade receivables	21,380	
Bank	34,802	
	199,643	
Current liabilities		
Trade payables	17,211	
Corporation tax	58,196	
Dividends	29,000	
	104,407	
		95,236
		815,236
Shareholders' equity		
Ordinary shares of £1 each fully paid		400,000
6% Preference shares of £1 each fully paid		100,000
General reserve		120,000
Retained earnings		195,236
		815,236

CHAPTER TWENTY-ONE

1 $\dfrac{GP}{Sales} \times 100 = \dfrac{67,000}{213,000} = 31.46\%$

$\dfrac{NP}{Sales} \times 100 = \dfrac{28,000}{213,000} = 8.45\%$

$\dfrac{Expenses}{Sales} \times 100 = \dfrac{39,000}{213,000} = 18.31\%$

$\dfrac{COS}{Ave\ stock} = \dfrac{146,000}{20,000} = 7.3\ times$

---

3 Fradtly plc is low geared (21.09%), Anthea's business is highly geared, while Wharma Plc is a low geared company.

5 55.1%

7 $\dfrac{CA}{CL} = \dfrac{60,500}{31,000} = 1.95:1$

$\dfrac{CA - stock}{CL} = \dfrac{26,500}{31,000} = 0.85:1$

$\dfrac{Debtors \times 365}{Credit\ sales} = \dfrac{26,500}{450,500} \times 365 = 22\ days\ (21.47)$

$\dfrac{Creditors \times 365}{Credit\ purchases} = \dfrac{19,460 \times 365}{291,900} = 25\ days\ (24.33)$

9 (a) 125.23% (b) 24.4% (c) 31.2% (d) 4.27 times (e) 3.2:1 (f) 1.15:1 (g) 28 days (h) 52 days

11 (a) 33.93% (b) 10.89% (c) 23.04% (d) 19.74% taken on opening capital (e) 1.25:1 (f) 0.57:1 (g) 24 days (h) 42 days

Gross margin has deteriorated from 35.62% to 33.93%, a fall of almost 5%. This means that Chris is now earning £33.93 on every £100 of sales. This could be due to more expensive purchases if selling prices have stayed the same, or a reduction in selling prices if cost of sales have remained the same. Last year there were 63 pence on every £1 of cost of sales current liabilities. The cover has decreased this year to 57 pence – has the overdraft increased? Debtors' collection has deteriorated by 3 days. Is it time to look at credit control?

13 (a) **Summarised trading and profit and loss accounts for the year ended 30 June 20*8**

	Jim Flack		Josie Chan	
	£	£	£	£
Sales		230,000		896,000
Less cost of sales				
Stock	12,400		32,000	
Purchases	58,600		515,000	
	71,000		547,000	
Stock	11,600	59,400	30,000	517,000
Gross profit		170,600		379,000
Expenses		84,600		126,000
Net profit		86,000		253,000

Debtors' collection period = $\dfrac{\text{debtors} \times 365}{\text{revenue}}$ 106 days

Gearing ratio = $\dfrac{\text{fixed cost capital}}{\text{total capital}} \times 100$ 6.48%

CHAPTER TWENTY-TWO

1 Rajpoot Ltd

Cash budget for the three months ending 30 October 20*9

	August £	September £	October £
Receipts – cash sales	90,963	106,125	116,230
Payments – creditors	29,650	35,050	38,400
wages	19,100	28,000	21,500
rent & rates	2,800	2,800	2,800
other expenses	5,700	5,500	5,300
machine purchase		84,000	
	57,250	155,350	68,000
Balance b/fwd	2,100	35,813	(13,412)
Receipts	90,963	106,125	116,230
	93,063	141,938	102,818
Payments	57,250	155,350	68,000
Balance c/fwd	35,813	(13,412)	34,818

3 Hunter Ltd

Cash budget for the three months ending 30 April

	February £	March £	April £
Receipts – debtors	21,000	28,000	30,000
Payments – purchases	12,000	9,000	10,000
expenses	20,000	22,000	18,000
purchase of office machinery	24,000		
	56,000	31,000	28,000
Balance b/fwd	3,200	(31,800)	(34,800)
Receipts	21,000	28,000	30,000
	24,200	(3,800)	(4,800)
Payments	56,000	31,000	28,000
Balance c/fwd	(31,800)	(34,800)	(32,800)

5 Singh Ltd

Cash budget for the three months ending 30 June

	April £	May £	June £
Receipts – cash sales	40,000	50,000	56,000
Payments – cash purchases	1,500	1,250	1,750
creditors	19,000	28,500	23,750
expenses	16,000	24,000	20,000
	36,500	53,750	45,500
Balance b/fwd	(1,500)	2,000	(1,750)
Receipts	40,000	50,000	56,000
	38,500	52,000	54,250
Payments	36,500	53,750	45,500
Balance c/fwd	2,000	(1,750)	8,750

Summarised balance sheets at 30 June 20*8

	£	£	£
Fixed assets		200,000	450,000
Current assets			
Stock	11,600		30,000
Debtors	14,000		80,000
Bank	2,400		4,000
	28,000		114,000
Creditors	16,000		67,000
		12,000	47,000
		212,000	517,000
Capital		142,000	332,000
Add profit		86,000	253,000
		228,000	585,000
Less drawings		16,000	68,000
		212,000	517,000
Gross margin		74.17%	42.3%
Net margin		37.39%	28.24%
ROCE		60.56%	76.2%
Overheads to turnover		36.78%	14.06%
Stock turnover		4.95 times	16.68 times
Current ratio		1.75:1	2.43:1
Liquid ratio		1.03:1	1.79:1
Debtors' days		23 days	33 days
Creditors' days		100 days	34 days

In terms of turnover, Josie's business is almost four times bigger than Jim's. Jim's gross profit margin is 75% greater than Josie's is. His net profit margin is 32% greater. Josie's control of her overheads is the better of the two (over 60% better). Josie gains a better return on the capital employed could be due to economies of scale that may be available to a larger business. Josie's stock turn is over three times greater than Jim's, thus releasing cash and profits more rapidly. Jim has proportionately fewer resources tied up in his current assets than Josie. Both debtor days and creditor days seem satisfactory, although Jim should be careful not to alienate his creditors. At present, his creditors have to wait, on average, over three months for payment. In the future they may be tempted to put him under pressure to settle more quickly than at present.

15 Bredgol plc

Gross margin = $\dfrac{\text{gross profit}}{\text{revenue}} \times 100$ 49.37%

Net profit margin = $\dfrac{\text{profit before interest and tax}}{\text{revenue}} \times 100$ 17.19%

Return on capital employed = $\dfrac{\text{PBIT}}{\text{Capital employed}} \times 100$ 16.75%

Net current asset ratio = $\dfrac{\text{current assets}}{\text{current liabilities}}$ 0.85 : 1

Liquid asset ratio = $\dfrac{\text{current assets} - \text{inventory}}{\text{current liabilities}}$ 0.74 : 1

Rate of stockturn = $\dfrac{\text{cost of sales}}{\text{average stock*}}$ 11.87 times

* closing stock used

7 Pierre

Cash budget for the three months ending 30 September

	July £	August £	September £
Receipts – cash sales	3,000	3,250	3,200
Debtors	58,900	57,000	61,750
	61,900	60,250	64,950
Payments – cash purchases	3,800	4,200	3,900
– creditors	27,000	28,800	34,200
– wages	13,000	12,500	12,500
– other expenses	8,300	8,500	8,500
– shop fittings	14,000		
	66,100	54,000	59,100
Balance b/fwd	(350)	(4,550)	1,700
Receipts	61,900	60,250	64,950
	61,550	55,700	66,650
Payments	66,100	54,000	59,100
Balance c/fwd	(4,550)	1,700	7,550

9 Tommy Chan

Cash budget for the three months ending 31 December

	October £	November £	December £
Receipts – cash sales	26,100	30,600	38,700
– debtors	2,400	2,900	3,400
	28,500	33,500	42,100
Payments – purchases	1,500	2,400	3,500
– creditors	10,800	11,700	13,500
– wages	4,500	6,000	6,500
– rent	200	225	225
– other expenses	3,400	1,600	980
	20,400	21,925	24,705
Balance b/fwd	670	8,770	20,345
Receipts	28,500	33,500	42,100
	29,170	42,270	62,445
Payments	20,400	21,925	24,705
Balance c/fwd	8,770	20,345	37,740

INDEX

abridged final accounts 237
account books 43
accounting
    concepts 209-13
    functions 27, 264
accounting bases 212
accounting equation 3-5, 3d, 4
accounting policies 212-13
accounting principles (concepts) 209-13
accounting ratios *see* ratios
accounts 42d
    see also final accounts; ledger accounts; nominal
        accounts; profit and loss accounts; trading
        accounts
    bookkeeping 42-50
accruals 143-5, 148, 167-9
accruals concept 209-10, 212
acid test ratio 250, 256
adjustments 199
    see also accruals; drawings; prepayments; provision
adverse variances 268d
appropriation of profits 226
articles of association 222, 222d
assets 1d, 3
    see also fixed assets; stock
    in accounting equation 4-5
    current 4, 148, 162
    intangible 237
    net 10-11, 10d, 16-17, 27, 35
    net current 250
auditors' report 237-8
authorised share capital 222d
average collection period ratio 250-1, 256

bad debts
    debiting 187-8
    provision for 138, 188-94
    recovery 194-5
balance sheets 1-7, 10, 16
    accruals 144
    closed off accounts 158, 160
    errors affecting 78, 80
    examples 13, 36-8
    at incorporation 223
    limited companies 220-7, 235, 236
    outstanding revenue 147-8
    sole traders 220
balancing figures 65-6
bank accounts 111-19, 111, 112
    cash books 58, 87-8
    statements 49, 97, 112, 112
bank balances 97
bank charges 112d
bank deposits 114
bank reconciliation statements 115-19

bank statements 49, 97, 112, 112
bank transactions 58, 111-19, 111, 112
bookkeeping *see* double-entry bookkeeping
books of prime entry
    bad debts 188
    cash transactions *see* cash books
    credit transactions 52-8, 53, 54, 55, 56, 86
    journals 55-8, 77-8, 80, 86
bounced (dishonoured) cheques 113d, 131
budgetary control 268-9
budgeting, benefits and limitations 264-5
budgets 264d, 265-8
business entity concept 211
business profits 11-13

capital 2d, 3
    see also share capital
capital expenditure 16d, 18, 28, 46, 175
capital receipts 17d, 18
capital reserves 227
carriage inwards 22d
carriage outwards 22d
cash
    banking 111
    checking 110
cash balances 97, 110
cash books 58, 87-8
    checking 110-19
    three column 106-7
    two column 92-100
cash budgets 265-7
cash discounts 103, 104-5
cash flows 244
    see also cash budgets
cash in hand 97, 97d
cash receipts and lodgement books 100
cash transactions 58, 87-8, 92-100, 228
    see also cheque transaction
cash withdrawals 99
casting 76d
cheque clearance 114d
cheque payments books 100
cheque transactions 92, 111, 112, 113, 114
    see also cash transactions
closing stock 19, 162, 163-4
closure of accounts
    see also final accounts
    accrued and prepaid expenses 167-70
    nominal accounts 155-60
    stock 161-7
commission, errors of 74
commission receivable 148
companies *see* limited companies
comparison, using ratios 254-6
compensating errors 74, 75

complete reversal of entries error 74, 75
concepts of accounting 209-13
consistency concept 211
contra entries 98-9, 98d, 136-8
control accounts 127-38
corporation tax 218
cost of sales 19-20, 19d
credit balances 70, 133-4
credit customers 46d
credit entries 49, 65, 74-5, 92, 156
credit notes 54, 55
credit purchases 52
credit suppliers 46d
credit transactions 49, 52-8, 53, 54, 55, 56
credit transfers 113d
creditors
    schedule of 128d, 132
    trade 2d, 144
creditors' payment period ratio 251, 256
current assets 4, 148, 162, 165
current liabilities 4d, 148
current ratio 250, 256

debentures 233-6
debit balances 70, 135
debit entries 49, 65, 74-5, 92, 165
debtors
    see also bad debts
    cash discounts 103
    credit customers 133-4
    sales ledgers 104, 130, 133-4, 187
    schedule of 128d, 130
    trade 2d, 144
debtors' collection period ratio 250-1, 256
debts see bad debts; debtors
depreciation 175-81, 175d, 184-5, 213
direct debits 112d
directors 217d
directors' reports 237
discounts 103-7
    see also trade discounts
dishonoured cheques 113d, 131
dividends 217d, 219, 219d, 221
double-entry bookkeeping 42-50, 53
    books of prime entry 52-9
    control accounts 127-38
    trial balances see trial balances
doubtful debts, provision for 138, 188-94
drawers (cheque payments) 111d
drawings 11d, 28, 46, 211
dual aspect concept 42, 212

errors
    bank transactions 113
    checking procedures 110-19
    in personal ledgers 127, 138
    stock records 162
    in trial balances 73-81, 138
errors of commission 74
errors of omission 74, 75
errors of original entry 74
errors of principle 74, 75
evaluation using ratios 254-6
expenditures
    capital 16d, 18, 28, 46, 175
    and losses 10

revenue 16d, 18, 26, 175
expenses
    accrued 144-5
    balance sheets 146
    debit balances 70
    non-cash 184
    prepaid 145-6, 167, 169-70
    provision for 177d

favourable variances 268d
final accounts 16, 33-8, 33d
    adjustments see accruals; adjustments; drawings;
        prepayments; provision
    balance sheets 36-8, 147-8, 158, 160
    limited companies 237
    preparing 155-70
    profit and loss accounts 28, 29, 34, 36, 38, 157,
        159
    sole traders 217-18
    suspense account entries 76
    trading accounts 18-20, 29, 34, 38, 157, 159
    use of trial balance 73, 75, 154-5, 157,
        158-9
financial year 5d
    see also closure of accounts
finite life 175d
fixed assets 3d
    in accounting equation 4-7
    depreciation 175-82, 184-5
    limited companies 231-2, 237
    sale or disposal 182-3
fixed dividends 221

gearing ratio 251-2, 256
general ledgers 47, 49
    bad and doubtful debts 187, 190
    depreciation 179-80
    discounts 105, 106-7
    fixed assets 177
    nominal accounts 47, 154d, 155-9
    posting to 52, 54, 88
    real accounts 47, 154d, 155
    stock accounts 162-3, 164
general reserves 224d, 226, 227
going concern concept 209
gross profit margin ratio 247, 255
gross profit mark-up ratio 247, 255
gross profits 16d, 26
    errors affecting 78, 80

horizontal layout (balance sheets) 2-3, 163

income statements, limited companies 217-18, 234,
    236
incorporation 221d, 222
infinite life 175d
intangible assets 237
interim dividends 219d
inventory turnover ratio 248-9, 256
investments, as fixed assets 237
issued share capital 222d

journals
    bad debts 188
    entries 55-8, 86
    errors 77-8, 80

ledger accounts 85-8
  balancing 67-73
  correcting errors 80
  posting to 52
ledgers 42d, 47
  see also general ledgers; ledger accounts; purchases
    ledgers; sales ledgers
  private 155d
  for stock 162-3, 164
liabilities 1d
  in accounting equation 4
  current 4d, 148
  non-current (debentures) 233
liability, limited 216d, 217
liability accounts 47
limited companies 216d
  articles of association 222, 222d
  balance sheets 220-7, 235, 236
  capital 223-4
  debentures 233-6
  description 216-17
  final accounts and reports 237-8
  fixed assets 231-2, 237
  general reserves 226
  income statements 217-20
  incorporation 221
  memorandum of association 222
  revenue reserves 224d, 227
  share capital 221, 222d
  shares 216d, 221, 228-30
limited liability 216d, 217
limited liability companies *see* limited
    companies
liquid assets 3d
liquid capital ratio 250, 256
liquidation 216d, 221
liquidity 244, 251
loans 251
  see also debentures
lodgements 114d
long-term liabilities 4d
losses, definition 10

management function of accounting 27, 264
master budgets 268
materiality concept 211-12
memorandum accounts 127d, 128
memorandum of association 222d
memorandum columns, cash books 106, 106d
money transactions see cash transactions; cheque
    transactions
motivation, and budgeting 264

net asset method, profit calculation 17, 27, 37
net assets 10-11, 10d, 16-17, 27, 35
net book value 177d
net current asset ratio 250, 256
net current assets 250
net profit margin ratio 247-8, 255
net profits 26d, 29
  errors affecting 78, 79, 80, 81
  and tax 246
net realisable value 166-7
nominal accounts 47, 154d, 155-9, 175
nominal ledgers see general ledgers
nominal value 216d

non-cash expenses 184
  see also depreciation
non-current assets 237
non-current liabilities (debentures) 233

objectivity 212
omission, errors of 74, 75
opening stock 19, 163-4
ordinary shares 221
original cost valuations 6
original entry
  see also books of prime entry
  errors of 74
outstanding revenue 146-8
overcast totals 76
overdrafts, interest 112d
overheads 247, 248
overheads in relation to turnover ratio 248

paid up capital 222d
par-value, shares 231
payees (cheque payments) 111d
paying in slips 111-12
personal accounts 47
personal ledgers
  see also purchases ledgers; sales ledgers
  errors 127, 138
personal use (drawings) 11d, 28, 46, 211
policies, accounting 212-13
posting, in ledgers 52, 54, 55, 88
preference shares 221
prepayments 145-6, 167, 169-70
prime entry see books of prime entry
principle, errors of 74, 75
principles, accounting 209-13
private ledgers 155d
private limited companies 217
private transactions 211
  see also drawings
profit and loss accounts 16, 26-9, 26d
  accruals 143-4
  bad debts 188
  closing off 157-8, 159
  depreciation 177-8, 179-80
  doubtful debts 190-1, 193-4
  errors affecting 78
  final accounts 28, 29, 34, 36, 38, 157, 159
  limited companies 224
  outstanding revenue 147
  sensitive content 155
profits 10-13, 10d
  calculation 17-23, 26-9
  calculation period 16
  general reserves 224d, 226, 227
  gross 16d, 26, 78, 80
  limited companies 223-4, 225, 226
  net 26d, 29, 78, 79, 80, 81
  reinvestment 35, 224-5
  retained 11d, 224d, 226
proposed dividends 219d
provision
  for depreciation account 177-8, 179-80
  for doubtful/bad debts 138, 188-94
  for known expenses 177d
prudence principle 165, 211
public limited companies 217

purchase returns 21d
purchase returns account 55, 156
purchases
   credit 52
   revenue expenditure 18, 43d
purchases accounts 47
   see also purchases ledgers
   closure 156
purchases day book (purchases book/journal) 52, 53, 86
purchases ledgers 47, 49
   see also personal ledgers
   closing accounts 156
   control accounts 132-3
   debit balances 135
   discounts 105
   posting to 52, 55
   schedule of creditors 128d
purchases returns day book (purchases returns book/journal) 54-5, 55, 86

quick asset ratio 250, 256

rate of stock turnover ratio 248-9, 256
ratios 243-5, 244d
   analysis 254-6
   financial 248, 250-1
   investment 251-2
   limitations 257
   profitability 246-8
   utilisation of resources 248-9
real accounts 47, 154d, 155, 175
realisable value 166-7
realisation concept 210
receipts 16d, 18, 100
reconciliation statements 115-19
recovery of bad debts 194-5
reducing balance method, depreciation 179-81
registered share capital 222d
reinvestment of profits 35, 224-5
rent receivable 148
reserves 224-5, 227
   see also profits
retained earnings/profits 11d, 224d, 226, 227
return on capital employed ratio 246, 256
returns in/inwards 21
returns out/outwards 21
revaluation reserves 231-3
revenue, not received 146-8
revenue expenditure 16d, 18, 26, 175
revenue receipts 17d, 18
revenue reserves 224d, 227

sales 43d
   cost of 19-20, 19d
   fixed assets 182-3
   revenue income 43
sales accounts 47, 156
   see also sales ledgers
sales day book (sales book/journal) 54, 54, 86
sales invoices 54, 56, 86
sales ledgers 47, 49, 54, 105
   see also personal ledgers
   closure of accounts 156
   control accounts 128-31, 129

credit balances 133-4
credit customers 47
debtors 104, 130, 133-4, 187
schedule of debtors 128d, 130
trade discounts 59
sales returns 21d
sales returns account 55, 156
sales returns day book (sales return book/journal) 55, 56
schedule of creditors 128d, 132
schedule of debtors 128d, 130
security, cash and cheques 98, 99
set-offs (contra entries) 98-9, 98d, 136-8
share capital 221, 222d
share premium accounts 227-8
shareholders 216, 221
   dividends 219
   reporting to 237-8
shareholders' equity 227-30
shares 216d, 221, 228-30, 231
sole traders
   balance sheets 220
   capital 223-4
   disadvantages 216
   final accounts 217-18, 253
source documents 86
   cash books 58, 97
   journals 56
standing orders 112d
stewardship function of accounting 27d
stock 3, 19d, 161-70
stock accounts 162-4
stock turnover ratio 248-9, 256
stock valuation 162, 165-7, 213
straight line method, depreciation 176-9
subsidiary books see books of prime entry
suspense accounts 75-6, 77, 80, 81

'T' accounts 67, 85
tax
   corporation 218
   and net profit 246
three column cash books 106-7
trade creditors 2d, 144
trade debtors 2d, 144
trade discounts 58-9, 103
trading accounts 16d, 17-23, 29
   accruals 143
   final accounts 18-20, 29, 34, 38, 157, 159
   outstanding revenue 147
   sensitive content 155-6
   and stock accounts 162-4
transactions, entry 45, 46, 52-9
trial balances
   and accruals 143-4
   debits and credits 65-73
   errors 73-81, 138
   for final accounts 73, 75, 154-5, 157, 158-9
two-column cash books 92-100

undercast totals 76, 77
unpresented cheques 115

valuation
   fixed assets 231-3

stock 162, 165-7, 213
variances, in budgets 268-9
vertical layout (balanced sheet)
   7, 7

wages
  account 168
  payments 99-100
working capital ratio 250, 256